BASIC Exercises for the ATARI

BASIC Exercises for the ATARI®

Jean-Pierre Lamoitier

SYBEX®

Berkeley • Paris • Düsseldorf

Cover art by Daniel Le Noury
Layout and design by Sharon Leong

Library of Congress Card Number: 82-63019
ISBN 0-89588-101-2
Printed in the United States of America
10 9 8 7 6 5 4 3 2 1

Acknowledgements

The author would like to thank Mark S. Bilk, who contributed many improvements to this book and provided valuable assistance with program development and verification, and Donna Scanlon who provided valuable organizational assistance.

Contents

Introduction

BASIC has become the most widely used programming language for small computers, and, as such, is an important tool for all computer users.

The most effective way of learning a programming language is through actual practice. This book has been designed to teach BASIC through graduated exercises. It is written for all readers who have a minimum scientific or technical background and who want to learn through actual experience, by studying realistic examples, how to program in BASIC.

All the programs in this book are written in Atari® BASIC. They will execute directly on an Atari® 400™ or an Atari® 800™.

Each exercise is presented in a progressive manner and includes: statement of the problem to be solved, analysis of the problem, solution with flowchart and comments, corresponding program, and sample run. This systematic presentation allows readers to check their understanding and progress at every step. Further, this method teaches the reader how to solve a problem in a "top-down" manner: sub-problems are identified and solved separately, leading to a modular program that is easy to read and modify.

Beyond the opportunity to learn BASIC programming in an effective manner, *BASIC Exercises for the Atari* offers a wealth of information and demonstrates valuable techniques for use in a broad range of applications. The following are brief descriptions of the topics covered in each chapter:

> *Chapter 1—Introductory Lesson:* A quick look at how a BASIC program is developed using a pertinent example from the income tax form 1040.
>
> *Chapter 2—Flowcharting:* How to get a solid, organized start on writing any BASIC program. The rest of the book shows the importance of working with a good flowchart.
>
> *Chapter 3—Integers:* Pursues programming in earnest with an unusual set of exercises using whole numbers. The applications range from ancient mathematics (Egyptian fractions) to modern computer science (integer base conversions).
>
> *Chapter 4—Geometry:* Shows how BASIC can be used to program some fairly complicated formulas from analytic geometry, and how to apply such computations to a practical problem in fence building. Also shows how to put together a simple, useful program to enable you to use your terminal to plot curves.

Chapter 5—Data Processing: More complex business-oriented exercises on sorting, merging files and report generation, including such useful routines as a simple program that tells the day of the week for any date.

Chapter 6—Scientific Programming: Using common formulas from algebra and calculus, this chapter contains exercises for evaluating polynomials and integrals and solving equations. Includes insights into an important issue in small computer programming: the validity and range of accuracy of numerical results.

Chapter 7—Finance: Includes exercises involving sales and growth forecasting, loan payments and interest computations, as well as more advanced income tax applications.

Chapter 8—Games: A little light programming after the solid core of the previous chapters. An exercise in increasing the level of computer involvement in playing a game. The use of random numbers in BASIC, demonstrated in the program for Craps.

Chapter 9—Operations Research: Offers more advanced exercises emphasizing the use of arrays and subscripts in BASIC: task scheduling, project management (PERT), and optimal trip planning.

Chapter 10—Statistics: All the usual in statistics—mean, variance, and standard deviation, plus two more exotic measurements, skewness and kurtosis. An exercise in linear regression and a program that measures the behavior of the BASIC random number generator, RND.

Chapter 11—Miscellaneous: Two final exercises illustrating the power of a systematic approach to the preparation of BASIC programs.

The author hopes that this book will encourage all readers to learn BASIC by actually using it, and welcomes all comments and suggestions for improvements.

CHAPTER 1

Your First Program in BASIC

Introduction

Anyone can learn to program a computer in BASIC by working through some practical exercises. This chapter will demonstrate that programming is not just for professionals. Starting with a simple exercise, you will be taught the rudimentary instructions and rules of the BASIC language and shown ways to improve upon a program after it has been written. No prior knowledge of BASIC is needed to understand the information presented in this chapter.

Although you can build up your command of BASIC by reading a textbook, it is more interesting to learn BASIC by creating actual programs. This method provides invaluable programming experience. If you work through the exercises presented in this chapter and each subsequent chapter, you will gain a sound working knowledge of BASIC.

1.1 Computing Taxable Income

As our first exercise, we will calculate taxable income from the following formula, which is commonly used in figuring income taxes:

TAXABLE INCOME = GROSS INCOME − N*1000

where N stands for the number of dependents.

This can be accomplished in a few lines of BASIC as follows:

```
40 INPUT G,N          Read in gross income and N.
50 T=G-N*1000         Calculate gross income - N × 1000.
60 PRINT T            Print out the result.
70 END
```

Although simple, this program brings up several points about the format of BASIC instructions:

- Each line has a line number.
- Each line carries an instruction.
- The read instruction, i.e., the INPUT instruction, is used to get information into the computer.
- In the instruction on line 50, multiplication is represented by an asterisk.
- The program is terminated by an END instruction, but this is optional.

If the program we have just written is run on a computer, the following dialogue between the program and the user will take place:

```
?21160,5              This is typed by the user.
16160                 This is typed by the computer.
```

When the computer executes an INPUT instruction, the computer types out a question mark to indicate to the user that it is waiting for some input.

In the previous dialogue, the user typed 21160 and 5. In the program, since the variable names that follow INPUT are G and N, the first value typed in, 21160, was assumed by the computer to be for G, and the second value, 5, was assumed to be for N. Using these values, the computer then carried out the calculation indicated on line 50 of our program and printed the result, 16160.

This result is mathematically correct, but the meaning of the dialogue is obscure. Let's change the program to present a better picture of what is going on, and print some explanatory text. For text to be printed, the text should be placed in double quotes and written after a PRINT instruction. The improved program now reads:

```
10 PRINT "GROSS INCOME ";
20 INPUT G
30 PRINT "DEPENDENTS ";
40 INPUT N
50 T=G-N*1000
60 PRINT
70 PRINT "TAXABLE INCOME IS ";T
80 END
```

The semicolon suppresses an otherwise automatic carriage return and linefeed at these points.

Now, the dialogue between the user and the computer is more easily understood:

```
GROSS INCOME ?21160
DEPENDENTS ?5

TAXABLE INCOME IS 16160
```

When the program waits for data, it displays a "?".

In many BASICs the first four instructions, 10 through 40, could be combined into one instruction by writing:

```
40 INPUT "GROSS INCOME, NUMBER OF DEPENDENTS? ";G,N
```

ATARI BASIC, however, does not permit print strings in input statements.

1.2 Another Way to Calculate Taxable Income

If we look at a real Internal Revenue Service (IRS) Form 1040 for 1981, we will find that the GROSS INCOME, G, of the program above is actually:

Adjusted Gross Income (line 31 of the Form 1040)

Looking a little closer, we see that this adjusted gross income is the difference between:

Total Income (line 21 of the Form 1040)

and

Total Adjustments (line 30 of the Form 1040)

Reading further through the Form 1040, we also come upon a more detailed calculation for the TAXABLE INCOME, T:

T = G − D − N∗1000

where:

G is adjusted gross income.
D is total deductions.
N is number of dependents (as before).

After we incorporate this new information, our refined program reads:

```
10 PRINT "TOTAL INCOME  ";
15 INPUT I
20 PRINT "TOTAL ADJUSTMENTS  ";
25 INPUT A
30 G=I-A
40 PRINT "TOTAL DEDUCTIONS  ";
45 INPUT D
50 PRINT "NUMBER OF DEPENDENTS  ";
55 INPUT N
60 T=G-D-N*1000
65 PRINT
70 PRINT "THE TAXABLE INCOME IS  ";
75 PRINT T
80 END
```

The dialogue between the computer and the user would now look like this:

```
TOTAL INCOME  ?27624
TOTAL ADJUSTMENTS  ?1737
TOTAL DEDUCTIONS  ?4727
NUMBER OF DEPENDENTS  ?5

THE TAXABLE INCOME IS  16160
```

In this example, each variable in the program has a name associated with it. In computer science jargon, this name is called an "identifier." Let us go back and list the identifiers used in this program:

I Total Income
A Total Adjustments
D Total Deductions
G Adjusted Gross Income
N Number of Dependents
T Taxable Income

Using single-letter names as identifiers is in keeping with the standard BASIC limitation (common in "Home Computer" BASICs) that identifiers may only be a single letter or a letter and a digit. ATARI BASIC, however, has been extended to accept names up to 114 characters long (the maximum line length). On the ATARI, the readability of the program can be improved then, by assigning more descriptive names, for example:

I → INCOMTOT
A → ADJUSTOT
D → DEDUCTOT
G → GROSSINC
N → NOFDEPEN
T → TAXINCOM

Conclusion

This elementary example shows how to design a simple program in BASIC. To undertake the writing of more ambitious programs, we must first learn techniques for analyzing a program and designing a "flowchart." These two skills will be developed in the next chapter.

The example on computing taxable income that we presented in this chapter will be pursued and expanded in Chapter 7 to compute the actual tax due.

CHAPTER 2

Flowcharts

Introduction

In the first chapter of this book, we learned the rudiments of the BASIC language and saw how to write a simple program. In the following chapters, the exercises will become more complex and the method we learned for writing programs (i.e., writing out the program directly) will no longer be feasible. As more complex problems are presented, it will be necessary to analyze the problem first, and then draw a "flowchart" before the program listing is coded. Indeed, experience has shown that flowcharting is an invaluable aid in programming, especially for the beginner.

The goal of this chapter is to demonstrate the proper technique for constructing a flowchart. The following chapters will provide many opportunities for applying the information learned here and for practicing the techniques of flowcharting.

Later on, with experience, it will become possible to reduce the amount of time spent designing flowcharts, but this practice is not advisable for the beginner.

2.1 The Purpose of the Flowchart

The flowchart is a graphic representation of the procedure proposed to solve the problem. At the present state of the art, the flowchart is only useful to the programmer, as it is incomprehensible to computers. Because of this, we might question the value of the flowchart. However, the flowchart provides a means to verify that some crucial part of the problem was not overlooked when the problem was analyzed. The flowchart may also facilitate communication between the various people working on a programming project. All in all, for the beginner, a detailed flowchart constitutes a first stage that promotes good programming.

2.1.1 Different Types of Flowcharts

In practice there are three types of flowcharts:

1. *A system flowchart:* principally used in data processing applications. This flowchart shows the connections between files and programs.

2. *A conceptual flowchart:* often used to present a macroscopic view of large programs that involve the interaction of multiple algorithms. Such flowcharts are of limited use for small programs.

3. *A detailed flowchart:* constitutes a complete and precise representation of the planned procedure. This type of flowchart removes all potential ambiguities and makes programming easier.

Note, however, that the flowchart should always be as independent of the programming language as possible.

2.1.2 Standards

Flowcharting standards and symbols have been promulgated by ANSI, the American National Standards Institute. Templates for drawing all of the standard flowcharting symbols are produced by IBM® and other companies, and are generally available. A table of the principal symbols used in flowcharting programs appears on the following page.

We should note here that there are many methods that can be used to describe algorithms, programs and systems. To list a few: metalanguage, pseudocode, structure charts, data flow diagrams, Warnier diagrams, "input-process-output" (IPO), hierarchical IPO (HIPO), etc. Many of these methods have great merit and warrant further study, but understanding them is an

THE ELEMENTS OF A FLOWCHART:

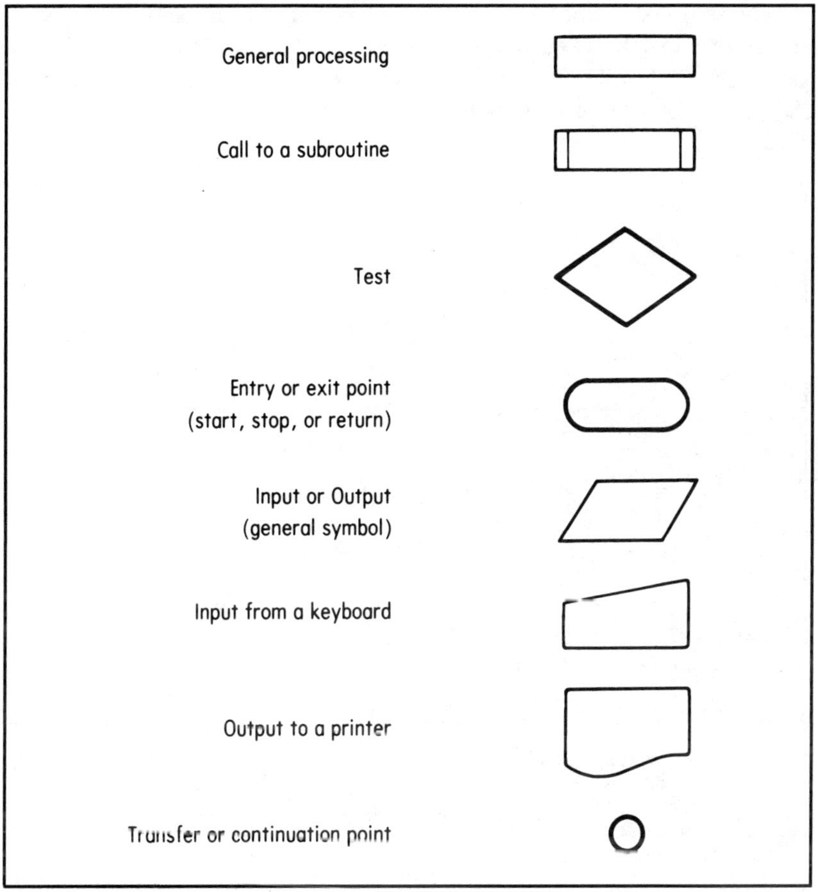

involved process that presupposes a good acquaintance with programming. For the beginning programmer, the flowcharting method has the advantage of being very accessible and widely understood.

We will begin our exposition of flowcharting with a simple "mini-flowchart," which allows us to ascertain that in programming, solutions are not unique. We will then go on to study more complicated situations.

2.2 The Maximum of Two Numbers, A and B

We want X to assume the value of the larger of two numbers A and B. How can we obtain a solution while minimizing the number of instructions that must be written?

First solution: We compare A and B. If A ⩾ B, we store the value of A in X, otherwise, we store the value of B in X. This method can be represented by means of a flowchart (see Figure 2.1) that consists of a diamond in which the comparison "A ⩾ B" is located, and two rectangles that correspond to the "assignments." The corresponding sequence of BASIC instructions is listed in Figure 2.2.

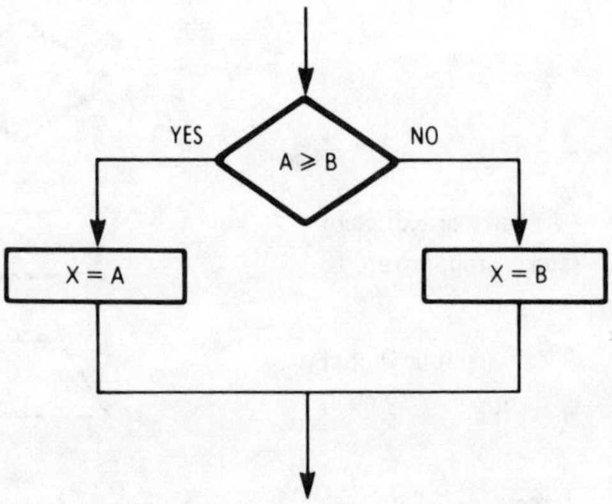

Figure 2.1: First Flowchart Example: Finding the Larger of Two Numbers

```
100 IF A>=B THEN 130
110 X=B
120 GOTO 140
130 X=A
```

Figure 2.2: Program Written from First Flowchart

If we use a more advanced BASIC, we can write:

100 IF A >= B THEN X = A ELSE X = B

Second solution: To avoid the branching on line 120, we change the flowchart shown in Figure 2.1 by moving one of the assignment instructions. This gives us the flowchart shown in Figure 2.3. The corresponding BASIC is shown in Figure 2.4.

In this solution we have omitted a GOTO instruction, and, therefore, have somewhat simplified the program. With an advanced BASIC we have:

100 X = A

101 IF B > A THEN X = B

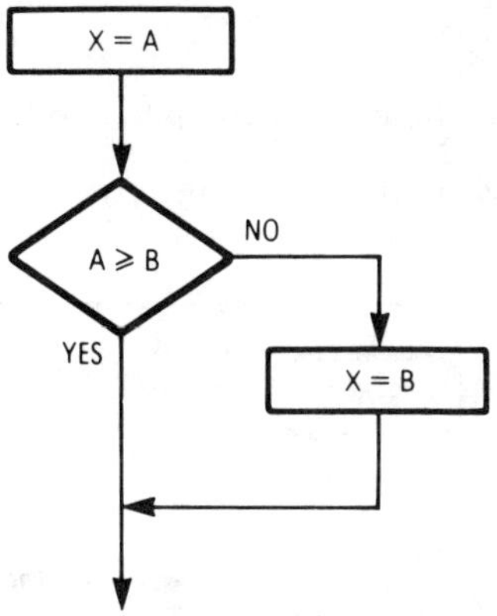

Figure 2.3: A More Efficient Flowchart

```
100 X=A
110 IF A>=B THEN 130
120 X=B
```

Figure 2.4: A Shorter Program

Third solution: Unfortunately only a few BASIC interpreters include the functions MAX and MIN. If these functions are available, we only need to write:

100 X = MAX (A,B)

At the present time the functions MAX and MIN are only rarely available on home computers.

Note: When these two functions are available, they often accept an arbitrary number of parameters. For example, we could write:

Y = MAX(X,3,Z,C)

or even

Y = MIN(X + Z, V*W, K*SIN(A))

2.3 Example of a Complete Flowchart: The Largest Element of an Array

Assume we want to find the largest number in an array, A, of 100 numbers. The method we propose is the following:

— Set X = A(1)

— Give I the values 2, 3, 4, successively, up to 100

— Compare X and A(I)

— If X< A(I) transfer the value of A(I) into X, otherwise, continue.

When we finish, X will contain the largest value. This method is represented in the flowchart shown in Figure 2.5.

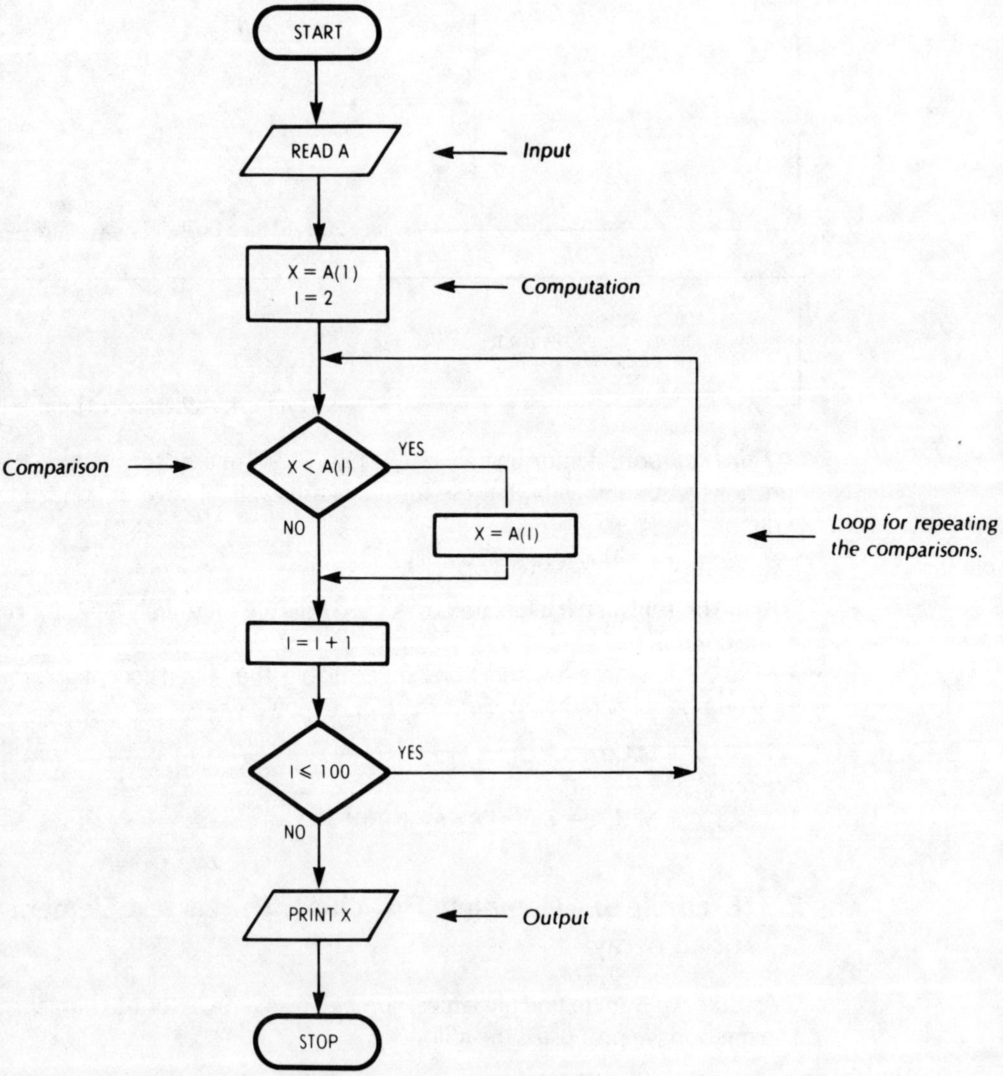

Figure 2.5: Flowchart for Finding the Largest Element of an Array

The diagram in Figure 2.5 illustrates the following conventions:

— Input or output instructions are enclosed in a parallelogram.

— Computational instructions are enclosed in a rectangle.

— Comparison instructions are enclosed in a diamond.

We also note an expression that may seem odd to a person who has not been involved with programming:

I = I + 1

Expressed in its most general form, a computational instruction may be written:

variable = <expression>

This instruction means that the numerical value of the expression will be computed and assigned for storage to the variable on the left of the equal sign. For this reason, an instruction of this form is called an "assignment statement." The character "=" acts here as the symbol for assignment. However, within a diamond, the instruction:

I = 100

means "compare I to 100 and see if they have the same value." Under no circumstances does this imply that the value 100 is to be stored in I. In other words, in a diamond the character "=" acts as the symbol for comparison.

2.4 How to Verify a Flowchart

If a program is derived from an erroneous flowchart, it will not yield the proper results. We should be as certain as possible that the flowchart is correct before we enter into the programming phase.

To do this, we can "desk check" the flowchart. This is done by simulating the operations of a computer and tracing the paths of the flowchart, step-by-step, to insure that the ordering is correct, and checking (by hand) the calculations involved.

Let us go back to the previous flowchart shown in Figure 2.5 and imagine a smaller array of, for example, five numbers.

At the outset, we set X = A(1), so X will take the value 3 (see Figure 2.6).

I	1	2	3	4	5
A(I)	3	2	4	−1	6

Figure 2.6: Array of Five Elements

Now we will go once around the loop. The table given in Figure 2.7 shows how the contents of X change as a function of I.

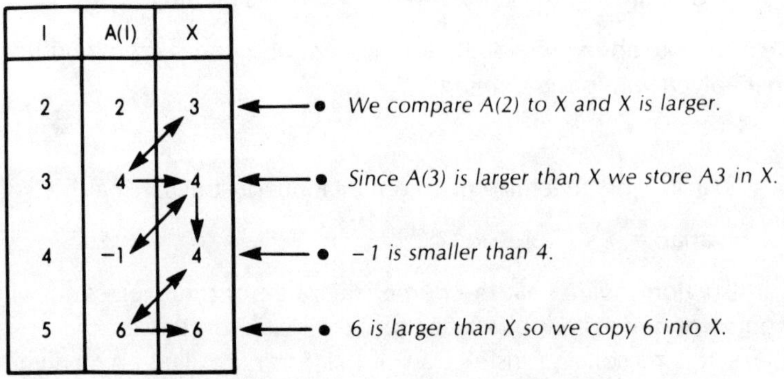

Figure 2.7: Comparing the Elements

We observe that by using this method, X is indeed being converted into the largest element of the array. Therefore, we can go ahead and program this flowchart.

Note: This method can only be used with fairly simple flowcharts.

The flowchart in Figure 2.5 can be translated into BASIC in various ways. An example of one way is shown in Figure 2.8.

```
100 DIM A(100)
110 FOR I=1 TO 100
120 READ Y:A(I)=Y
130 NEXT I
140 X=A(1)
150 FOR I=2 TO 100
160 IF X>=A(I) THEN 180
170 X=A(I)
180 NEXT I
190 PRINT "THE LARGEST ";
195 PRINT "ELEMENT IN THE ";
197 PRINT "ARRAY = ";X
200 DATA ...
210 DATA ...
410 END
```

Figure 2.8: Largest-Element Program

This is not the best possible version, but it is easy to understand:

- Lines 110 to 130 read in the entire array.
- Lines 140 to 180 correspond to the search for the largest element in the array.
- Lines 200, 210, etc., would normally hold the actual values of the 100 elements to be read into the array.

Note that ATARI BASIC will not permit a subscripted variable in a READ statement, so an extra variable (y) is used in line 120.

Criticism of this program: This program will not work unless the array contains exactly 100 elements. It is often preferable to read a number, N, initially, that is the actual number of elements in the array. We can then provide a program that adapts itself to handle an array of any size, N, up to 100. The program given in Figure 2.9 is much better from this point of view.

```
100 DIM A(100)
105 READ N
110 FOR I=1 TO N
120 READ Y:A(I)=Y
130 NEXT I
140 X=A(1)
150 FOR I=2 TO N
160 IF X>=A(I) THEN 180
170 X=A(I)
180 NEXT I
190 PRINT "THE LARGEST ";
195 PRINT "ELEMENT IN THE ";
197 PRINT "ARRAY =";X
200 DATA 5
210 DATA 3,-2,34,5,0
410 END

RUN
THE LARGEST ELEMENT IN THE ARRAY = 34
```

Figure 2.9: Modified Largest-Element Program

Comments: Looking in detail at this program we see that:

- Instruction 105 reads the number, N, of elements in the array.
- Line 200 holds the value 5 corresponding here to 5 elements.
- Line 210 holds the values of the 5 elements.
- This version of the program is limited by the instruction DIM A(100) to 100 elements. By modifying this instruction the program can be adapted to have a larger or smaller maximum capacity.

- — This type of organization makes the program less expensive to modify and easier to read.

Note: It is a general rule with FOR loops that the terminal value should be a variable rather than a constant.

2.5 Decision Points

On a flowchart, a decision point has one entry and two or three exits. Figure 2.10 illustrates this point. The symbol "?" is used as a symbol for comparison.

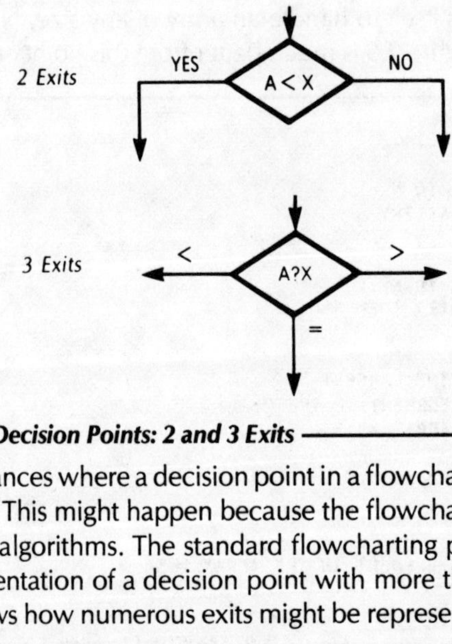

Figure 2.10: Decision Points: 2 and 3 Exits

There are instances where a decision point in a flowchart could have more than three exits. This might happen because the flowchart must represent a general class of algorithms. The standard flowcharting procedure does not specify a representation of a decision point with more than three exits, but Figure 2.11 shows how numerous exits might be represented.

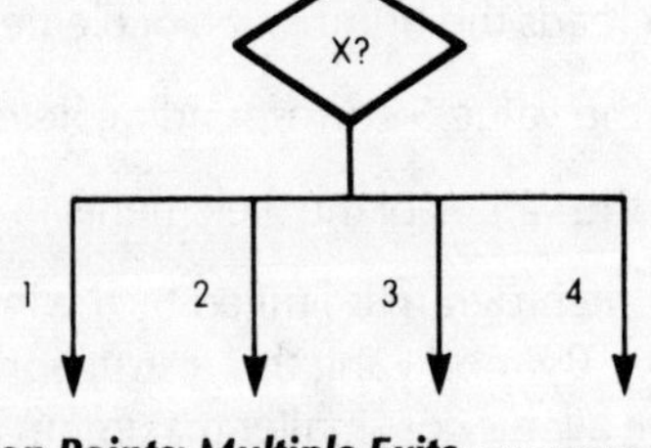

Figure 2.11: Decision Points: Multiple Exits

2.6 A "Flip-Flop" Technique for Branching

How can we flowchart a loop so that the left side of the flowchart is executed on each odd passage through the loop and the right side is executed on each even passage? This alternation should be continued until the conditions are right for leaving the loop (see Figure 2.12).

A simple method that might accomplish this task would be to use an auxiliary variable. The value of this auxiliary variable could control this "flip-flop" function. For example, the value 0 could be assigned to a variable S before entering the loop. In the loop a test on B would select the left branch if B is zero. In the left branch an instruction, B = 1, would be inserted, so that on the next test, the right branch would be taken. In this branch, a B = 0 will be placed, which will cause a switch back to the left side for the next run through. This method is incorporated into the flowchart displayed in Figure 2.13.

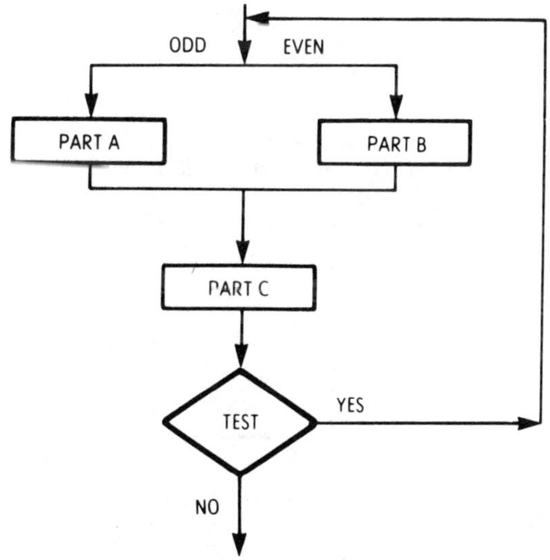

Figure 2.12: Conceptual Flowchart for Flip-Flop Branching

The flowchart is easily turned into BASIC, as the code in Figure 2.14 shows. The line numbers are included for purposes of the example.

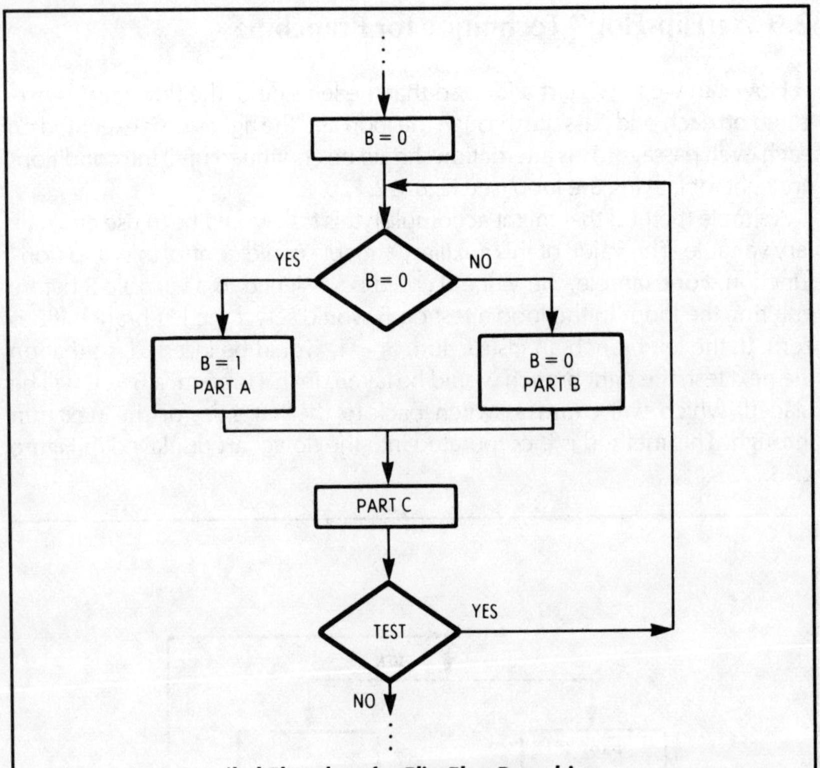

Figure 2.13: Detailed Flowchart for Flip-Flop Branching

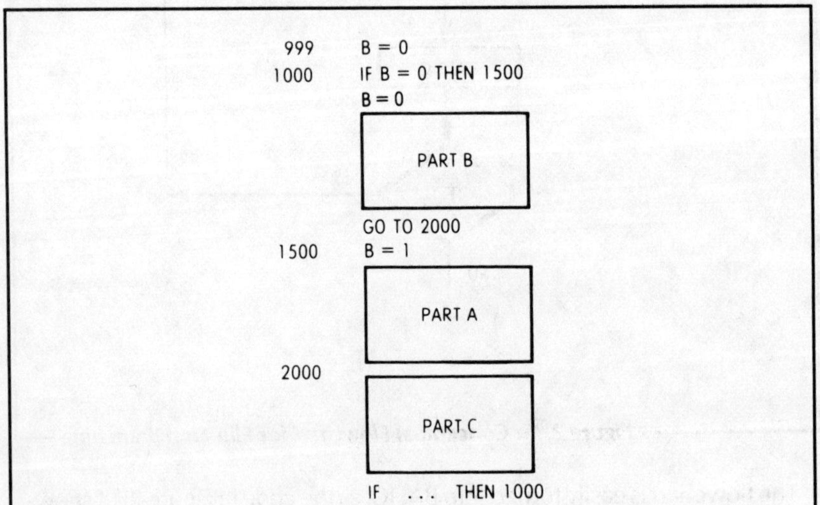

Figure 2.14: Flip-Flop Branching Program

Note: As points of interest to the reader:

1. Figure 2.15 shows how the last example could be written in FORTRAN 77.
2. Figure 2.16 shows how it could be written in CBASIC[1].

(*Note* that for this example we have not included all of the line numbers that are required by CBASIC; they are not needed to understand the example.)

```
999    B = 0
1000   IF (B.EQ.0)      THEN
                               B = 1
                               part A
                        ELSE
                               B = 0
                               part B
                        ENDIF
       part C
       IF (...)         GOTO 1000
```

Figure 2.15: Flip-Flop Branching in FORTRAN 77

```
999    B = 0
1000   IF B = 0         THEN
                               B = 1
                               part A
                        ELSE
                               B = 0
                               part B
       part C
       IF(...)          THEN 1000
```

Figure 2.16: Flip-Flop Branching in CBASIC

(1)CBASIC is a registered trademark of Software Systems, Inc. It denotes an extended BASIC, which operates under the CP/M monitor, available on compatible INTEL 8080, INTEL 8085, and Zilog Z80 based systems.

2.7 The Implementation of a P-Stage Round Robin

For this example, we want the first cycle through the flowchart to follow branch one, the second cycle to follow branch two, the pth cycle to follow branch p, and the p + 1st cycle to follow branch 1, and so on, indefinitely. In more mathematical terms, the ith cycle should be through branch i modulo p (see Figure 2.17).

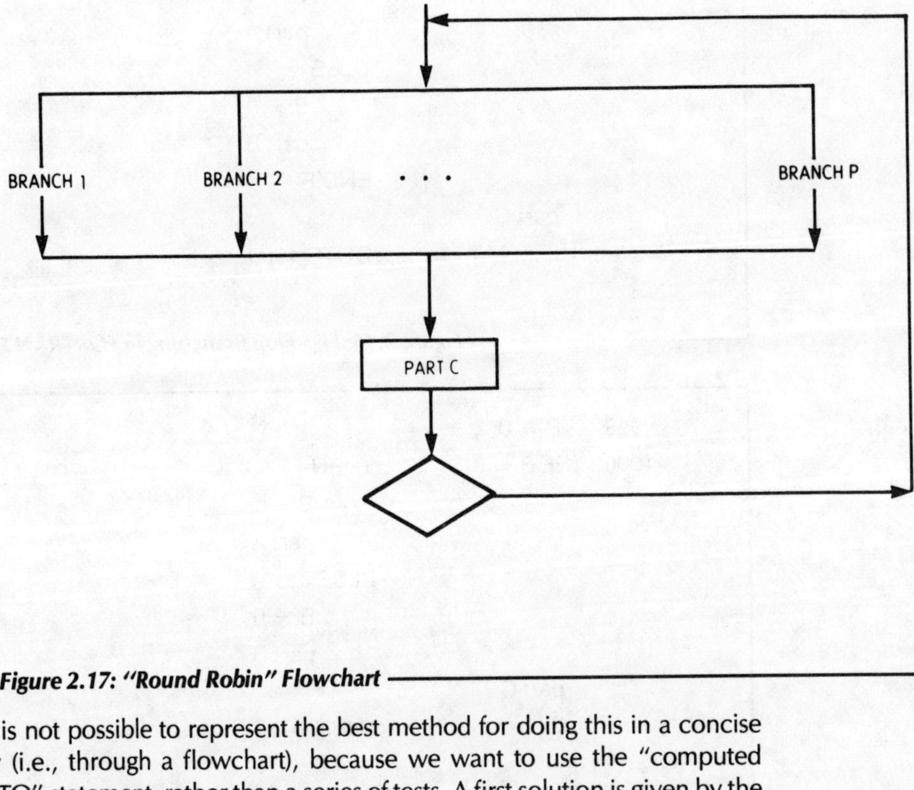

Figure 2.17: "Round Robin" Flowchart

It is not possible to represent the best method for doing this in a concise way (i.e., through a flowchart), because we want to use the "computed GOTO" statement, rather than a series of tests. A first solution is given by the code sketched in Figure 2.18.

Note that we can go through the sequence properly, with a centralized section of code at the common exit that uses a single assignment, B = B + 1, and a test for handling the recycling. This implementation is sketched in Figure 2.19.

```
999  B = 1
1000 ON B GOTO 1100, 1300, 1500, 1600
1100 B = 2
        Branch 1
     GOTO 1800
1300 B = 3
        Branch 2
     GOTO 1800
1500 B = 4
        Branch 3
     GOTO 1800
1600 B = 1
        Branch 4
1800
     part C
     IF ... THEN 1000
```

Figure 2.18: "Round Robin" Program

```
999  B = 1
1000 ON B GOTO 1100, 1300, 1500, 1600
1100 Branch 1
     GOTO 1800
1300 Branch 2
     GOTO 1800
1500 Branch 3
     GOTO 1800
1600 Branch 4
1800 B = B + 1
     IF B > 4 THEN B = 1
        part C
     IF ... THEN 1000
```

Figure 2.19: More Efficient "Round Robin" Program

Conclusion

In this chapter we have covered the rudiments of flowcharting. Section 2.7, however, presented a more advanced branching technique that is not required knowledge for the beginning programmer but can be useful when more complex problems are attempted.

As we study the exercises in the following chapters, we will be able to perfect our general knowledge of flowcharts and, above all, learn how to construct them.

CHAPTER 3

Exercises Using Integers

Introduction

This chapter will present exercises that demonstrate the use of whole numbers in BASIC. The corresponding flowcharts, some more complicated than others, will provide the reader with additional insights into the nature of problem solving. If you experience difficulty with some of the exercises in this chapter, do not spend a great amount of time trying to complete them; instead, move on to the following chapters and return to this chapter again at a later time.

The solutions given for the exercises presented here are valid for "standard" BASIC interpreters. Most of the words and symbols in all BASIC interpreters are the same, although there are exceptions. Various computer manufacturers may vary a particular instruction or symbol. Some BASIC interpreters may include features not available in other interpreters. For example, it is now becoming common practice for some BASIC interpreters to accept "true" integers: A%, B%. (This is not, however, true of ATARI.) The % tells the BASIC interpreter to store and treat this variable as a computer integer (usually 16 bits), rather than a "floating point" number, which is encoded in 32 bits. It is important to keep in mind that although features may vary, the concept remains the same.

The convention followed in these exercises is that the value of the integer variables will never exceed 32,767[(1)]. This constraint allows the use of "integer" BASICs to reduce execution time and use less memory. However, not all systems have integer variables and, furthermore, such standard functions as SIN, COS, SQR, etc., are rarely available for integer variable arguments.

One difficulty often encountered when completing exercises using integers is the need to carry out "integer division" and calculate remainders. For example, we might want to determine the value of Q and R such that:

```
A = B*Q + R
```

To do this, we must perform the integer division A/B for which BASIC has no special operator. In this case, we would use the function INT and write:

```
Q = INT (A/B)
R = A - Q*B
```

To obtain the quotient Q and the remainder R when integer variables are available, we simply write:

```
Q% = A%/B%
R% = A% - B%*Q%
```

Or, if we are only interested in the remainder, we write:

— With ordinary variables:

```
R = A - B*INT(A/B)
```

— With integer variables:

```
R% = A% - B%*(A%/B%)
```

3.1 Integers Satisfying $A^2 + B^2 = C^2$

Exercise: Find all integers A and B between 1 and 100 such that $A^2 + B^2$ is a perfect square.

In order to solve this problem, we will complete the following tasks:

— Analyze the problem.

— Decide on a method to use, and draw a flowchart.

— Write the corresponding BASIC program.

---

(1) This is usually the maximum integer that can be represented on most micro- and minicomputers that have only 16-bit integer arithmetic. Larger integers are available on "megaminis" or main frame computers.

Analysis: Before we begin our analysis, it should be noted that solutions that differ only by a permutation are to be considered identical.

For example:

A = 3		A = 4
B = 4	and	B = 3
C = 5		C = 5

constitute two identical solutions.

To avoid repeating identical solutions, we will seek solutions such that B>A. Thus, let us determine if $I^2 + J^2$ is a perfect square by giving the variable I a value from 1 to 99 and the variable J a value from I + 1 to 100. Two different approaches can be used to obtain the solution.

First approach: Increment a variable K starting from J + 1. Then,

If $I^2 + J^2 = K^2$ we have found a solution.

If $I^2 + J^2 > K^2$ increment K by one and try again.

If $I^2 + J^2 < K^2$ there is no solution for I and J.

Second approach: Calculate:

$$K = \sqrt{I^2 + J^2}$$

If K is an integer, we have a solution; if it is not an integer, there is no solution for I and J. To determine whether or not K is an integer, we simply compare K with INT(K).

These two approaches are indicated in the flowcharts drawn in Figures 3.1 and 3.2 (respectively). In both of these flowcharts we see:

— An outer loop varying I from 1 to 99

— An inner loop varying J from I + 1 to 100.

Using the two flowcharts shown in Figures 3.1 and 3.2, we can easily construct the programs shown in Figures 3.3 and 3.4.

It is necessary to become aware of the degree of precision invoked when using floating point computations in ATARI BASIC. Let's examine line 40 of the program in Figure 3.4. Here we compare the value K, known to be the product of the floating point arithmetic operation SQR(I*I+J*J), with INT(K), known to be an integer. We must be careful when testing for equality between these two values for K, since we have entered the area of potential round-off errors. For example, the SQR function may have computed the value of K to be 51.0000001 or 50.9999999; this is very close to the correct value and sufficiently accurate for most practical purposes. On the other

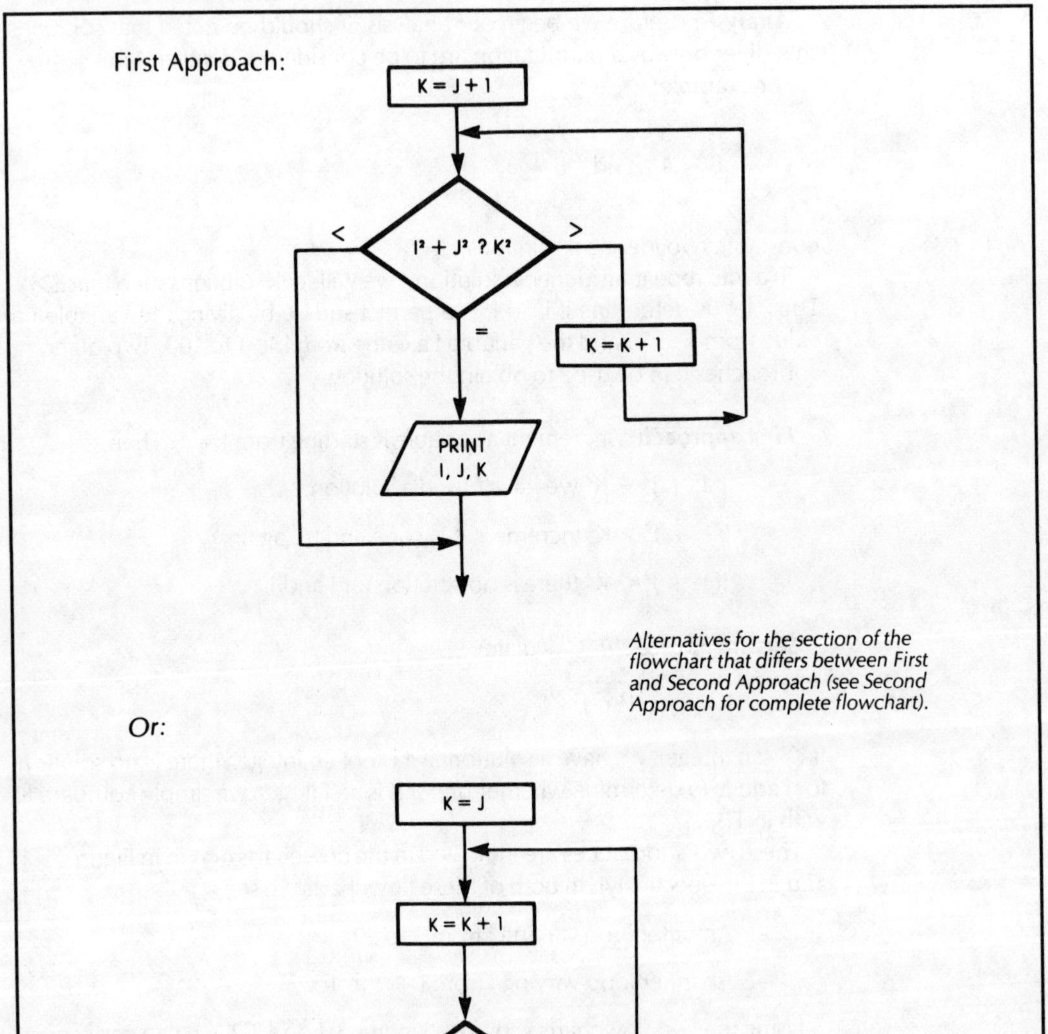

Figure 3.1: Flowchart Segments: Integer Solutions for $A^2 + B^2 = C^2$

Second Approach:

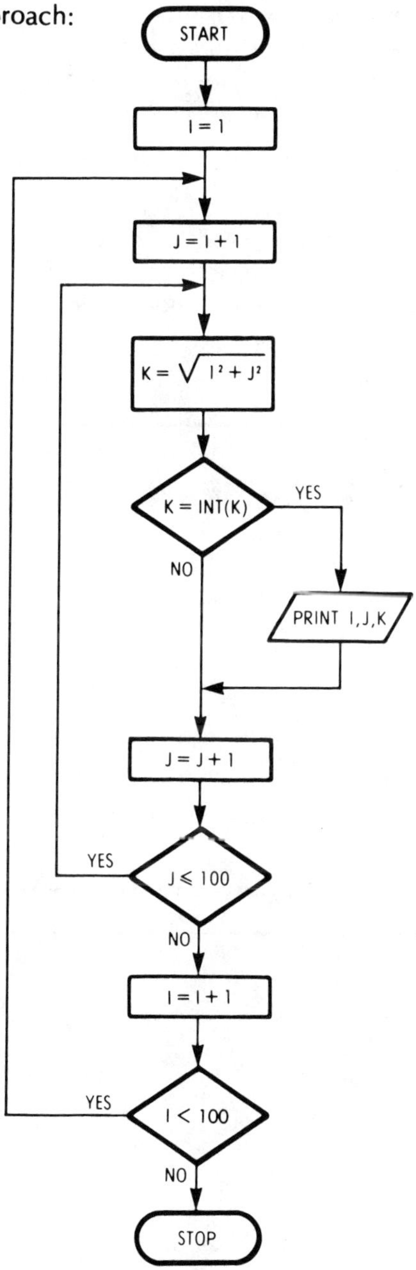

Figure 3.2: Complete Flowchart: Integer Solutions for $A^2 + B^2 = C^2$

hand, the INT function has changed all digits following the decimal point to zero (i.e., 51.0000000 or 50.0000000). The instruction in line 40 will find these two values unequal and, consequently, our program will fail to show $24^2 + 45^2 = 51^2$ as a possible solution. Therefore, to resolve the round-off errors, line 40 in Figure 3.4 becomes:

```
40    IF ABS(K - INT(K + .5)) > 1E - 7 THEN 60
```

The program in Figure 3.3, using the first approach, avoids these difficulties. Throughout the program, only positive integer exponents of integers are used. Also, given the limited range of the values of A and B, the highest number to be represented is 20,000—a number well within the nine digits of precision supplied by ATARI BASIC.

Note: The topic of round-off errors is discussed in detail in Chapter 6.

```
5 N=100
10 FOR I=1 TO N
20 FOR J=I+1 TO N
30 S=I*I+J*J
40 K=J
50 K=K+1
60 K2=K*K
70 IF K2<S THEN 50
80 IF K2>S THEN 100
90 PRINT " ";I;" ";J;
95 PRINT " ";K
100 NEXT J
110 NEXT I
120 END
```

Figure 3.3: Program Using the First Approach

```
5 N=100
10 FOR I=1 TO N-1
20 FOR J=I+1 TO N
30 K=SQR(I*I+J*J)
40 IF K<>INT(K) THEN 60
50 PRINT " ";I;" ";J;
55 PRINT " ";INT(K)
60 NEXT J
70 NEXT I
80 END
```

Figure 3.4: Program Using the Second Approach

```
3 4 5
5 12 13
6 8 10
7 24 25
8 15 17
9 12 15
9 40 41
10 24 26
11 60 61
12 16 20
12 35 37
13 84 85
14 48 50
15 20 25
15 36 39
16 30 34
16 63 65
18 24 30
18 80 82
20 21 29
20 48 52
20 99 101
21 28 35
21 72 75
24 32 40
24 45 51
24 70 74
25 60 65
27 36 45
28 45 53
28 96 100
30 40 50
30 72 78
32 60 68
33 44 55
33 56 65
35 84 91
36 48 60
36 77 85
39 52 65
39 80 89
40 42 58
40 75 85
40 96 104
42 56 70
45 60 75
48 55 73
48 64 80
48 90 102
51 68 85
54 72 90
56 90 106
57 76 95
60 63 87
60 80 100
60 91 109
63 84 105
65 72 97
66 88 110
69 92 115
72 96 120
75 100 125
80 84 116
```

Figure 3.5: Output of Integer Solutions for $A^2 + B^2 = C^2$

The output shown in Figure 3.5 is produced by a program that displays output in a linear fashion. This method makes reading and understanding the output very inconvenient. To reduce the excessive length of the printout, we can display multiple solutions per line. For example, we can add an output-control variable B that will cause the program to print three sets of numbers across the page, before advancing to the next line. To do this, we must slightly modify the earlier flowcharts, as shown in Figure 3.6. This modification leads to the listing and output displayed in Figures 3.7 and 3.8, respectively. Since ATARI BASIC lacks the usual TAB( ) command for cursor positioning, vertical alignment of output is accomplished by embedding the numbers (varying from one to three digits) in strings of fixed length.

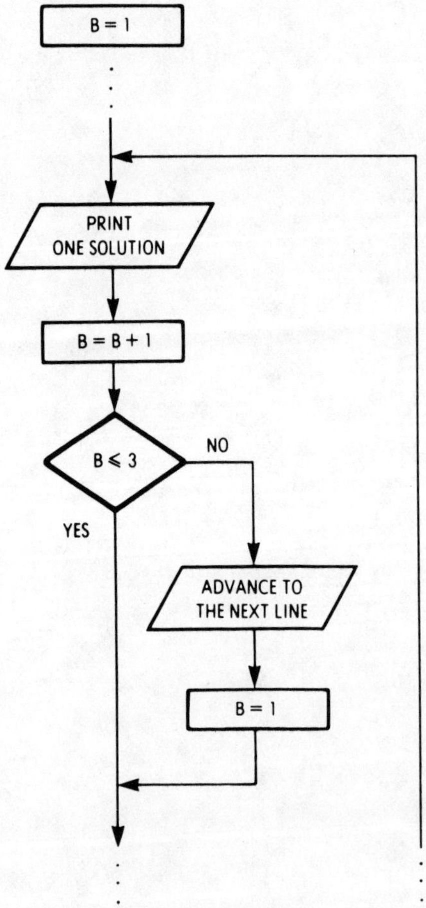

Figure 3.6: Flowchart for Improving Output Format

```
90 DIM V$(10)
100 N=100
105 B=1
110 FOR I=1 TO N
120 FOR J=I+1 TO N
130 S=I*I+J*J
140 K=J
150 K=K+1
160 K2=K*K
170 IF K2<S THEN 150
180 IF K2>S THEN 200
191 V=I:W=2:GOSUB 1000
192 V=J:W=4:GOSUB 1000
193 V=K:W=4:GOSUB 1000
195 IF B<=2 THEN PRINT " I ";
196 B=B+1
197 IF B<=3 THEN 200
198 PRINT
199 B=1
200 NEXT J
210 NEXT I
400 END
1000 REM .    SUBROUTINE TO RIGHT-
1010 REM .    JUSTIFY  A VALUE,V, IN
1020 REM .    A FIELD OF WIDTH W AND
1025 REM .    PRINT IT.
1030 V$="          "
1040 V$(W-LEN(STR$(V))+1,W)=STR$(V)
1045 PRINT V$(1,W);
1050 RETURN
```

Figure 3.7: Program Modified for Improved Output Format

```
 3  4   5 I  5  12  13 I  6  8  10
 7 24  25 I  8  15  17 I  9 12  15
 9 40  41 I 10  24  26 I 11 60  61
12 16  20 I 12  35  37 I 13 84  85
14 48  50 I 15  20  25 I 15 36  39
16 30  34 I 16  63  65 I 18 24  30
18 80  82 I 20  21  29 I 20 48  52
20 99 101 I 21  28  35 I 21 72  75
24 32  40 I 24  45  51 I 24 70  74
25 60  65 I 27  36  45 I 28 45  53
28 96 100 I 30  40  50 I 30 72  78
32 60  68 I 33  44  55 I 33 56  65
35 84  91 I 36  48  60 I 36 77  85
39 52  65 I 39  80  89 I 40 42  58
40 75  85 I 40  96 104 I 42 56  70
45 60  75 I 48  55  73 I 48 64  80
48 90 102 I 51  68  85 I 54 72  90
56 90 106 I 57  76  95 I 60 63  87
60 80 100 I 60  91 109 I 63 84 105
65 72  97 I 66  88 110 I 69 92 115
72 96 120 I 75 100 125 I 80 84 116
```

Figure 3.8: Improved Output Format

3.2 Armstrong Numbers

Numbers that are equal to the sum of the cubes of their digits are known as Armstrong numbers. For example, 153 is an Armstrong number, since

$$153 = 1^3 + 5^3 + 3^3$$

Exercise: Write a program that outputs all Armstrong numbers between 1 and 2,000.

Analysis: To determine whether or not a number is an Armstrong number, we must take each of the digits making up the number (e.g., 1, 5 and 3) and then calculate the sum of the cubes of those digits.

To obtain the ones digit, we compute the remainder of the number, after it has been divided by ten. For example, if I is the number, we calculate:

```
Q = INT(I/10)
R = I - 10*Q
```

and R is now the ones digit.

To get the tens digit, we repeat the same calculation using Q:

```
Q1 = INT(Q/10)
R = I - 10*Q1
```

and R is now the tens digit.

This same process is repeated until we get a zero quotient. If we limit ourselves to numbers up to 2,000, we will never exceed four digits.

Rather than calculating Q1, Q2, Q3 and so on, the operation may be carried out as follows:

1. Set K = I and S = 0
2. Compute Q = INT(K/10)
   R = K − 10*Q
   Set S = S + R^3
   Set K = Q for the next iteration
   If K>0 go back to 2; if not, go to 3.
3. Check to see if S = I

This leads us to the flowchart shown in Figure 3.9.

The listing given in Figure 3.10 corresponds to the flowchart in Figure 3.9. The sample output displayed in Figure 3.11 shows that Armstrong numbers are not numerous.

R is one the digits of I. We add R cubed to S (S is the sum of the cubes of the previous digits).

When K = 0 we have gone through all the digits of 1.

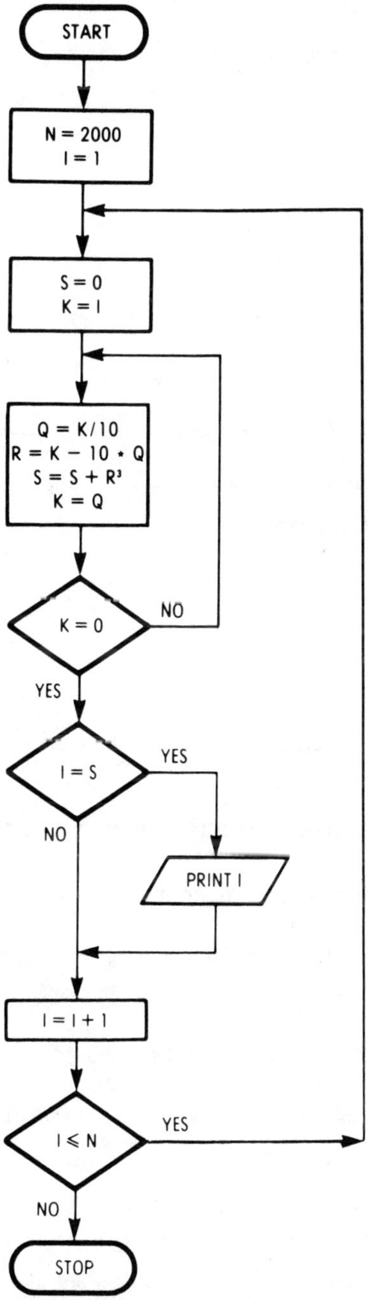

Figure 3.9: Flowchart for Determining Armstrong Numbers

```
10 N=2000
20 PRINT "ARMSTRONG NUMBERS"
25 PRINT "BETWEEN 1 AND 2000"
30 PRINT
40 FOR I=1 TO N
50 S=0
60 K=I
70 Q=INT(K/10)
80 R=K-10*Q
90 S=S+R*R*R
100 K=Q
110 IF K<>0 THEN 70
120 IF I<>S THEN 130
125 PRINT I
130 NEXT I
140 END
```

Figure 3.10: Armstrong Numbers Program

```
ARMSTRONG NUMBERS
BETWEEN 1 AND 2000

1
153
370
371
407
```

Figure 3.11: Output of Armstrong Numbers

3.3 Partitioning a Fraction into Egyptian Fractions

A fraction that has a numerator of 1 is said to be an Egyptian fraction[(2)] (for example, $\frac{1}{3}$, $\frac{1}{10}$ etc).

A fraction that has a numerator that is smaller than its denominator is called a proper fraction.

Exercise: Partition a proper fraction into a sum of Egyptian fractions.

Analysis: We propose to use the Fibonacci maximal algorithm[(3)] to solve this problem.

[(2)]Such fractions were used by the ancient Egyptians, because they lacked practical methods for handling other types of fractions.

[(3)]Fibonacci: Leonardo da Pisa, known by the name of Fibonacci, was born in Pisa around 1175 and published this algorithm in 1202.

Let us assume that you are given the fraction $\frac{A}{B}$ to decompose. To determine the first fraction of the decomposition we will use the largest Egyptian fraction that has a value lower than $\frac{A}{B}$. We will subtract this fraction from $\frac{A}{B}$ and continue this process until a 0 remainder is encountered.

In this example:

$$A = 2 \qquad B = 3 \qquad \frac{A}{B} = \frac{2}{3}$$

the largest Egyptian fraction occurring here is $\frac{1}{2}$, i.e.:

$$\frac{A}{B} - \frac{1}{2} = \frac{2}{3} - \frac{1}{2} = \frac{1}{6}$$

This gives the desired partition:

$$\frac{2}{3} = \frac{1}{2} + \frac{1}{6}$$

The decomposition is not always as simple as in the previous example. For example, for the fraction $\frac{8}{11}$ we obtain:

$$\frac{8}{11} = \frac{1}{2} + \frac{1}{5} + \frac{1}{55} + \frac{1}{110}$$

Exercise: Construct a program that partitions a fraction into Egyptian fractions using the Fibonacci algorithm. Pay particular attention to formatting the output. We will soon discuss the limitations of this program and some precautions to be taken.

Solution: At first this problem appears to be very simple. We must:

- Find the largest Egyptian fraction less than $\frac{A}{B}$.
- Calculate the remainder fraction.

If we start with the calculation C = INT($\frac{B}{A}$), then

$$\frac{1}{C} \geqslant \frac{A}{B}$$

In this calculation, C will be very close to the desired denominator. So we just make C = C + 1 until

$$\frac{1}{C} < \frac{A}{B}$$

and then we will have the desired fraction. The remainder fraction is given by

$$\frac{A}{B} - \frac{1}{C} = \frac{A*C - B}{B*C}$$

On the basis of this analysis, we can sketch an initial flowchart. We are also ready to make one important observation: this computation can give rise to some integer variables that are large enough to cause overflow and meaningless output. The representation of integers used in any computer is of limited precision, so we must provide tests to insure that we do not exceed the precision of the computer system that we are using. In general, these tests would have to be made after every multiplication A*B or B*C; but, since B > A, we need only test the second multiplication. This brings us to the flowcharts shown in Figures 3.12 and 3.13. The algorithm we have designed will terminate successfully when the new A is zero and unsuccessfully if the new B exceeds the precision of the machine.

Note: As in the previous problems, integer variables can be used on systems that permit them. However, with microcomputers they generally have fewer significant digits than floating point numbers. Therefore, it is preferable to work with ordinary variables.

We will divide our program shown in Figure 3.14 into two parts:

1. a main program that carries out the input/output and some conditional tests.
2. a subprogram that searches (on each "iteration") for the largest admissible Egyptian fraction and computes the remainder fraction for the following iteration.

By dividing the program into two parts we have increased the number of program statements. It does, however, make the program easier to write and follow.

The flowchart shown in Figure 3.12 includes a variable L, which takes on one of two values: 0 or 1. By assigning L a value of 0 at the beginning of the program, we will avoid printing the plus sign (+) in front of the first fraction that is found. Subsequently, the variable is set to 1, and the output of each following fraction is preceded with a plus sign.

Comments on the program: The precision with which a number may be represented is fixed for any given computer. The maximum integer number possible in a computer is a constant. The program should include a parameter mechanism that can be used to protect the integrity of the output. By varying the setting of the parameter, the program may execute on computers that have different capacity limitations. Listed below are two ways to accomplish the setting of this parameter. We may either:

1. Indicate the largest integer admissible in the system using an assignment instruction or a READ/DATA instruction. (We have chosen the READ/DATA method.)

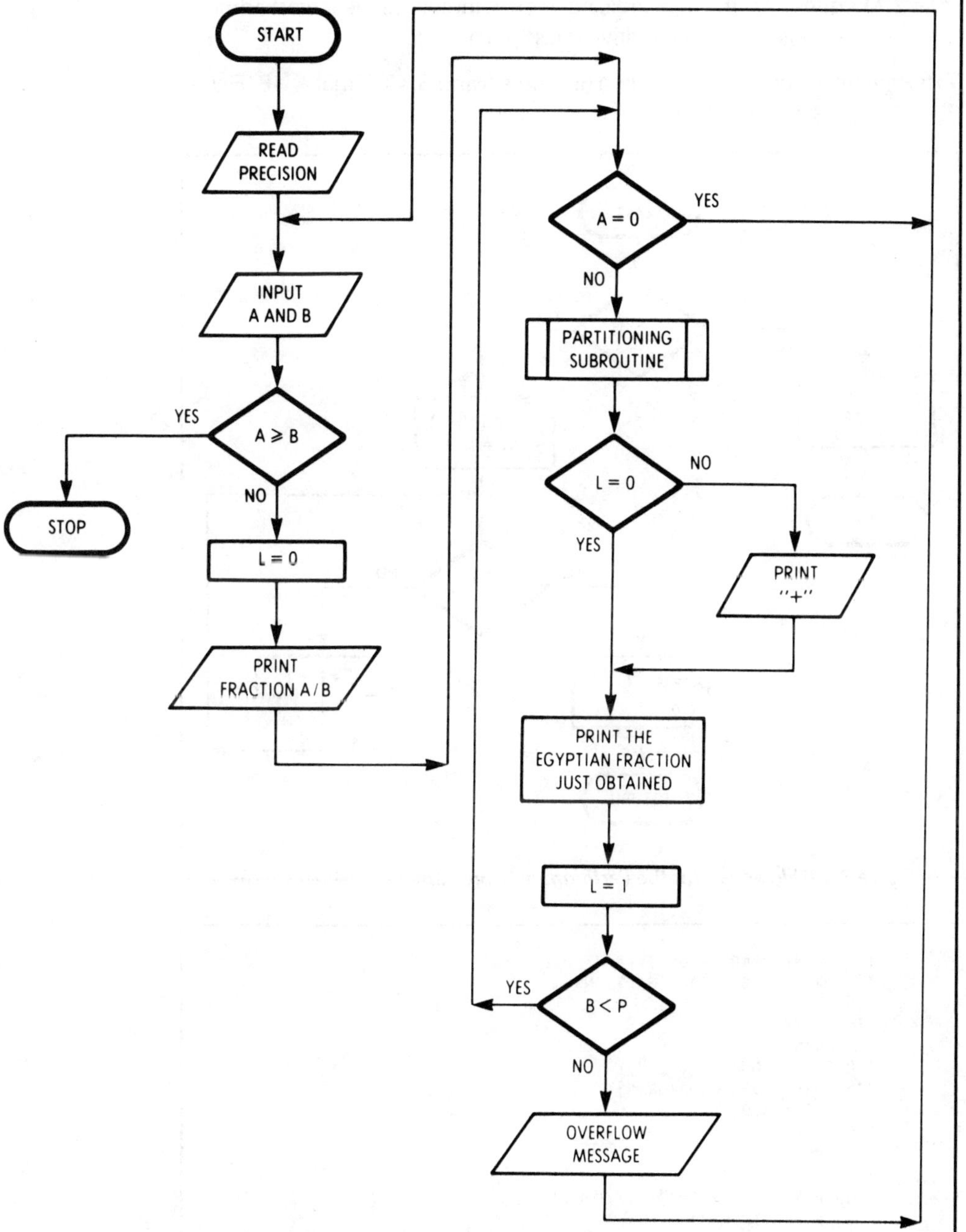

Figure 3.12: Main Flowchart for Partitioning Fractions

or:

2. Request that the user indicate at execution time the largest admissible integer. (This alternative is less practical.)

To terminate the program, input two numbers A and B, such that A ≥ B. Figure 3.15 shows a sample dialogue.

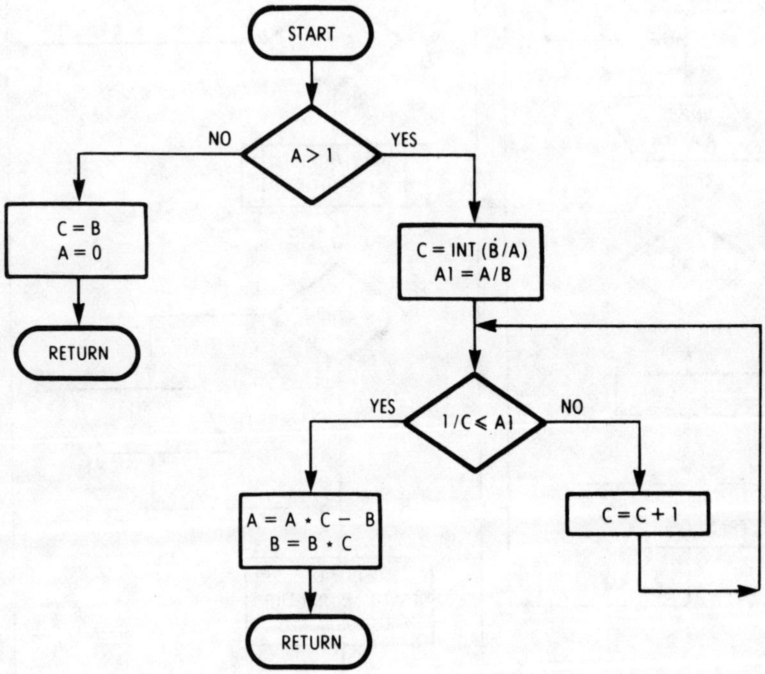

Figure 3.13: Flowchart for the Partitioning Subroutine

```
100 PRINT "PARTITION INTO ";
101 PRINT "EGYPTIAN FRACTIONS"
105 READ P
110 PRINT
120 PRINT
130 PRINT "NUMERATOR, ";
135 PRINT "DENOMINATOR ";
140 INPUT A,B
150 IF A>=B THEN 800
160 L=0
170 PRINT
180 PRINT "FRACTION ";A;"/";B;" = ";
190 IF A=0 THEN 110
```

Figure 3.14: Egyptian Fractions Program (continues)

```
200 GOSUB 500
210 IF L=0 THEN 230
220 PRINT " + ";
230 PRINT "1/";C;
235 L=1
240 IF B<P THEN 190
300 PRINT
303 PRINT "NEXT DENOMINATOR ";
305 PRINT "TOO BIG TO COMPUTE"
310 GOTO 110
500 IF A>1 THEN 600
510 C=B
520 A=0
530 RETURN
600 C=INT(B/A)
605 A1=A/B
610 IF 1/C<=A1 THEN 640
620 C=C+1
630 GOTO 610
640 A=A*C-B
650 B=B*C
670 RETURN
700 DATA 999999999
800 END
```

Figure 3.14: Egyptian Fractions Program

```
PARTITION INTO EGYPTIAN FRACTIONS


NUMERATOR, DENOMINATOR ?2,3

FRACTION 2/3 = 1/2 + 1/6

NUMERATOR, DENOMINATOR ?3,7

FRACTION 3/7 = 1/3 + 1/11 + 1/231

NUMERATOR, DENOMINATOR ?7,13

FRACTION 7/13 = 1/2 + 1/26

NUMERATOR, DENOMINATOR ?16,17

FRACTION 16/17 = 1/2 + 1/3 + 1/10 + 1/128 + 1/32640
NEXT DENOMINATOR TOO BIG TO COMPUTE


NUMERATOR, DENOMINATOR ?3,2
```

Figure 3.15: Output of Egyptian Fractions

Suggestion: Design another interactive version of this program that will allow the user to partition a proper fraction without having to do the arithmetic for each step. In response to the input of each successive Egyptian fraction, the program will compute and display the resulting remainder fraction.

3.4 Prime Numbers

One way to find prime numbers is to search for those odd numbers, starting with the number three, that cannot be divided by any other number except themselves and one. We will first explain this method and then go on to study a more refined method.

First method: Write a program that prints the first N primes. N will vary between 10 and 60. Later, focus on improving the output format.

Solution: The overall structure of the program corresponds to the flowchart shown in Figure 3.16. The instructions are as follows:

— Print the numbers 1, 2 and 3.

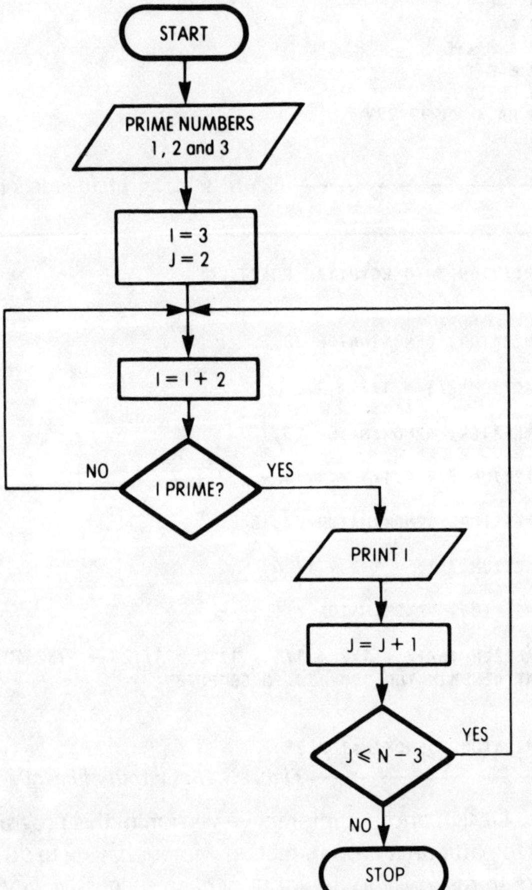

Figure 3.16: Flowchart for Finding Prime Numbers

— Then, find the other prime numbers, successively, by incrementing I by 2's since after 2 all prime numbers are odd.

To determine if I is prime, we will conduct successive tests using odd numbers until one of the following circumstances occurs:

— We get a zero remainder, which means that I is not prime.

— We get a non-zero remainder and a quotient less than or equal to the divisor, which means that I is prime.

Therefore, to answer the question, "Is I prime?", we must carry out the steps shown in the section of the flowchart displayed in Figure 3.17. We can then design a more detailed flowchart and write the program (see Figure 3.18). Figure 3.19 shows a sample output of this program.

Second method: Starting with the number five, all primes are of the form 6n ± 1, with n being an integer. Furthermore, we may choose all divisors from the set of primes already found. Write a program that takes these two observations into account.

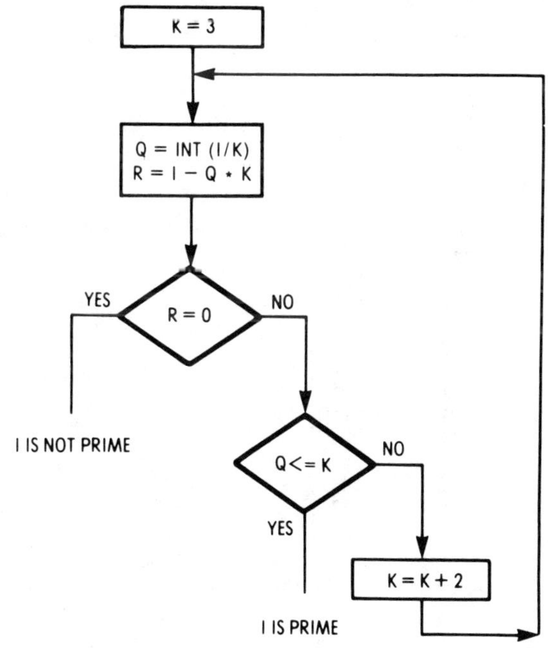

Figure 3.17: Detailed Flowchart Segment: Finding Prime Numbers

```
100 N=60
110 PRINT :PRINT "THE FIRST ";
115 PRINT N;" PRIME NUMBERS ";
117 PRINT "ARE:":PRINT
120 PRINT 1,2,3
130 I=3
140 FOR J=1 TO N-3
150 I=I+2
160 K=3
170 Q=INT(I/K)
180 R=I-Q*K
190 IF R=0 THEN 150
200 IF Q<=K THEN 230
210 K=K+2
220 GOTO 170
230 PRINT I,
234 REM PRINT IN THREE COLUMNS
235 IF J-3*INT(J/3)=0 THEN PRINT
240 NEXT J
250 END
```

Figure 3.18: Prime Numbers Program

```
THE FIRST 60 PRIME NUMBERS ARE:

1       2       3
5       7       11
13      17      19
23      29      31
37      41      43
47      53      59
61      67      71
73      79      83
89      97      101
103     107     109
113     127     131
137     139     149
151     157     163
167     173     179
181     191     193
197     199     211
223     227     229
233     239     241
251     257     263
269     271     277
```

Figure 3.19: Output of Prime Numbers

Solution: In order to confine the search for possible divisors to the primes already found, we must be able to store or save the primes. This requires using an array, and the dimensions of that array will limit the maximum number of primes that can be investigated. To use the fact that the numbers are all of the form 6n ± 1, we should note that the numbers we are seeking are not divisible by 2 or 3; hence, we need only check for divisors from 5 upward. We will divide our work into two sections:

1. a main program that initializes the first few entries in the array T of trial divisors, then computes the values of the variable A, and calls a subroutine.

2. a subroutine that checks to see if the value of the variable A is prime, and, if it is prime, stores it in the array T. (When T is full, its contents are printed out.)

This discussion leads us to the flowcharts presented in Figures 3.20 and 3.21.

The program is shown in Figure 3.22 and the sample output is displayed in Figure 3.23.

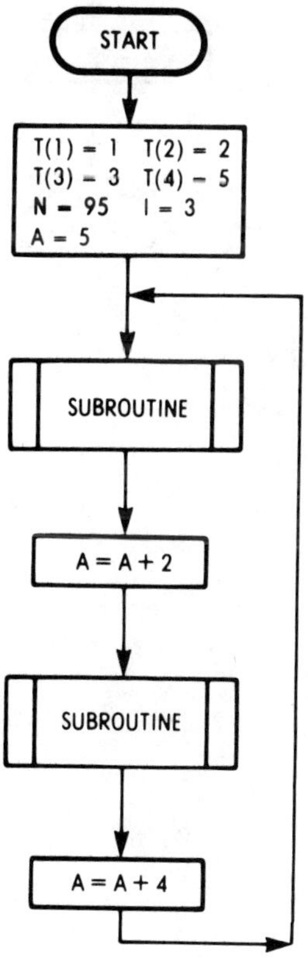

Figure 3.20: Flowchart: Second Approach to Finding Prime Numbers

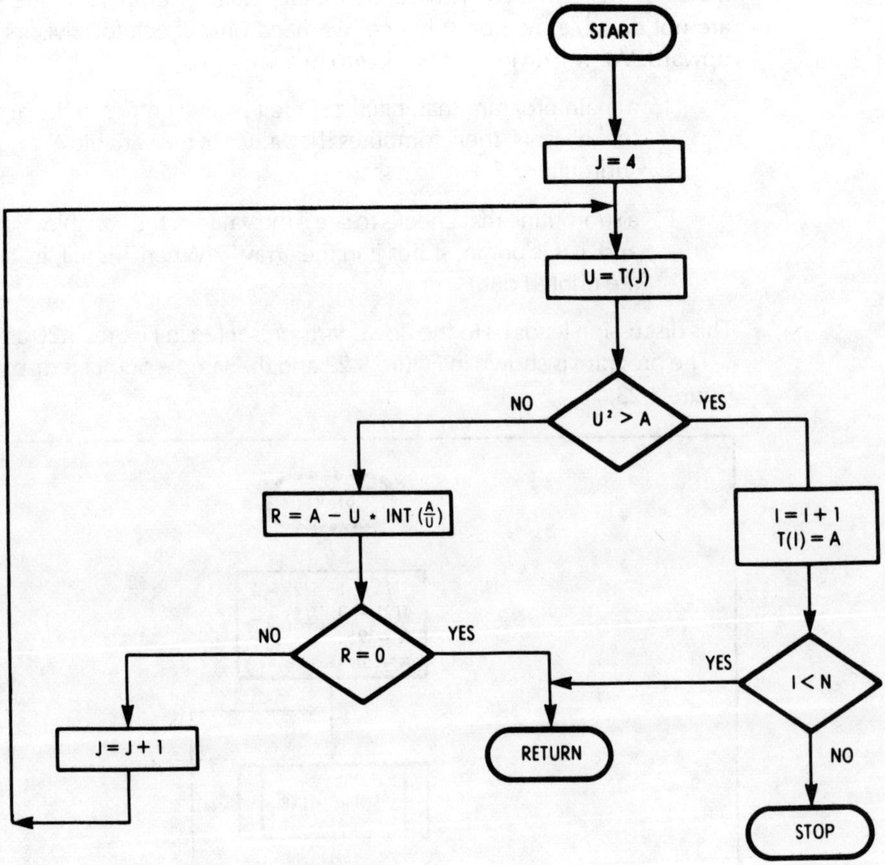

Figure 3.21: Flowchart: Subroutine for Finding Prime Numbers

```
10 N=95
90 PRINT "THE FOLLOWING LIST";
95 PRINT " CONTAINS"
97 PRINT N;" PRIME NUMBERS:"
100 PRINT
104 POKE 201,7:REM . SET PRINTOUT TAB
105 REM .            INCREMENT = 7
110 PRINT 1,2,3,
140 DIM T(N)
150 T(1)=1:T(2)=2:T(3)=3:T(4)=5
160 A=5:I=3
170 GOSUB 500
180 A=A+2
190 GOSUB 500
200 A=A+4
210 GOTO 170
495 REM
500 REM .          SUBROUTINE
505 J=4
510 U=T(J)
520 IF (U*U>A) THEN 560
530 R=A-INT(A/U)*U
540 IF R=0 THEN RETURN
550 J=J+1:GOTO 510
560 I=I+1
570 T(I)=A
635 PRINT A,
650 REM FORMAT OUTPUT INTO 5 COLUMNS
660 IF I-5*INT(I/5)=0 THEN PRINT
670 IF I<N THEN RETURN
680 END
```

Figure 3.22: Second Prime Numbers Program

```
THE FOLLOWING LIST CONTAINS
95 PRIME NUMBERS:

1       2       3       5       7
11      13      17      19      23
29      31      37      41      43
47      53      59      61      67
71      73      79      83      89
97      101     103     107     109
113     127     131     137     139
149     151     157     163     167
173     179     181     191     193
197     199     211     223     227
229     233     239     241     251
257     263     269     271     277
281     283     293     307     311
313     317     331     337     347
349     353     359     367     373
379     383     389     397     401
409     419     421     431     433
439     443     449     457     461
463     467     479     487     491
```

Figure 3.23: Prime Numbers Output, Second Approach

3.5 Decomposition into Prime Factors

Dividing a number into prime factors means finding all of the prime number divisors for that number.

Elementary approach: Starting with the number two, we will look for divisors. When we find a proper divisor, we will print it out. If a divisor does not work or no longer works, we will go on to the next number.

If we encounter a quotient that is smaller than the divisor, then one of the following is true.

- If the dividend is the given number, then the given number is prime.
- If the dividend is less than the given number, then this dividend is a prime number and a divisor for that number.

Exercise: Design a program that carries out this factorization and continues to ask for another number until it receives either a negative number or a zero.

Solution: The general structure of the program is shown in the flowchart in Figure 3.24.

Let us now work out the "FACTORIZATION" section of the flowchart in detail. To implement this factorization, we can use the following algorithm:

1. Save N in N1.
2. Set the values 2, 3, 4, 5, etc. (successively), for I:
   2a. Check to see if I is a divisor of N:
   Let Q be the value of the quotient:
   If I is a proper divisor, then print I; set N = Q, and go to 2a.
   If I is not a divisor, then go to 2b.

   2b. If Q > I, increment I and go back to 2. If the quotient Q ≤ I then:
   If N = 1, the process terminates.
   If N = N1, then N is prime.
   If N < N1, then N is a divisor, and must be printed.

This approach is illustrated in the flowchart in Figure 3.25 from which we derive (with no difficulty) the actual program shown in Figure 3.26. The sample dialogue is shown in Figure 3.27.

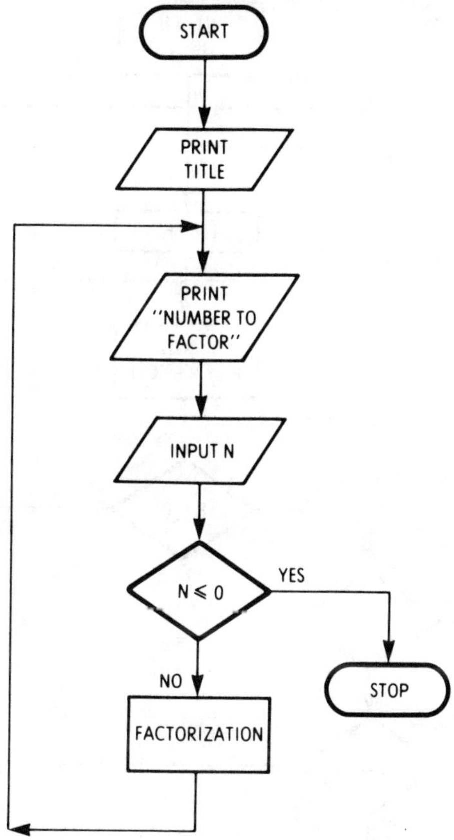

Figure 3.24: Conceptual Flowchart for Factorization

An advanced approach: The purpose of this exercise is to take the previous program example and, by providing additional information, obtain the improved output display that appears in Figure 3.28.

Solution: We begin by modifying the flowchart in Figure 3.25 to print only when the divisor is completely divided out. (The section of the flowchart enclosed in the dashed rectangle in Figure 3.25 should be replaced by the section of the flowchart that appears in Figure 3.29.)

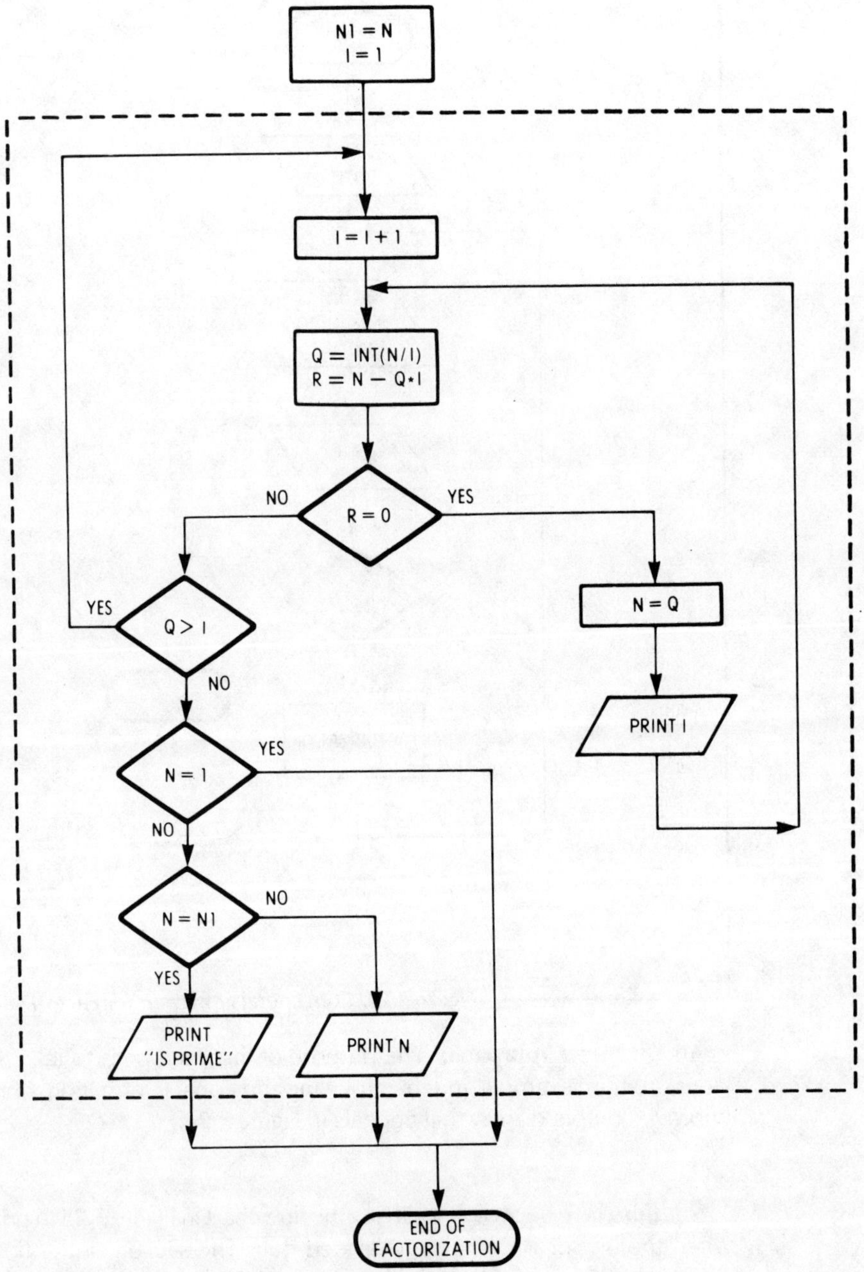

Figure 3.25: Flowchart for the Factorization Subroutine

```
120 PRINT "DECOMPOSITION INTO";
125 PRINT " PRIME FACTORS"
130 PRINT
140 PRINT "THE NUMBER TO FACTOR ";
145 INPUT N
150 IF N<=0 THEN END
160 N1=N
170 I=1
180 I=I+1
200 Q=INT(N/I)
210 R=N-Q*I
220 IF R<>0 THEN 290
230 N=Q
240 PRINT " ";I;" ";
250 GOTO 200
290 IF Q>I THEN 180
300 IF N=1 THEN 350
310 IF N<>N1 THEN 340
320 PRINT "      IS PRIME."
330 GOTO 350
340 PRINT " ";N;" ";
350 PRINT
360 GOTO 130
370 END
```

Figure 3.26: Factorization Program

```
DECOMPOSITION INTO PRIME FACTORS

THE NUMBER TO FACTOR ?12
 2  2  3

THE NUMBER TO FACTOR ?8192
 2  2  2  2  2  2  2  2  2  2  2  2  2

THE NUMBER TO FACTOR ?65784
 2  2  2  3  2741

THE NUMBER TO FACTOR ?1217
      IS PRIME.


THE NUMBER TO FACTOR ?0
```

Figure 3.27: Output from the Factorization Program

```
DECOMPOSITION INTO PRIME FACTORS

THE NUMBER TO FACTOR  ?65784
  IS DIVISIBLE BY 2     3      TIMES.
  IS DIVISIBLE BY 3     1      TIMES.
  IS DIVISIBLE BY 2741  1      TIME.


THE NUMBER TO FACTOR  ?1217
   IS PRIME.


THE NUMBER TO FACTOR  ?35427
  IS DIVISIBLE BY 3     1      TIMES.
  IS DIVISIBLE BY 7     2      TIMES.
  IS DIVISIBLE BY 241   1      TIME.


THE NUMBER TO FACTOR  ?8192
  IS DIVISIBLE BY 2      13     TIMES.


THE NUMBER TO FACTOR  ?19
   IS PRIME.


THE NUMBER TO FACTOR  ?14
  IS DIVISIBLE BY 2      1      TIMES.
  IS DIVISIBLE BY 7      1      TIME.


THE NUMBER TO FACTOR  ?0
```

Figure 3.28: Desired Output from the Advanced Approach to Factorization

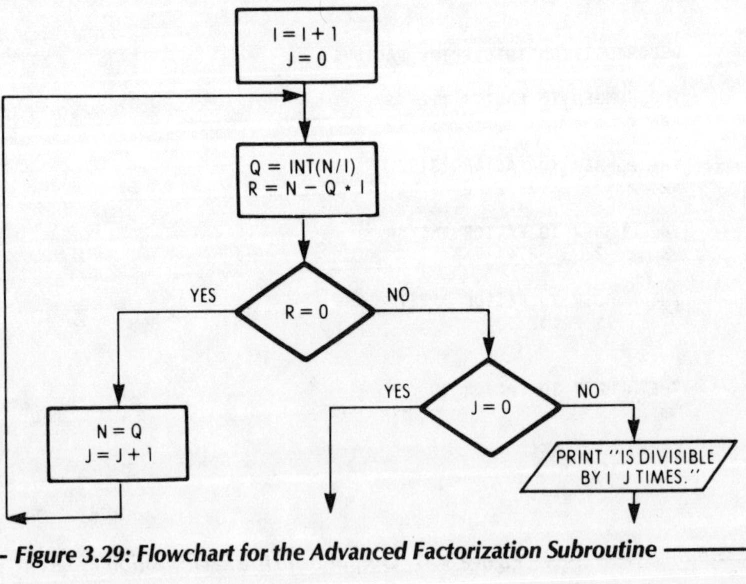

Figure 3.29: Flowchart for the Advanced Factorization Subroutine

We can now use the previous program to design a new program. In addition to the modifications indicated in Figure 3.29, we will modify the print instructions to obtain a printout like the one in Figure 3.28.

```
120 PRINT "DECOMPOSITION INTO";
125 PRINT " PRIME FACTORS"
130 PRINT
135 POKE 201,6:REM SET COLUMN WIDTH
140 PRINT "THE NUMBER TO FACTOR  ";
145 INPUT N
150 N1=N
160 IF N<=0 THEN END
170 I=1
180 I=I+1
190 J=0
200 Q=INT(N/I)
210 R=N-Q*I
220 IF R<>0 THEN 260
230 N=Q
240 J=J+1
250 GOTO 200
260 IF J=0 THEN 290
270 PRINT "  IS DIVISIBLE BY ";
275 PRINT I,
277 PRINT J,"TIMES."
280 GOTO 180
290 IF Q>I THEN 180
300 IF N=1 THEN 350
310 IF N<>N1 THEN 340
320 PRINT "   IS PRIME."
330 GOTO 350
340 PRINT "  IS DIVISIBLE BY ";
345 PRINT N,"1","TIME."
350 PRINT
360 GOTO 130
370 END
```

Figure 3.30: Advanced Factorization Program

3.6 Conversion from Base Ten to Another Base

Representing numbers in different number systems (base 10, base 8, base 2, etc.) is, for "the man on the street," an exercise in mathematics with no practical value. However, quite the contrary is true for people who are involved with programming. A task of this sort has real application, especially for those programming in assembly language.

The principle of conversion includes the following steps:

— Carry out successive divisions by the new base until a quotient is obtained that is less than the new base.

As an example, let us look at the conversion of 83 (base 10) into base 8.

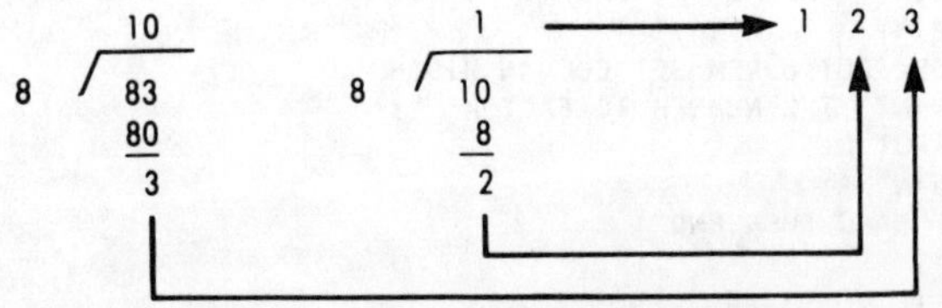

— The ones digit corresponds to the first remainder. The next digit corresponds to the remainder after the quotient has been divided by the base again. The most significant digit is the first quotient less than the base.

Thus: 83 (base 10) is 123 (base 8)
83 (base 10) is 146 (base 7)

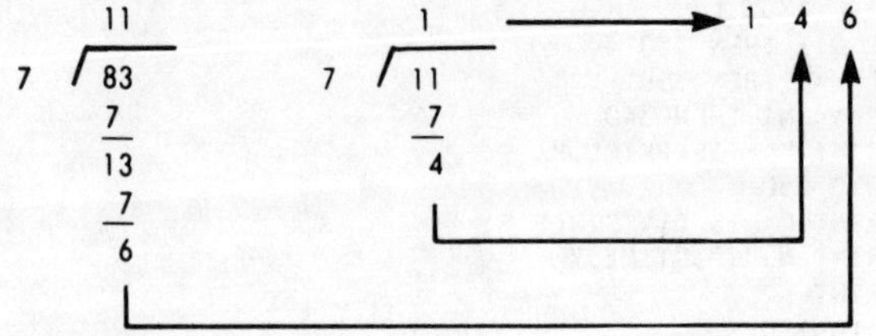

3.6.1 Conversion to a Base Less Than Ten

Exercise: Write a program that prints a conversion table for a range of numbers between two numbers F and L, as specified by the user. The conversion will be made from base 10 to some other base, B, which is less than 10.

Solution: As we shall see a little later on, the construction of this program has much in common with that of the preceding programs. For example:

— the use of "integer division"

— the computation of remainders

— the use of arrays.

To set off the general structure of the algorithm proper in a clear fashion, we will, as before, break the program into two parts: the main program, that will handle the necessary inputs and outputs, and a subroutine, that will handle the actual base conversion.

The conceptual flowchart shown in Figure 3.31 is quite straightforward.

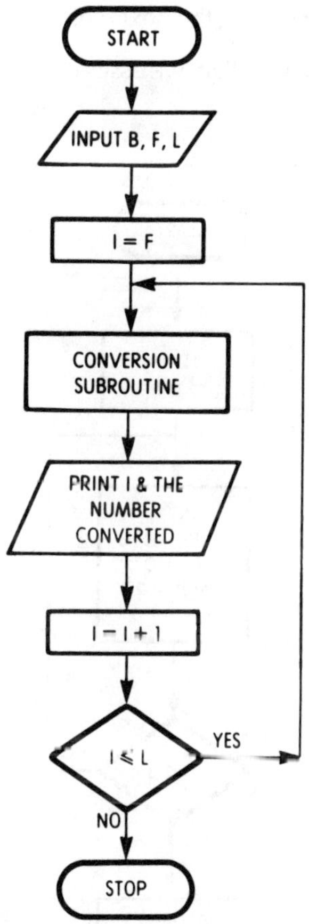

Figure 3.31: Conceptual Flowchart for Base Conversion

On the other hand, the flowchart shown in Figure 3.32 requires some explanation. For example:

- When starting a conversion, we often do not know in advance the number of digits the converted number will have. Thus, we should store the digits in the order that we compute them.

— The proposed approach will give the ones digit first, then the tens digit (or, more exactly, the coefficient of the base to the power 1), and so on. To store each digit in the array A, we initially set J = 1, and then increment J for each digit as it is found:

A(J) = R
J = J + 1 (for storing the next digit)

However, for the last digit, we assign:

A(J) = Q

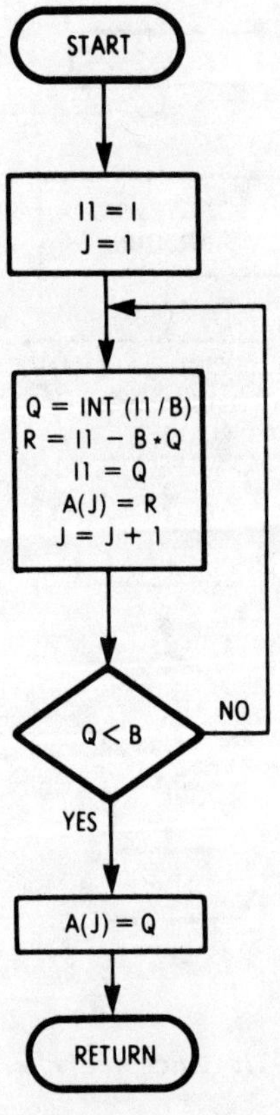

Figure 3.32: Detailed Flowchart for Base Conversion

We now understand the flowchart presented in Figure 3.32, showing the conversion subroutine and can go on to write the complete program. When printing out the converted number, we must operate in the opposite order from the order in which the digits were obtained. For example, if the converted number is 127, then table A would contain:

A(1) = 7
A(2) = 2
A(3) = 1 and J = 3

To print this out in the proper order, we would write the following instructions:

FOR D = J TO 1 STEP −1	
PRINT A(D);	*To keep on the same line.*
NEXT D	
PRINT	*To move onto the next line.*

The program appears in Figure 3.33 and the sample run appears in Figure 3.34.

```
95 DIM A(15)
100 PRINT "THE NEW BASE  ";
110 INPUT B
120 PRINT "FIRST AND LAST NUMBER TO"
125 PRINT "CONVERT  ";
130 INPUT F,L
135 POKE 201,8:REM SET COLUMN WIDTH
140 FOR I=F TO L
150 PRINT
160 GOSUB 1500
170 REM PRINT A TABLE ENTRY
180 PRINT " ";I,
190 FOR D=J TO 1 STEP -1
200 PRINT " ";A(D);" ";
210 NEXT D
220 NEXT I
230 END
1500 I1=I
1510 J=1
1520 Q=INT(I1/B)
1530 R=I1-Q*B
1535 I1=Q
1540 A(J)=R
1545 J=J+1
1550 IF Q>=B THEN 1520
1560 A(J)=Q
1570 RETURN
1580 END
```

Figure 3.33: Conversion Program for Bases Less Than 10

```
THE NEW BASE  ?2
FIRST AND LAST NUMBER TO
CONVERT  ?260,280

260      1  0  0  0  0  0  1  0  0
261      1  0  0  0  0  0  1  0  1
262      1  0  0  0  0  0  1  1  0
263      1  0  0  0  0  0  1  1  1
264      1  0  0  0  0  1  0  0  0
265      1  0  0  0  0  1  0  0  1
266      1  0  0  0  0  1  0  1  0
267      1  0  0  0  0  1  0  1  1
268      1  0  0  0  0  1  1  0  0
269      1  0  0  0  0  1  1  0  1
270      1  0  0  0  0  1  1  1  0
271      1  0  0  0  0  1  1  1  1
272      1  0  0  0  1  0  0  0  0
273      1  0  0  0  1  0  0  0  1
274      1  0  0  0  1  0  0  1  0
275      1  0  0  0  1  0  0  1  1
276      1  0  0  0  1  0  1  0  0
277      1  0  0  0  1  0  1  0  1
278      1  0  0  0  1  0  1  1  0
279      1  0  0  0  1  0  1  1  1
280      1  0  0  0  1  1  0  0  0
```

Figure 3.34: Output—Conversion to Base 2

3.6.2 Conversion to a Base Greater Than Ten

Exercise: Extend the program to convert and print a conversion table for a base greater than 10. In this case, represent the "digit" 10 by the letter A, 11 by the letter B, and so on.

Solution: For this problem we will use character strings. For example, we can create a string, B$, such that:

```
B$ = "0123456789ABCDEF"
```

To obtain the proper "digit" to print for the value A(L) (of the preceding example), we simply extract the character in position A(L) + 1 of the string B$. (The digit 0 corresponds to the first character of B$.) In most BASICs, but not ATARI, this is done by using string functions, such as SUBSTR or MID$ (the function used depends upon the BASIC system used). In some BASICs, we could write:

```
PRINT MID$ (B$,A(L) + 1,1);
```

to print out the appropriate character. The results are represented in the program shown in Figure 3.35. A sample run is shown in Figure 3.36.

```
10    REM BASE CONVERSION PROGRAM
50    DIM A(15)
90   B$ = "0123456789ABCDEFGHIJKLMN"
100   INPUT "THE NEW BASE? ";B
120   PRINT "FIRST AND LAST";
125   PRINT " NUMBER TO"
130   INPUT "CONVERT? ";F,L
140   FOR I = F TO L
150   PRINT
160   GOSUB 1500
170   REM PRINT A TABLE ENTRY
180   PRINT " ";I; TAB( 7);
190   FOR D = J TO 1 STEP  - 1
200   PRINT  MID$ (B$,A(D) + 1,1);
210   NEXT D
220   NEXT I
230   STOP
1480  REM BASE CONVERSION
1500 I1 = I
1510 J = 1
1520 Q =  INT (I1 / B)
1530 R = I1 - Q * B
1535 I1 = Q
1540 A(J) = R
1545 J = J + 1
1550  IF Q >  = B THEN 1520
1560 A(J) = Q
1570  RETURN
1580  END
```

Figure 3.35: Conversion Program for Bases Greater Than 10 in Microsoft-type BASIC

```
THE NEW BASE? 16
FIRST AND LAST NUMBER TO
CONVERT? 1023,1035

 1023 3FF
 1024 400
 1025 401
 1026 402
 1027 403
 1028 404
 1029 405
 1030 406
 1031 407
 1032 408
 1033 409
 1034 40A
 1035 40B
```

Figure 3.36: Sample Output from Conversion Program

ATARI case: Some systems, including ATARI, do not provide the functions SUBSTR or MID$. Instead, they provide another feature: after declaring a maximum length for the string B$ at the beginning of the program, a substring may be extracted by writing the expression:

B$(I,J)

in which I represents the position of the first character in the substring and J represents the position of the last character in the substring. In a system with this feature we write:

A1 = A(L) + 1
PRINT B$(A1,A1)

to print out a single character. The program and output, shown in Figures 3.37 and 3.38, illustrate this approach.

```
10 REM BASE CONVERSION PROGRAM
20 REM AUTHOR: J. P. LAMOITIER
30 DIM A(15),B$(30)
40 B$="0123456789ABCDEFGHIJKLMNOPQR"
95 PRINT "THE NEW BASE  ";
100 INPUT B
110 PRINT
120 PRINT "FIRST AND LAST NUMBER TO"
122 PRINT "CONVERT  ";
123 INPUT F,L
125 PRINT
130 PRINT "BASE 10   BASE ";B
135 POKE 201,12
140 FOR I=F TO L
150 PRINT
160 GOSUB 1500
170 REM PRINT A TABLE ENTRY
180 PRINT " ";I,
190 FOR D=J TO 1 STEP -1
195 A1=A(D)+1
200 PRINT B$(A1,A1);
210 NEXT D
220 NEXT I
230 END
1480 REM BASE CONVERSION
1500 I1=I
1510 J=1
1520 Q=INT(I1/B)
1530 R=I1-Q*B
1535 I1=Q
1540 A(J)=R
1545 J=J+1
1550 IF Q>=B THEN 1520
1560 A(J)=Q
1570 RETURN
1580 END
```

Figure 3.37: Conversion Program for ATARI

```
THE NEW BASE  ?16

FIRST AND LAST NUMBER TO
CONVERT  ?12,20

BASE 10   BASE 16

 12         0C
 13         0D
 14         0E
 15         0F
 16         10
 17         11
 18         12
 19         13
 20         14
```

Figure 3.38: Output from Revised Conversion Program

Conclusion

The exercises of varying difficulties presented in this chapter illustrate the usefulness of constructing flowcharts section by section. If possible, it is best to proceed from the general structure of the problem, progressively elaborating the flowchart(s) until the point is reached where a program follows easily.

For any particular problem, the solution is, in general, not unique in either the method or the program used. The programs presented in this book are not necessarily designed to be efficient; instead, they are designed to be easily understood and to correspond very closely to a flowchart. As you gain experience, you may reduce the time spent drawing flowcharts by proceeding directly from a conceptual flowchart to the design of a program.

CHAPTER 4

Elementary Exercises in Geometry

Introduction

Euclidean geometry has few numerical applications, but analytic geometry offers many opportunities for such calculations. This chapter will present elementary exercises from analytic geometry which will highlight the capabilities of a computer.

The exercises were designed for their practical application and simplicity. The flowcharts and programs presented with the exercises are straightforward and easy to construct. The calculations involved in performing the exercises, however, must be accurate, which is sometimes a difficult task if performed manually. On the other hand, a computer can be used to perform the calculations rapidly and with a high degree of accuracy.

After completing the exercises in this chapter, the advanced programmer may go on to design exercises that are more complex or better-suited to a particular application.

4.1 The Area and Perimeter of a Triangle

To calculate the area of a given triangle we will first measure the length of each side of the triangle and then apply Hero's formula:

$$A = \sqrt{S (S - A) (S - B) (S - C)}$$

where A, B, and C are the lengths of the three sides and

$$S = \frac{A + B + C}{2}$$

Exercise: Given A, B, and C, write a program that computes the perimeter and area of the triangle.

Solution: Since we know A, B, and C, the calculation is straightforward. The perimeter is computed using P = A + B + C. Then, the half-perimeter is calculated, and Hero's formula is applied. In the program shown in Figure 4.1, P first represents the perimeter and then the half-perimeter.

A sample run is provided in Figure 4.2.

```
10 PRINT "THE LENGTHS OF ";
12 PRINT "THE SIDES OF A"
15 PRINT "TRIANGLE  ";
20 INPUT A,B,C
30 P=A+B+C
40 PRINT "PERIMETER = ";P
45 PRINT
50 P=0.5*P
60 S=SQR(P*(P-A)*(P-B)*(P-C))
70 PRINT "AREA = ";S
80 END
```

Figure 4.1: Program for Computing the Area of a Triangle

```
THE LENGTHS OF THE SIDES OF A
TRIANGLE  ?4,5,7
PERIMETER = 16

AREA = 9.79795897
```

Figure 4.2: Sample Run for Program Computing the Area of a Triangle

Comments: To learn more about the conventions of BASIC, let us take a closer look at the program in Figure 4.1:

Line 10: A semicolon or comma placed at the end of the line supresses the automatic carriage return and line-feed, allowing the input to be typed on the same line.

Line 40: PRINT "PERIMETER = ";P. In this case, the semicolon is used to cause the numerical value of P to print out immediately next to the space following the equal sign.

Line 45: A PRINT instruction with no parameters produces a blank line. This practice avoids overcrowded or cramped printouts.

Line 50: After the value of the perimeter has been printed, P is no longer needed, thus, it can be used to store the half-perimeter needed for the next calculation.

Criticism of this program: If the lengths given for A, B, and C in the program shown in Figure 4.1 are not valid lengths for the sides of a triangle (for example, if the sides given were 10, 20 and 40), there would be no way for the computer to indicate this error. Instead, the program would attempt to find the square root of a negative number, which, in general, would be detected by the computer in some inconvenient way.

To remedy this problem, we need to insert a validity check: the length of the longest side should not exceed the sum of the lengths of the two other sides. A test for this condition could be added, or, more directly, we might check that:

$$(S - A)(S - B)(S - C) > 0$$

Figure 4.3 shows the program in Figure 4.1 after such a test has been added.

A sample run appears in Figure 4.4.

```
10 PRINT "THE LENGTHS OF THE ";
15 PRINT "SIDES OF A"
18 PRINT "TRIANGLE  ";
20 INPUT A,B,C
30 P=A+B+C
40 PRINT "PERIMETER = ";P
45 PRINT
50 P=0.5*P
```

Figure 4.3: Program with Data Validity Check (continues)

```
54 P1=(P-A)*(P-B)*(P-C)
56 IF P1>=0 THEN 60
57 PRINT "IMPOSSIBLE SET OF";
58 PRINT " SIDES"
59 GO TO 80
60 S=SQR(P*(P-A)*(P-B)*(P-C))
70 PRINT "AREA = ";S
80 END
```

Figure 4.3: Program with Data Validity Check

```
THE LENGTHS OF THE SIDES OF A
TRIANGLE  ?10,20,40
PERIMETER = 70

IMPOSSIBLE SET OF SIDES
```

Figure 4.4: Sample Run for Data Validity Check Program

4.2 Determination of a Circle Passing Through Three Given Points

Exercise: Given the Cartesian coordinates of three points M_1, M_2, and M_3, determine the circle that passes through the three points; i.e., find the coordinates of the center and the length of the radius.

Mathematical analysis: Let (X_1, Y_1), (X_2, Y_2) and (X_3, Y_3) be the coordinates of M_1, M_2, and M_3, respectively. The slope of the straight line that joins M_1 and M_2 is given by:

$$\frac{Y_2 - Y_1}{X_2 - X_1}$$

Thus, the slope of the perpendicular to this line is given by:

$$-\frac{X_2 - X_1}{Y_2 - Y_1}$$

The equation of the bisector of the segment M_1M_2 is:

$$Y = \frac{Y_1 + Y_2}{2} - \frac{X_2 - X_1}{Y_2 - Y_1}\left(X - \frac{X_1 + X_2}{2}\right)$$

Similarly, the equation of the bisector of the segment M_1M_3 is:

$$Y = \frac{Y_1 + Y_2}{2} - \frac{X_3 - X_1}{Y_3 - Y_1}\left(X - \frac{X_1 + X_3}{2}\right)$$

These two equations can be written in the form:

$$Y = K_2X + H_2$$

$$Y = K_3X + H_3$$

where:

$$K_2 = -\frac{X_2 - X_1}{Y_2 - Y_1}$$

$$K_3 = -\frac{X_3 - X_1}{Y_3 - Y_1}$$

$$H_2 = \frac{Y_1 + Y_2}{2} + \frac{X_2^2 - X_1^2}{2(Y_2 - Y_1)}$$

$$H_3 = \frac{Y_1 + Y_2}{2} + \frac{X_3^2 - X_1^2}{2(Y_2 - Y_1)}$$

Solving this set of simultaneous linear equations, we can write the coordinates of the center, I, of the circle as follows:

$$X_0 = \frac{H_3 - H_2}{K_2 - K_3}$$

$$Y_0 = \frac{K_3H_2 - K_2H_3}{K_3 - K_2}$$

From the coordinates (X_0, Y_0) of the center I we obtain the length, R, of the radius:

$$R = \sqrt{(X_1 - X_0)^2 + (Y_1 - Y_0)^2}$$

Flowchart: Constructing a flowchart for this problem is not difficult; we simply follow the order of the calculations (see Figure 4.5). Figure 4.6 shows the program. A sample run appears in Figure 4.7.

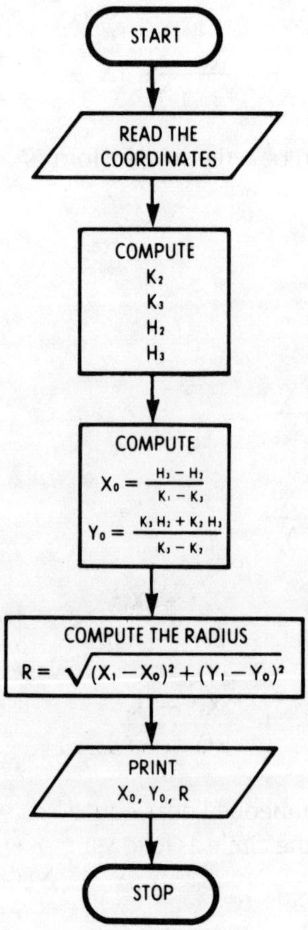

Figure 4.5: Flowchart for Finding the Circle that Passes Through Three Points

```
100 PRINT "DETERMINATION OF ";
102 PRINT "A CIRCLE PASSING "
104 PRINT "THROUGH 3 POINTS"
110 PRINT
120 REM THE COORDINATES OF THE
122 REM 3 POINTS MUST BE PLACED
124 REM IN A DATA INSTRUCTION
126 REM PRIOR TO EXECUTION
127 REM
```

Figure 4.6: Circle Program (continues)

```
130 READ X1,Y1,X2,Y2,X3,Y3
140 K2=-(X2-X1)/(Y2-Y1)
150 K3=-(X3-X1)/(Y3-Y1)
155 D=K3-K2
160 IF D=0 THEN 230
170 H2=0.5*(Y1+Y2+(X2*X2-X1*X1)/(Y2-Y1))
180 H3=0.5*(Y1+Y3+(X3*X3-X1*X1)/(Y3-Y1))
190 X0=(H2-H3)/D
200 Y0=(K3*H2-K2*H3)/D
210 R=SQR((X1-X0)^2+(Y1-Y0)^2)
220 PRINT "X0= ";X0;
222 PRINT "   Y0=";Y0;
224 PRINT "   R=";R
225 GOTO 250
230 PRINT "COLLINEAR POINTS, ";
235 PRINT "HENCE NO SOLUTION"
240 DATA 2,-1,0,1,2,3
250 END
```

Figure 4.6: Circle Program

```
DETERMINATION OF A CIRCLE PASSING
THROUGH 3 POINTS

X0= 2    Y0=1    R=1.99999999
```

Figure 4.7: Output from Circle Program

4.3 Computing the Length of a Fence

Often fields and plots of land have a geometrical form corresponding to a polygon (a rectangle, for example). Let us assume it is necessary to know the length of the perimeter, for example, in order to determine the cost of a fence for a specific plot of land.

Exercise: We have been given the Cartesian coordinates of each of the vertices (corners) of a polygonal field. We now want to write a program that computes the amount of fencing needed in order to enclose the field.

Solution: This exercise consists of calculating the length of each side and then computing the sum of the sides. If X(I),Y(I) are the coordinates of the vertex I, the length of the boundary between I and I + 1 is as follows:

$$\sqrt{(Y(I+1) - Y(I))^2 + (X(I+1) - X(I))^2}$$

Therefore, we first need to read the number of vertices, N, which is equal to the number of sides, and then read successively the pairs (X(I),Y(I)). After that we can do the computation.

We must not forget that the last side has as its ends the vertices N and 1. This information is shown in the flowchart in Figure 4.8.

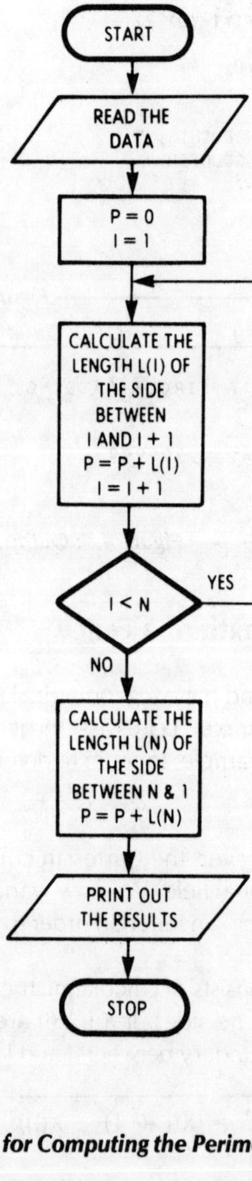

Figure 4.8: Flowchart for Computing the Perimeter of a Polygon

The program shown in Figure 4.9 is divided into several parts:

- a main program, which does not include any of the functions that appear in the flowchart.
- three subroutines, which do the following:
  - read the data
  - calculate the length of each side and the perimeter
  - print the data and results.

```
100 REM COMPUTATION OF THE
105 REM LENGTH OF A FENCE
110 REM
120 DIM X(100),Y(100),L(100)
130 PRINT "THE PERIMETER OF A";
140 PRINT " POLYGON":PRINT
150 GOSUB 400
160 GOSUB 500
170 GOSUB 600
180 DATA 5
190 DATA 1,3,4,6,8,6,11,5,11,0
200 END
390 REM READ THE VERTICES
400 READ N
410 FOR I=1 TO N
420 READ X,Y:X(I)=X:Y(I)=Y
430 NEXT I
440 RETURN
490 REM COMPUTE THE LENGTH
495 REM OF THE PERIMETER
500 P=0
510 FOR I=1 TO N-1
520 L(I)=SQR((X(I)-X(I+1))^2+(Y(I+1)-Y(I))^2)
530 P=P+L(I)
540 NEXT I
550 L(N)=SQR((X(N)-X(1))^2+(Y(N)-Y(1))^2)
560 P=P+L(N)
570 RETURN
590 REM PRINT OUT THE RESULTS
595 POKE 201,8:REM TABS EVERY 8 COLS.
600 POKE 201,8:REM TABS EVERY 8 COLS.
605 PRINT "VERTEX","X","Y","LENGTH"
610 PRINT
620 FOR I=1 TO N
630 PRINT " ";I,X(I),Y(I),L(I)
640 NEXT I
650 PRINT
660 PRINT
675 PRINT ,"    PERIMETER = ";P
680 RETURN
690 END
```

Figure 4.9: Perimeter Program

This type of organization was not really necessary for the short, simple program presented here. It was used to serve as a guide for handling longer programs.

Note: In the program the symbol ^ is used to indicate powers of a number. Another equivalent form is ↑. Other BASICs use **.

Figure 4.10 shows a sample run.

```
THE PERIMETER OF A POLYGON

VERTEX  X       Y           LENGTH

1       1       3           4.24264065
2       4       6           3.99999995
3       8       6           3.16227764
4       11      5           4.99999993
5       11      0           10.44030646


                PERIMETER = 26.84522463
```

Figure 4.10: Output from Perimeter Program

4.4 Plotting a Curve

A printer or a typewriter may sometimes be used to plot data when an actual plotter is not available. The problem is to find a method that will produce reasonably good graphs.

Exercise: Write a program for plotting curves in the following stages:

1. Determine the easiest way to plot a curve Y = F(X) with X varying between two given values XMIN and XMAX. How can the operation be performed to minimize round-off errors?
2. Construct a flowchart; then write the program.
3. Try to plot different functions such as:

$e^{\frac{-X}{2}} \cos 2X$ for X from 0 to 10

$e^{\frac{-x^2}{2}}$ for X from -2 to $+2$

$\frac{\sin x}{x}$ for X from -3π to $+3\pi$ (plotted by Figure 4.12)

Solution: First, keep in mind that with a printer it is impossible, except in special cases, to "roll back" the paper. However, we want to be able to increment X. The simplest method is to choose the Y-axis to be horizontal and pointing toward the right and the X-axis to be vertical and pointing toward the bottom of the page (as shown in Figure 4.11).

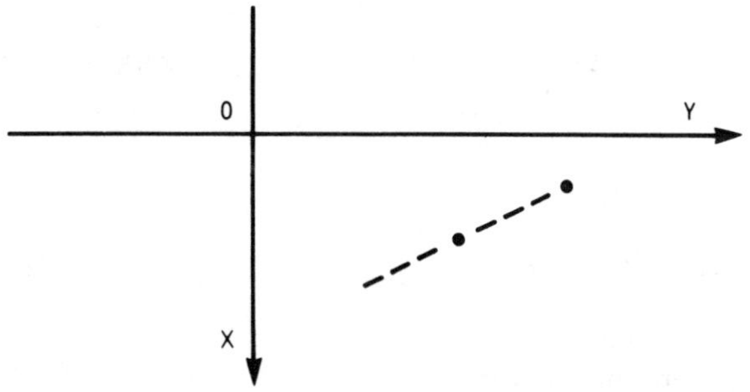

Figure 4.11: Orientation of X- and Y-Axes for Plotting a Curve

The following problems must be addressed:

- scaling the axes
- finding a way to determine for a given value of Y, the number of blanks to issue before printing a point.

These two questions require rounding the data to the nearest print position because the standard printer or typewriter can only move an integral number of columns. For example, if we needed to advance a distance of YDIST = 8.60 spaces, we would actually have to advance the printer or typewriter nine spaces. If on the other hand, YDIST = 8.40, the typewriter or printer would advance only eight spaces. Thus, in computing the column number, the following calculation is necessary:

```
YCOL = INT(YDIST + .5)
```

to obtain the appropriate rounding.

Second, before drawing the flowchart we must determine the position of the axes and the scaling factor: how do we pass from the theoretical Y to the actual Y on the terminal?

As Y varies from YMIN to YMAX, YDIST must vary proportionately from 1 to L (the maximum number of characters per line). The (linear) relation is:

$$\text{YDIST} = \frac{\text{Y} - \text{YMIN}}{\text{YMAX} - \text{YMIN}}(\text{L} - 1) + 1$$

or

$$\text{YDIST} = \underbrace{\left(\frac{\text{L} - 1}{\text{YMAX} - \text{YMIN}}\right)}_{\text{A}} * \text{Y} + \underbrace{\left(\frac{-\text{YMIN}\,(\text{L} - 1)}{\text{YMAX} - \text{YMIN}} + 1\right)}_{\text{C}}$$

which is of the form

$$\text{YDIST} = \text{A} * \text{Y} + \text{C}$$

with A and C constant.

Applying the rounding formula:

```
YCOL = INT (YDIST + .5) = INT (A * Y + C + .5)
YCOL = INT (A * Y + B)
```

which is used in the program in Figure 4.12. Notice that the constants, A and B, are calculated only once (outside the loop) to save time.

AXCOL is the column number of the X axis, (i.e., the line Y = 0). If it is off the paper (lines 240–250), then it is flagged (set = –1) and not plotted (line 620). Lines 630–635 plot the Y axis when (and if) X = 0. (See Figure 4.13.)

```
100 REM PROGRAM TO PLOT CURVES
105 REM ON THE TERMINAL
107 REM
110 REM THE FUNCTION Y=F(X) IN THE
115 REM SUBROUTINE AT LINE 140
120 REM DEFINES THE CURVE TO PLOT
130 GOTO 154
140 REM THE FUNCTION TO PLOT
142 IF X=0 THEN Y=1:GOTO 150
145 Y=SIN(X)/X
150 RETURN
152 REM
154 PI=3.14159
155 XMIN=-3*PI
160 XMAX=3*PI
165 XINC=0.2*PI
170 YMIN=-0.4
175 YMAX=1.2
```

Figure 4.12: Curve-Plotting Program (continues)

```
180 L=37:REM MAX COLUMNS PER LINE
185 DIM BL$(L),PR$(L)
190 FOR I=1 TO L:BL$(I)=" ":NEXT I
200 A=(L-1)/(YMAX-YMIN)
210 B=-YMIN*A+1.5
230 AXCOL=INT(B)
240 IF 0<=AXCOL AND AXCOL<=L THEN 500
250 AXCOL=-1
500 REM PLOT THE FUNCTION
530 FOR X=XMIN TO XMAX STEP XINC
560 GOSUB 140
580 YCOL=INT(A*Y+B)
600 PR$=BL$
620 IF AXCOL<>-1 THEN PR$(AXCOL,AXCOL)="!"
630 IF X<>0 THEN 640
635 FOR I=1 TO L:PR$(I,I)="-":NEXT I
637 PR$(AXCOL,AXCOL)="0"
640 PR$(YCOL,YCOL)="*"
680 PRINT PR$
700 NEXT X
800 END
```

Figure 4.12: Curve-Plotting Program

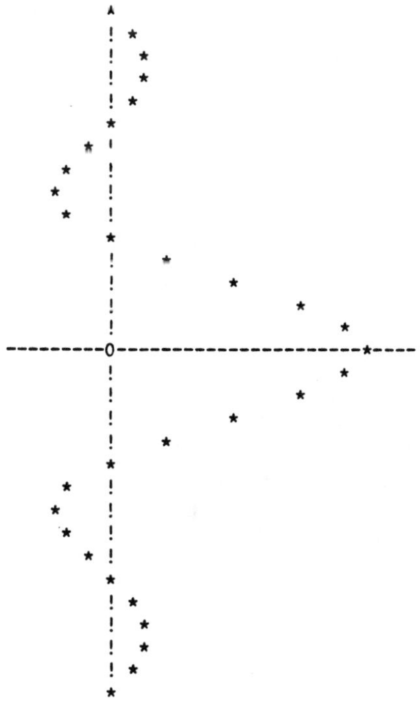

Figure 4.13: The Points of the Plotted Curve

Conclusion

After working out the preceding exercises, the reader might think that programming mathematical formulas can present few, if any, problems. This is the case if only assignment statements are needed and the flowcharts remain simple and linear. But programming mathematical formulas can become complicated, as was demonstrated in the example on plotting curves. This example involved more advanced analysis and additional thought when handling the output.

Later in this book we will encounter more complex programs that require significant subscript manipulation or involve numerous tests. The "Eight Queens" exercise in Chapter 11, concerning positions on a chessboard, is an example of such a complicated program.

CHAPTER 5

Exercises Involving Data Processing

Introduction

This chapter will present simple exercises in data processing that are both practical and educational. In data processing applications there is a continual need to SORT or MERGE arrays, files, etc. The exercises in this chapter answer that need. Later they can be incorporated into more ambitious programs. For example, the SORT sequence shown in Section 5.1 can be used to generalize the MERGE program discussed in Section 5.2 and also improve the telephone directory program provided in Section 5.3.

5.1 Shell Sort

There are many ways to arrange or sort data in the main memory. The simplest technique is known as the bubble sort. It will not be discussed here, but it is described in other texts. In this chapter we will utilize the Shell sort, because this method speeds up execution by reducing the number of comparisons that need to be made. Also, the Shell method is relatively simple to use. For example, if an array of N numbers needs to be sorted, a Shell sort would operate as follows:

1. Determine K such that:

   $2^K < N < 2^{K+1}$

   Then a variable D would be initialized to the value $2^K - 1$.

2. Perform the first step of the sort by varying the subscript I from 1 to N − D.

   2.1 Check for A(I) ⩽ A(I + D)
   If yes, go to the next step (3)
   If no, exchange A(I) and A(I + D)
   Set K = I and go to step 2.1

   2.2 Check for A(K − D) ⩽ A(K)
   If yes, go to the next step (3)
   If no, exchange A(K) and A(K − D),
   Set K = K − D and return to step 2.

3. Increment I and continue the comparisons. When I reaches the value N and D > 0, set D = INT $\frac{D - 1}{2}$ and return to step 2.

   When D = 0, the sort has been completed.

Exercise: First, design a flowchart for a SORT subroutine. Then, write a program that reads a non-sorted array and calls the SORT subroutine.

Solution: A program can be easily written using the previous description of the Shell technique. We must first understand, however, how to exchange two numbers.

To exchange Y and K we simply give Y the value of Z and Z the value of Y. Thus, we might be tempted to write:

```
500  Y = Z
510  Z = Y
```

But the value of Y was modified in the first instruction, so the second statement would not produce the expected result (i.e., the value of Z would remain unchanged). The contents of Y must be saved in an auxiliary variable

X, as in the following sequence:

```
490  X = Y
500  Y = Z
510  Z = X
```

This type of exchange occurs in the program shown in Figure 5.1 (lines 590 to 610) and also in the second program presented on preparing a telephone directory (in Section 5.5.2). A sample run for the program in Figure 5.1 appears in Figure 5.2.

```
100 DIM A(11)
110 N=11
120 PRINT "INITIAL LIST"
130 PRINT
140 FOR I=1 TO N
150 READ A:A(I)=A
160 PRINT A(I);" ";
170 NEXT I
180 GOSUB 500
190 PRINT
195 PRINT
200 PRINT "SORTED LIST"
210 PRINT
220 FOR I=1 TO N
230 PRINT A(I);" ";
240 NEXT I
250 END
500 D=1
510 D=2*D
520 IF D<=N THEN 510
530 D=INT((D-1)/2)
540 IF D=0 THEN 700
550 FOR I=1 TO N-D
560 J=I
570 L=J+D
580 IF A(J)<=A(L) THEN 640
590 X=A(J)
600 A(J)=A(L)
610 A(L)=X
620 J=J-D
630 IF J>0 THEN 570
640 NEXT I
650 GOTO 530
700 RETURN
800 DATA 3,-1,4,10,8,9,5,-10,-5
810 DATA 25,22
900 END
```

Figure 5.1: Sort Program

```
INITIAL LIST

3 -1 4 10 8 9 5 -10 -5 25 22

SORTED LIST

-10 -5 -1 3 4 5 8 9 10 22 25
```

Figure 5.2: Output from Sort Program

5.2 Merging Two Arrays

We want to merge two vectors[(1)] A and B, arranged in ascending order, into a third vector, C, also arranged in ascending order. For example, we have:

A = 3, 4, 6, 18
B = −1, 0, 5

and we want to obtain:

C = −1, 0, 3, 4, 5, 6, 18

Solution: Use three subscripts I, J and K for each of the vectors; each of these subscripts is initialized to 1.

If $A_I \leqslant B_J$ store A_I in C_K

Increment I and K

If $A_I > B_J$ store B_J in C_K

Increment J and K.

When one of the vectors A or B has been completely transferred to C, then the remainder of the other vector is copied into C.

Exercise: Design a flowchart showing the technique just described. Write a subroutine in BASIC to merge two vectors.

Questions:

a) What should be done if A and B are not sorted?

b) How can the program be adapted to merge two sorted sequential files?

Solution: The method we propose is shown in the conceptual flowchart presented in Figure 5.3. This flowchart, however, will need more work before

(1) An array of one dimension is often referred to as a "vector."

it will be useful for programming. The transformation of this flowchart into a more detailed flowchart (Figure 5.4) is easily done; it will use three separate subscripts:

I, the subscript for A

J, the subscript for B

K, the subscript for C

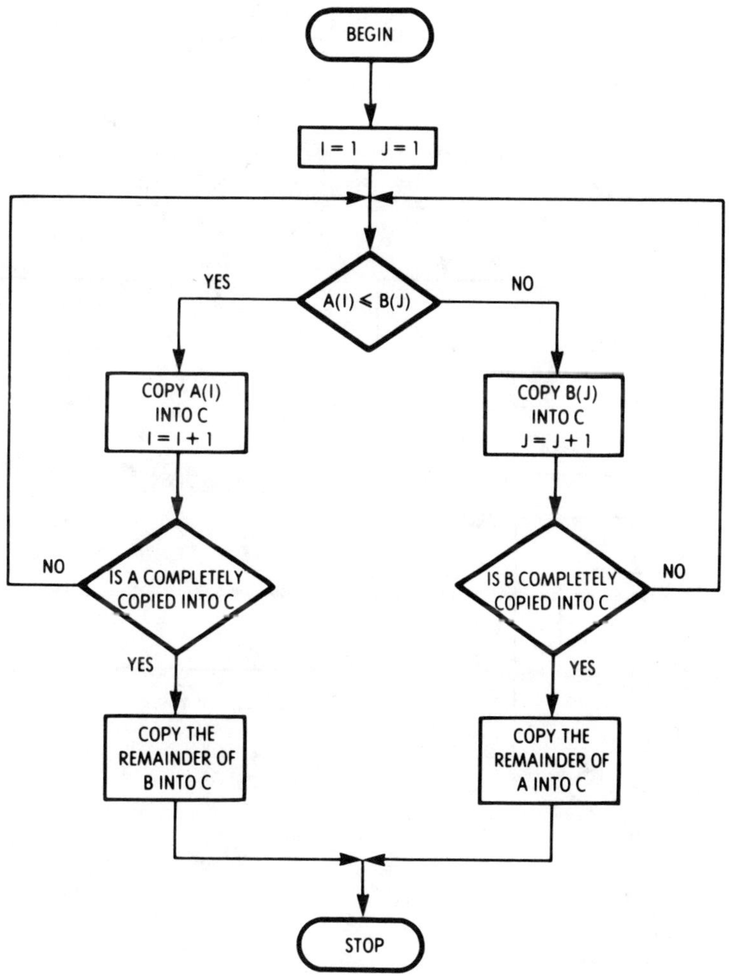

Figure 5.3: Flowchart for Merging Two Arrays

To avoid using a GOTO statement in the program, initialize K to zero, then place the instruction K = K + 1 at the beginning of the loop, rather than at the end. This works because K must be incremented no matter which way the first test goes (see Figure 5.4).

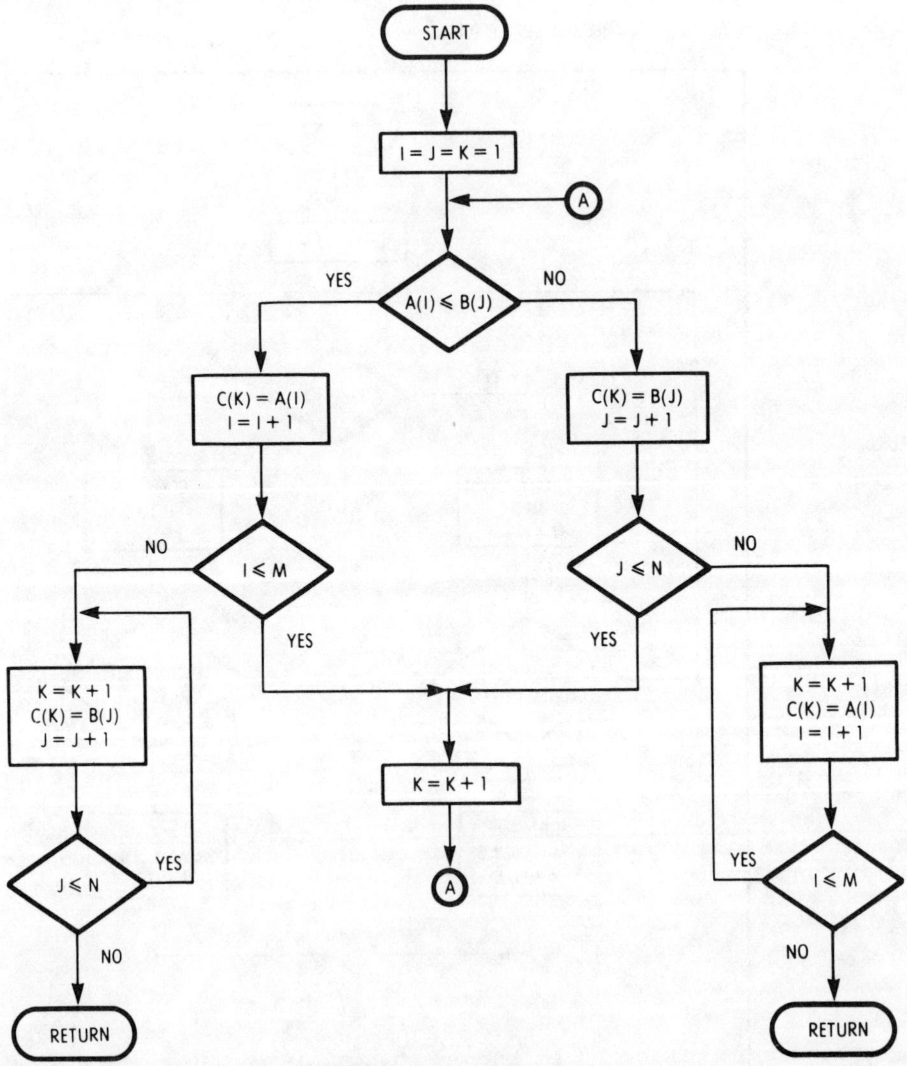

Figure 5.4: More Detailed Flowchart for Merge Program

Similarly, the two small loops at the end of the main loop can then be written with an auxiliary subscript variable, using the instructions FOR and NEXT (see Figure 5.5).

```
100 DIM A(100),B(100),C(200)
120 READ M
130 PRINT "LIST A:"
140 FOR I=1 TO M
150 READ A:A(I)=A
153 PRINT " ";A(I);" ";
157 NEXT I
160 PRINT
170 PRINT
180 REM READ LIST B
190 PRINT "LIST B:"
200 READ N
210 FOR I=1 TO N
220 READ B:B(I)=B
223 PRINT " ";B(I);" ";
227 NEXT I
230 PRINT
240 PRINT
250 GOSUB 300
260 PRINT "MERGED LIST:"
270 FOR I=1 TO M+N
280 PRINT " ";C(I);" ";
285 NEXT I
290 END
295 REM ROUTINE TO MERGE A & B
300 I=1:J=1:K=1
310 IF A(I)>=B(J) THEN 350
320 C(K)=A(I):I=I+1
330 IF I>M THEN 390
340 K=K+1:GOTO 310
350 C(K)=B(J):J=J+1
360 IF J<=N THEN 340
365 REM COPY REST OF A TO C
370 K=K+1:C(K)=A(I)
375 I=I+1
380 IF I<=M THEN 370
381 RETURN
385 REM COPY REST OF B TO C
390 K=K+1:C(K)=B(J)
395 J=J+1
400 IF J<=N THEN 390
401 RETURN
410 DATA 5
420 DATA 4,7,9,12,45
430 DATA 4
440 DATA -1,5,6,60
450 END
```

Figure 5.5: Merge Program

A sample run is shown in Figure 5.6. We might now begin to think about extending this program.

```
LIST A:
 4 7 9 12 45

LIST B:
 -1 5 6 60

MERGED LIST:
 -1 4 5 6 7 9 12 45 60
```

Figure 5.6: Output from Merge Program

First extension: Let us look at some ways to adapt the program to handle two unsorted vectors. The first way might be to combine the vectors into a single unsorted vector (C) and then to perform a sort. This method takes longer to sort than a second method, which is to sort each of the two vectors (A and B) first, and then to perform a merge.[(2)]

For these preliminary sorts we can use a section of code from the previous exercise (i.e., lines 500 through 700 of Figure 5.1). These instructions must be copied twice: the first time to sort the vector A, and the second time to sort the vector B. This is done because most BASIC compilers and interpreters do not provide subroutines that pass parameters.[(3)]

Second extension: The second extension involves merging two sequential files. The flowchart shown in Figure 5.3 is an excellent starting point for this extension. However, read and write instructions will have to be added. But, remember that the actual number of items in a file is rarely known in advance, so periodic checks must be provided to detect the end of the file.

This extension is sketched in the conceptual flowchart shown in Figure 5.7. The actual programming will be highly system dependent, because file manipulation is not standardized in BASIC.

[(2)] For more details, consult books specializing in SORT algorithms.

[(3)] The inability to handle subroutines with parameters is one of the limitations of BASIC. The fact that FORTRAN offers this feature is one of the most important differences between FORTRAN and BASIC.

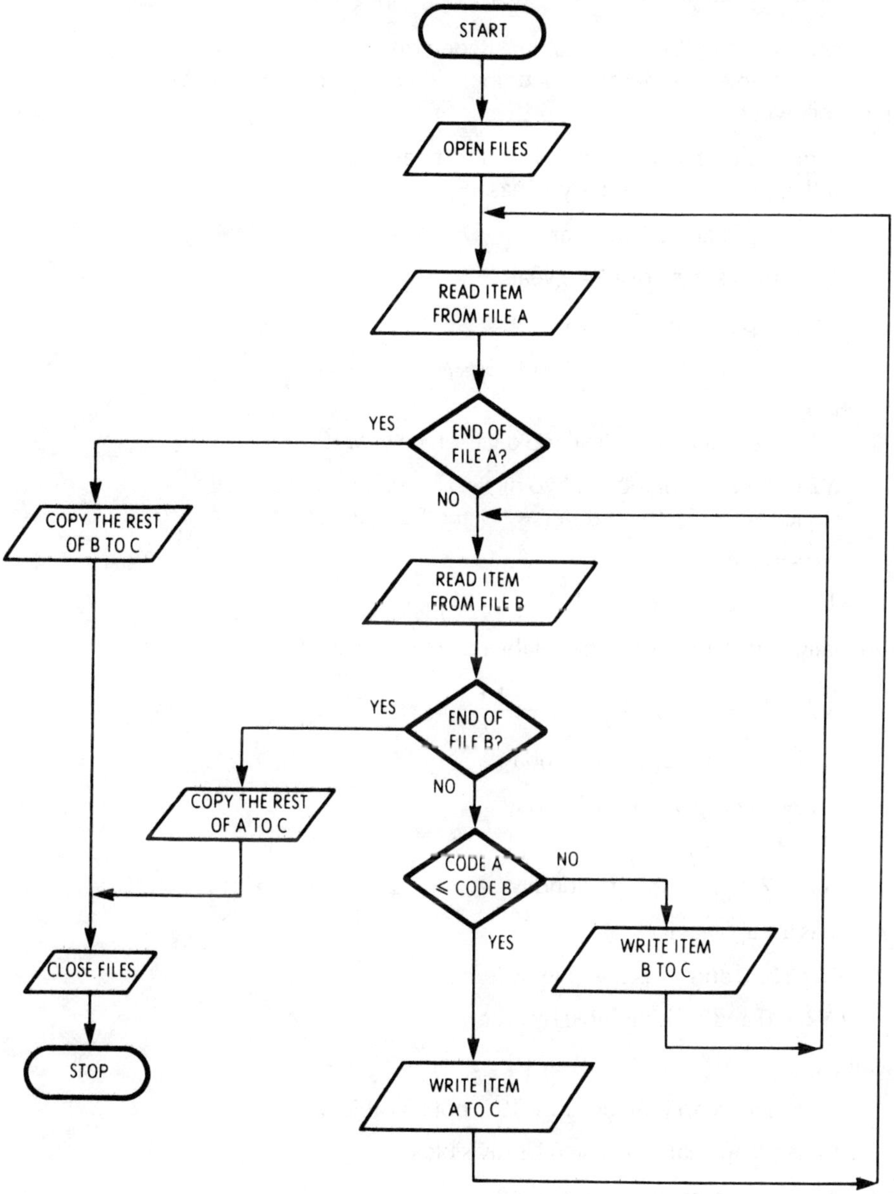

5.7: Flowchart for Merging Two Sequential Files

5.3 The Day of the Week

Given a date, i.e., the MONTH, DAY, YEAR, determine the corresponding day of the week. Numerous methods for doing this have been proposed. We suggest the following:

— Compute a correction term, N. In most cases, N = 0, but, if the month is January or February, N has the value:

1 if the year is a leap year

2 if the year is not a leap year.

— Next, compute the "Day Code," C:

C = INT(365.25*Y2) + INT(30.56*M) + D + N

where:

Y1 is the value of the first two digits of the year

Y2 is the value of the last two digits of the year, for example, for 1980 Y1 = 19 and Y2 = 80

M is the month

D is the day of the month.

— Finally, calculate the number of the day of the week, W, by:

$$W = C + 3 - 7*\text{INT}\left(\frac{C + 2}{7}\right)$$

W = 1 corresponds to Monday.

W = 2 corresponds to Tuesday.

⋮

W = 7 corresponds to Sunday.

Note: A year is a leap year if:

Either Y2≠0 and Y2 is divisible by four,

or Y2 = 0 and Y1 is divisible by four.

For example:

1900 is not a leap year, because 19 is not divisible by 4.

1984 is a leap year, because 84 is divisible by 4.

Note also that the computation for C does not incorporate Y1 and applies only to the twentieth century.

Exercise: Write a program that accepts a date, M, D, Y, and prints out the corresponding day of the week.

Solution: The proposed method translates easily into a flowchart (see Figure 5.8). (For convenience we have designed a program that continues to ask for a new date until the day input is either negative or zero.)

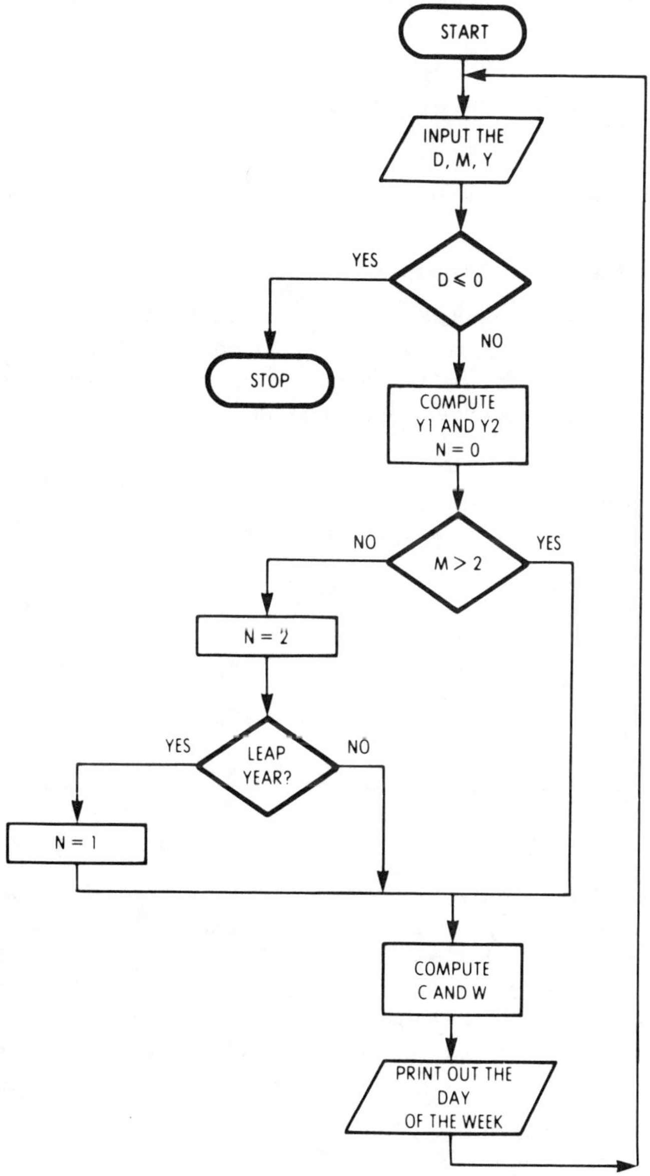

Figure 5.8: Flowchart for Finding the Day of the Week

However, before we can program we must first know:

— How to compute Y1 and Y2
— How to determine if Y is a leap year.

Note that Y1 is equal to the quotient of the "integer division of Y by 100," that is:

```
Y1 = INT(Y/100)
```

Y2 is the remainder of this integer division, and, thus:

```
Y2 = Y - 100*Y1
```

To determine whether or not Y2 is divisible by four, compute a remainder, R, as follows:

```
R = Y2 - 4*INT(Y2/4)
```

Note: This type of computation occurs throughout Chapter 3.

We are now able to write the computational part of the program up through the calculation of W. The next part of the problem is to determine how the output is presented. We will consider two cases.

First case: This method may be used if the system allows arrays of character strings (ATARI does not). In this case, the following instructions could be used to process the actual day of the week:

```
DIM D$(7)
D$(1) = "MONDAY"
:
:
D$(7) = "SUNDAY"
```

To print out the day of the week we write:

```
PRINT D$(W)
```

Second case: This method may be used if the system does not support string arrays. We may then assign a character string that is long enough to hold all the names of the days of the week. The day of the week with the most letters is WEDNESDAY, which contains nine letters. A string of length 9*7 or 63 characters would suffice to hold a uniform representation of each of the days. When this string has been suitably initialized, the substring containing the day of the week can be printed with an instruction of the following type:

```
PRINT MID$(D$,9*W-8,9)
```

or

```
PRINT D$(9*W-8,9*W)
```

for the ATARI BASIC system. Figure 5.9 shows the program and Figure 5.10 shows a sample dialogue.

```
90 DIM D$(63)
95 D$="MONDAY   TUESDAY  WEDNESDAY"
96 D$(28)="THURSDAY FRIDAY   "
97 D$(46)="SATURDAY SUNDAY   "
100 REM DAY-OF-WEEK COMPUTATION
110 REM W IS # OF WEEKDAY
115 REM (1 FOR MON.. 7 FOR SUN)
120 PRINT "DATE (MM,DD,YYYY)  ";
122 INPUT M,D,Y
125 IF D<=0 THEN END
130 Y1=INT(Y/100)
140 Y2=Y-100*Y1
150 N=0
160 IF M>2 THEN 300
165 N=2
170 IF Y2=0 THEN 220
180 R=Y2-4*INT(Y2/4)
190 IF R<>0 THEN 300
200 N=1
210 GOTO 300
220 R=Y1-4*INT(Y1/4)
230 IF R=0 THEN N=1
300 C=INT(365.25*Y2)+INT(30.56*M)+N+D
310 W=3+C-7*INT((C+2)/7)
320 PRINT D$(9*W-8,9*W)
330 PRINT
340 GOTO 120
```

Figure 5.9: Day of the Week Program

```
DATE (MM,DD,YYYY)  ?05,13,1981
WEDNESDAY

DATE (MM,DD,YYYY)  ?07,04,1981
SATURDAY

DATE (MM,DD,YYYY)  ?04,14,1983
THURSDAY

DATE (MM,DD,YYYY)  ?07,14,1982
WEDNESDAY

DATE (MM,DD,YYYY)  ?03,01,1982
MONDAY

DATE (MM,DD,YYYY)  ?00,00,00
```

Figure 5.10: Sample Output from Day of the Week Program

Note: In the program given in Section 5.4, we will define a user function to reduce the number of program statements needed.

Program for analysis: The program in Figure 5.11 shows another method that can be used to obtain the day of the week. Figure 5.12 is a sample run.

```
80 REM PROGRAM TO CALCULATE
85 REM THE DAY OF THE WEEK
90 DIM D$(63)
95 D$="MONDAY   TUESDAY  WEDNESDAY"
96 D$(28)="THURSDAY FRIDAY    "
97 D$(46)="SATURDAY SUNDAY    "
190 PRINT "DATE (MM,DD,YYY)  ";
200 INPUT M,D,Y
205 IF D<=0 THEN END
210 GOSUB 500
220 PRINT D$(9*Z-8,9*Z)
230 GOTO 190
500 IF Y<=1752 THEN 620
510 N=INT(0.6+1/M)
520 L=Y-N
530 P=M+12*N
540 C=L/100
550 Y1=INT(C)
560 Z1=INT(C/4)
570 Z3=INT(5*L/4)
580 Z4=INT(13*(P+1)/5)
590 Z=Z4+Z3-Y1+Z1+D+5
600 Z=Z-(7*INT(Z/7))+1
610 RETURN
620 PRINT "THE YEAR MUST ";
625 PRINT "BE AFTER 1752"
640 END
```

Figure 5.11: Another Approach to the Day of the Week Program

```
DATE (MM,DD,YYY)  ?5,13,1981
WEDNESDAY
DATE (MM,DD,YYY)  ?5,15,1981
FRIDAY
DATE (MM,DD,YYY)  ?4,12,1982
MONDAY
DATE (MM,DD,YYY)  ?3,15,1982
MONDAY
DATE (MM,DD,YYY)  ?1,12,1982
TUESDAY
DATE (MM,DD,YYY)  ?6,6,1982
SUNDAY
DATE (MM,DD,YYY)  ?4,13,1700
THE YEAR MUST BE AFTER 1752
```

Figure 5.12: Sample Output from Second Day of the Week Program

Questions: Looking at the program in Figure 5.11, let us consider the following questions:

1. What does instruction 510 do?
2. How is line 530 to be interpreted?
3. Can the number of program statements be reduced without modifying the method used or increasing the number of program operations?

Answers:

1. In statement 510:

   — If M is equal to 1 or 2, then N takes the value INT(0.6 + 1) or INT(0.6 + $\frac{1}{2}$), which results in 1 in both cases.

   — If M is equal to 3, 4, etc., N takes the value 0.

   This section of the program is comparable to the previous program up to the point where the consequences of the leap year are taken into account.

2. In statement 530:

   — P corresponds to the number of the month if the month is March, April, etc., up to December. For January and February, P will take the values 13 and 14, respectively.

   — Y1 in statement 590 is such that the expression C − Y1 has a value V, such that V = 0 if the year is an even century. In any other year:

   $0 < V < 1$

3. Since the variables Y1, Z1, Z3 and Z4 are only used in the calculation of Z in statement 590, statements 560, 570 and 580 can be eliminated if 590 is written in the following way:

```
590  Z = INT(13*(P + 1)/5) + INT(5*L/4) - INT(C) + INT(C/4) + D + 5
```

5.4 The Time Elapsed Between Two Dates

To determine the interval between two dates, calculate the "day code" of each date and then find the difference. The result is the number of days between the given dates. This type of information is critical in the computation of interest.

Exercise: Utilizing the preceding program, develop a program that computes the time elapsed between two dates.

Solution: The value of subroutines can be truly appreciated in this problem. Because the day code must be calculated twice, it could be advantageous to build a day code subroutine. The flowchart shown in Figure 5.13 was constructed with this point in mind.

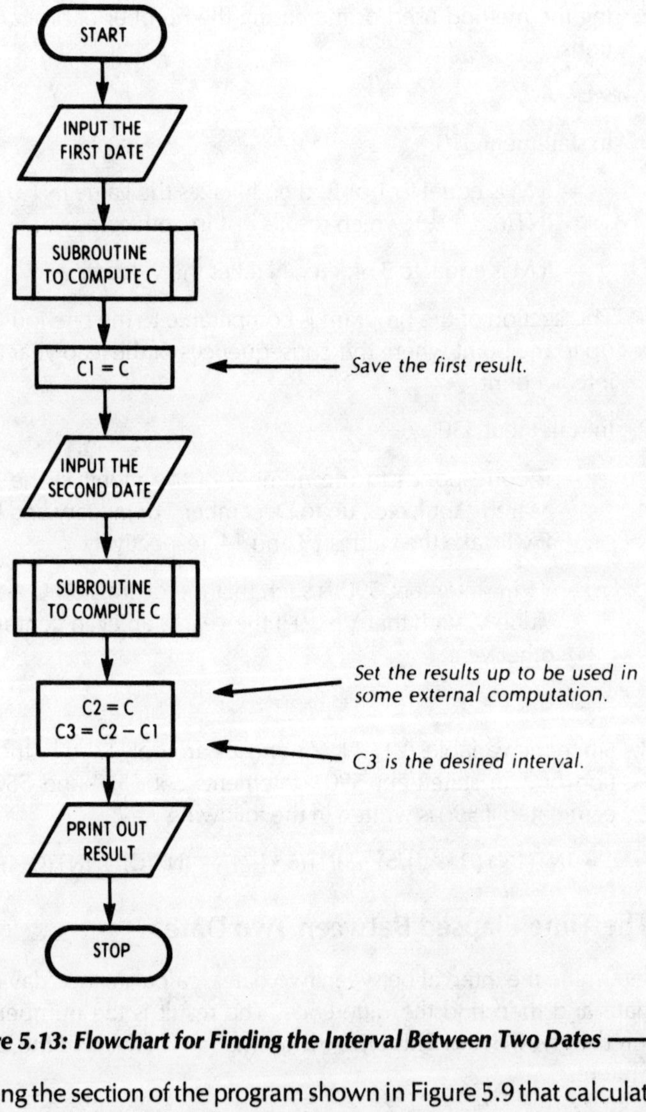

Figure 5.13: Flowchart for Finding the Interval Between Two Dates

By taking the section of the program shown in Figure 5.9 that calculates the day code, we can more easily write the progam in Figure 5.14. Figure 5.15 displays a sample of the program dialogue.

```
100 REM COMPUTATION OF INTERVAL
101 REM BETWEEN TWO DATES
110 PRINT "FIRST DATE ";
115 PRINT "(MM,DD,YYY)  ";
120 INPUT M,D,Y
130 GOSUB 500
140 C1=C
150 PRINT "SECOND DATE ";
155 PRINT "(MM,DD,YYYY) ";
160 INPUT M,D,Y
170 GOSUB 500
180 C2=C
185 PRINT
190 C3=C2-C1
195 PRINT "TIME ELAPSED ";
196 PRINT "BETWEEN DATES IS:"
197 PRINT
198 PRINT ,,C3;" DAYS"
200 END
500 A=Y:B=100
506 GOSUB 1000:Y2=F
510 N=0
520 IF M>2 THEN 570
525 N=2
530 IF Y2=0 THEN 550
535 A=Y2:B=4
536 GOSUB 1000:R=F
540 IF R<>0 THEN 570
545 GOTO 560
550 A=Y1:B=4
551 GOSUB 1000
552 IF F<>0 THEN 570
560 N=1
570 C=INT(365.25*Y2)+INT(30.65*M)+N+D
580 RETURN
590 END
1000 F=A-B*INT(A/B)
1010 RETURN
9999 END
```

Figure 5.14: Interval Program

```
FIRST DATE (MM,DD,YYY)  ?2,23,1981
SECOND DATE (MM,DD,YYYY) ?6,30,1982

TIME ELAPSED BETWEEN DATES IS:

                            492 DAYS
```

Figure 5.15: Sample Output from Interval Program

5.5 A Telephone Directory

BASIC has certain advantages over a language like FORTRAN. One example is BASIC's ability to handle character strings easily. The two exercises that follow show how character strings can be readily manipulated in practical applications.

5.5.1 Exercise 1: Creating a Directory

Exercise: Write a program that reads DATA statements, each of which should contain the following items: last name, first name, room number and telephone extension. The lines should be printed in a specified format. Assign the names L$, F$, R$ and T (respectively) to the items and assume that the data list is presented in alphabetical order.

Solution: The conceptual flowchart is quite simple as it only reads and prints and does no data manipulation. The most difficult part of this exercise is determining when the last DATA line has been read. There are two methods to do this:

1. Place a dummy entry to "flag" the end of the data statements.
2. Use the IF END instruction that is provided in some BASICs.

We will use the first method since it applies to all systems, whereas the second method is system-dependent.

At the end of the data list we add a special name, "ZZZ", which will be readily detected in our program and will mark the end of the data. This method is shown in the flowchart in Figure 5.16.

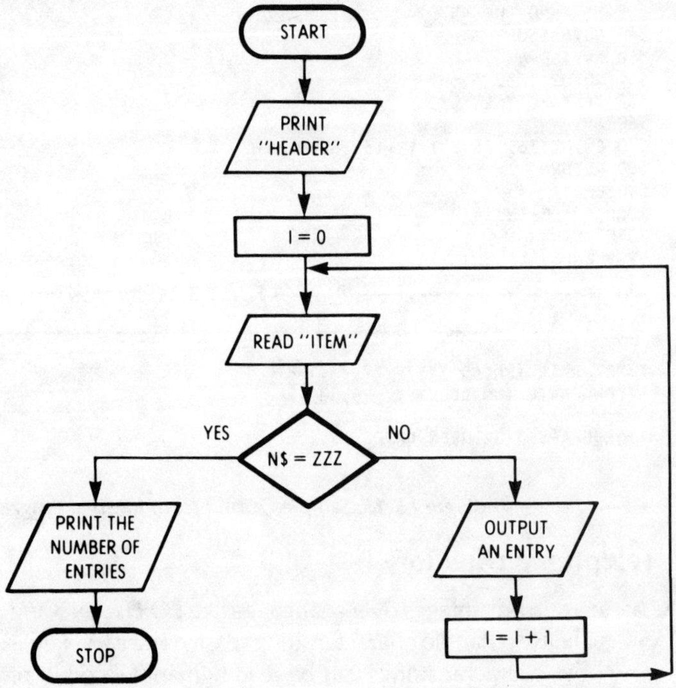

Figure 5.16: Flowchart for Creating a Telephone Directory

The flowchart in Figure 5.16 contains a variable I that "counts" the actual number of entries in the data list. Counting the number of lines of output this way makes it possible to intersperse page ejects at appropriate places, so that important lists can be presented in a neater and clearer way.

The program is shown in Figure 5.17 and the sample run in Figure 5.18. Although this program does not sort, it will nonetheless produce an ordered list if the DATA statements are already sorted. For this reason the lines are numbered by tens, so that lines may be inserted where they belong.

```
100 REM PHONE DIRECTORY PROGRAM
110 REM
120 DIM L$(20),F$(20),R$(20)
130 REM
140 REM
150 PRINT "       TELEPHONE DIRECTORY"
160 PRINT
170 PRINT "LAST       FIRST"
175 PRINT "NAME       NAME      ";
177 PRINT "ROOM      EXTENSION"
180 PRINT
190 I=0
200 READ L$,F$,R$,T
210 IF L$="ZZZ" THEN 250
220 PRINT L$,F$,R$,T
230 I=I+1
240 GOTO 200
250 PRINT
260 PRINT "NUMBER OF ENTRIES";
261 PRINT " = ";I
265 END
270 DATA DUBOIS,ANDREW,3,310
280 DATA DUBOIS,JOHN,3,340
290 DATA DUPONT,JOHN,5,400
300 DATA GABDEZ,LARRY,4,360
900 DATA ZZZ,Z,3,4
910 END
```

Figure 5.17: Telephone Directory Program

```
        TELEPHONE DIRECTORY

LAST      FIRST
NAME      NAME      ROOM     EXTENSION

DUBOIS    ANDREW     3         310
DUBOIS    JOHN       3         340
DUPONT    JOHN       5         400
GABDEZ    LARRY      4         360

NUMBER OF ENTRIES = 4
```

Figure 5.18: Sample Output from the Telephone Directory Program

With some minor modifications (at the READ instruction level) we could work with a sequential file. With such a file, the length of the directory would not have to be limited.

Note: Some versions of BASIC provide an IF END instruction to detect an end of file. This instruction avoids the necessity of providing a dummy record (here flagged by the name ZZZ). Under these circumstances the flowchart would take the form displayed in Figure 5.19.

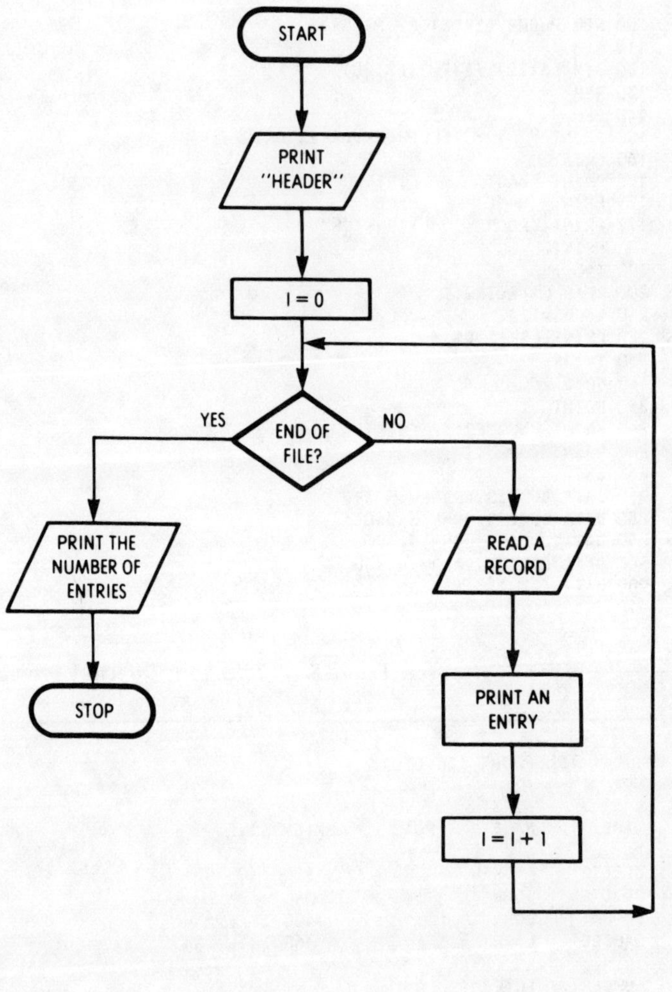

Figure 5.19: Flowchart Illustrating the "End-of-File" Option

5.5.2 Exercise 2: Creating a Directory

We now want to create a more ambitious program that presents a "menu" from which the user may choose one of the following commands:

- SORT on last name
- SORT on last name and first name
- SORT on first name only
- SORT on telephone extension
- LIST all persons at a specific extension.
- EXIT

To do the SORT in this context, we will modify some of the sorting techniques demonstrated in the exercise at the beginning of this chapter.

Exercise: Construct a program that reads the DATA statements in the program and then prints out the above "menu."

Depending upon the response given by the user, the program then performs the selected task and displays the menu once again.

Note: BASIC does not generally permit subroutines to pass parameters as other languages, such as ALGOL and FORTRAN, do; thus, we are going to have trouble constructing a SORT subroutine that operates the way we want it to in all cases. One solution is to pass the "SORT key" in a dedicated array.

Solution: This should present no major problems, provided we work methodically. Let us first construct a general flowchart without including any of the details. This flowchart is shown in Figure 5.20.

In order to use the same SORT subroutine for all of the sort options, we have set up the input arguments prior to the call. To do this we have chosen the following convention. Let us assume that the data are:

L$(I) Last name

F$(I) First name

R$(I) Room

T(I) Extension

A separate array B$(I) is first loaded with the elements to be sorted, and then the sort is carried out. For example, before a sort is performed on "Last

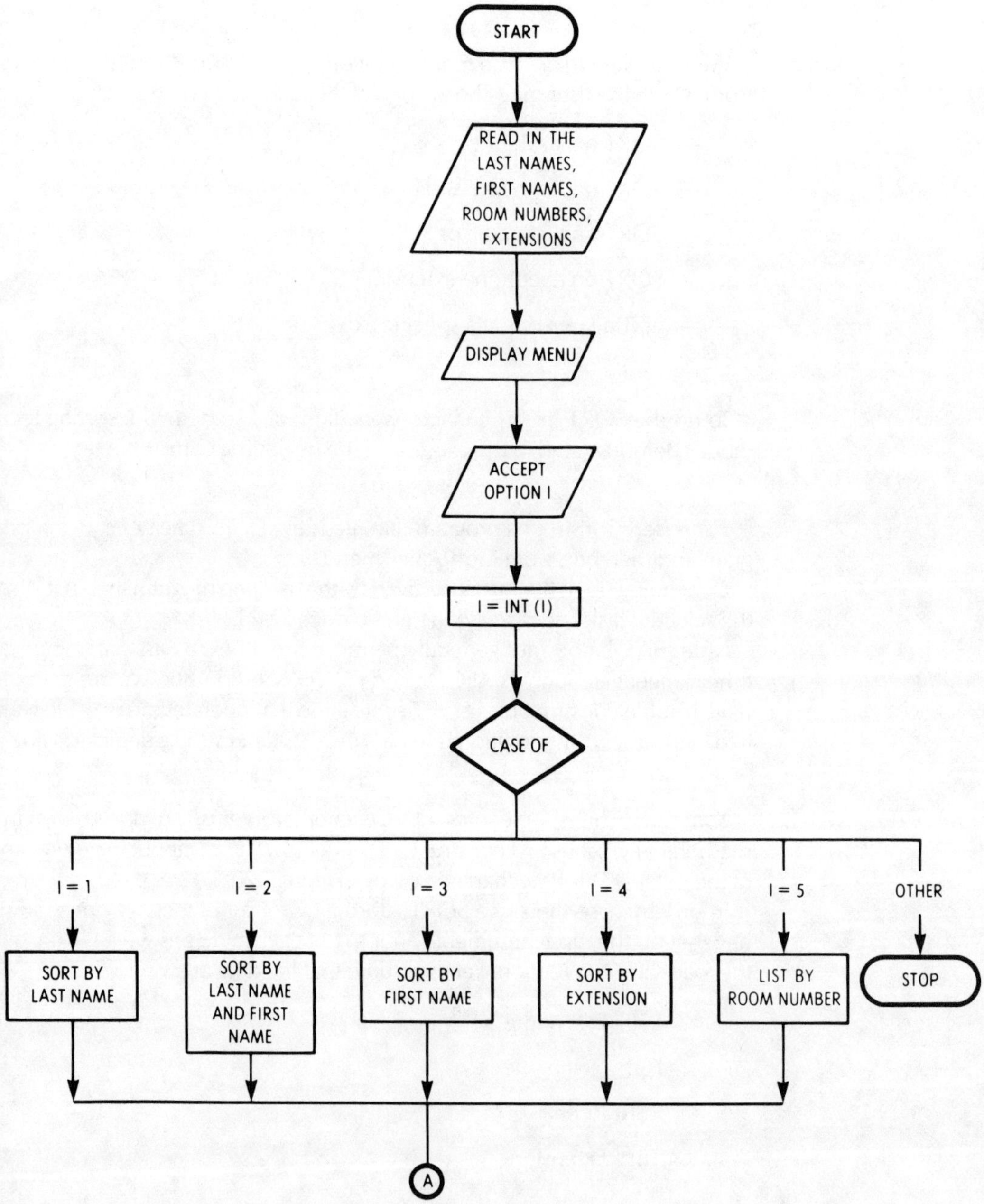

Figure 5.20: Flowchart for Sorting a Telephone Directory

name," we first execute the following:

B$ = L$

This statement presumes that we are going to do an alphabetic sort, which BASIC does without difficulty on ASCII strings.

To perform a sort on last name *and* first name, we load B$ with the concatenation L$ + F$. This could, however, present a problem. Consider the following case:

SMIT JAN

SMITH JOHN

On simple concatenation we have:

SMITJAN

SMITHJOHN

and the comparison will give:

SMITHJOHN < SMITJAN

To avoid this situation, we insert a "blank" character between the last name and the first name. A blank character in ASCII precedes the letter A in the collating sequence. After concatenation we will then have:

SMIT JAN

SMITH JOHN

so that the comparison will indeed produce the desired result. To insert the necessary blank character, we would write (with string arrays):

B$(I) = L$(I) + " " + F$(I)

a blank character

The ATARI code in lines 465–405 has the same effect. The telephone directory program is shown in Figure 5.21. Figure 5.22 displays sample dialogue.

```
100 REM PHONE DIRECTORY PROGRAM
110 REM
115 NN=15:REM MAX # OF NAMES
120 DIM L$(10*NN),F$(10*NN)
121 DIM R$(5*NN),T(NN)
122 DIM B$(21*NN),NA(NN)
124 DIM X$(20),Y$(20)
130 GOSUB 270
140 PRINT "SELECT DESIRED ";
141 PRINT "OPTION"
150 PRINT "1 = SORT BY ";
151 PRINT "LAST NAME"
160 PRINT "2 = SORT BY LAST ";
161 PRINT "AND FIRST NAME"
170 PRINT "3 = SORT BY ";
```

Figure 5.21: Telephone Directory Sort Program (continues)

```
171 PRINT "FIRST NAME"
180 PRINT "4 = SORT BY ";
181 PRINT "TELEPHONE EXTENSION"
190 PRINT "5 = LIST ALL ";
191 PRINT "PERSONS IN A ";
192 PRINT "GIVEN ROOM?"
193 PRINT "6 = EXIT"
195 TRAP 260
200 INPUT I:TRAP 40000
250 REM SELECT OPERATION
255 ON I GOTO 390,450,510,570,630,3000
260 GOTO 140
270 REM ********** LOAD DATA
272 REM SUBROUTINE
275 IP=1
277 NA(IP)=IP
280 SIZE=10
285 GOSUB 325:L$(BEG,FIN)=X$
290 IF Y$="ZZZ" THEN N=IP-1:GOTO 320
295 GOSUB 325:F$(BEG,FIN)=X$
300 SIZE=5
305 GOSUB 325:R$(BEG,FIN)=X$
310 READ T:T(IP)=T
315 IP=IP+1:GOTO 277
320 RETURN
325 REM ******** READ,TRUNCATE, & PAD
330 READ Y$
335 X$="          ":X$=X$(1,SIZE)
340 MIN=SIZE:IF LEN(Y$)<SIZE THEN MIN=LEN(Y$)
345 X$(1,MIN)=Y$(1,MIN)
350 REM ******* COMPUTE ARRAY INDICES
355 BEG=1+SIZE*(NA(IP)-1)
360 FIN=SIZE*NA(IP)
365 RETURN
390 REM *********** SORT ON LAST NAME
400 BSIZ=10
410 B$=L$
430 GOTO 1000
450 REM *********** SORT LAST & FIRST
451 REM NAMES
460 FOR I=1 TO N
465 BBEG=1+21*(I-1)
470 LBEG=1+10*(I-1):LFIN=10*I
480 B$(BBEG,BBEG+9)=L$(LBEG,LFIN)
482 B$(BBEG+10,BBEG+10)=" "
485 B$(BBEG+11,BBEG+20)=F$(LBEG,LFIN)
487 NEXT I
490 BSIZ=21
495 GOTO 1000
510 REM *********** SORT ON FIRST NAME
530 B$=F$
540 BSIZ=10
550 GOTO 1000
570 REM ********** SORT ON EXTENSION
580 FOR IP=1 TO N
584 Y$=STR$(T(IP)):SIZE=5:NA(IP)=IP
```

Figure 5.21: Telephone Directory Sort Program (continues)

```
590 GOSUB 335:B$(BEG,FIN)=X$
600 NEXT IP
605 BSIZ=5
610 GOTO 1000
630 REM ********** LIST ALL
631 REM PERSONS IN GIVEN ROOM
640 PRINT "WHICH ROOM  ";
660 INPUT Y$
670 SIZE=5:GOSUB 335
680 PRINT :PRINT "LIST OF ALL OCCU";
681 PRINT "PANTS OF ROOM ";X$
695 GOTO 1503
990 REM ********** SHELL SORT
1000 D=1
1010 D=2*D
1020 IF D<=N THEN 1010
1030 D=INT((D-1)/2)
1040 IF D=0 THEN 1500
1050 FOR I=1 TO N-D
1060 FOR J=I TO 1 STEP -D
1070 L=J+D
1072 BJBEG=1+BSIZ*(NA(J)-1)
1073 BJFIN=BSIZ*NA(J)
1074 BLBEG=1+BSIZ*(NA(L)-1)
1075 BLFIN=BSIZ*NA(L)
1080 IF B$(BJBEG,BJFIN)<=B$(BLBEG,BLFIN) THEN 1220
1180 X=NA(J)
1190 NA(J)=NA(L)
1200 NA(L)=X
1210 NEXT J
1220 NEXT I
1230 GOTO 1030
1490 REM ********* AND PRINT THE DATA
1500 X$=""
1503 J=0
1505 PRINT
1510 PRINT "LAST NAME  FIRST ";
1511 PRINT "NAME  ROOM  EXTENSION"
1520 FOR IP=1 TO N
1522 IF X$="" THEN 1527
1524 SIZE=5:GOSUB 350
1525 IF R$(BEG,FIN)<>X$ THEN 1560
1527 SIZE=10
1530 GOSUB 350:PRINT L$(BEG,FIN);" ";
1535 GOSUB 350:PRINT F$(BEG,FIN);"  ";
1537 SIZE=5
1540 GOSUB 350:PRINT R$(BEG,FIN);" ";
1545 PRINT T(NA(IP))
1550 J=J+1
1560 NEXT IP
1570 PRINT :PRINT "A TOTAL OF  ";J;
1571 PRINT " PERSONS FOUND":PRINT
1580 GOTO 140
2010 DATA DUPONT,PETER,BE,100
2020 DATA DURAND,JOHN,BE,110
2030 DATA LEFEBURE,RICHARD
```

Figure 5.21: Telephone Directory Sort Program (continues)

```
2031 DATA LABO,310
2040 DATA DUPONT,PAUL,FA,115
2050 DATA TALLOW,ARNOLD,COM,300
2060 DATA DUBOIS,AGNES,SEC,301
2070 DATA ZZZ
3000 END
```

Figure 5.21: Telephone Directory Sort Program

```
SELECT DESIRED OPTION
1 = SORT BY LAST NAME
2 = SORT BY LAST AND FIRST NAME
3 = SORT BY FIRST NAME
4 = SORT BY TELEPHONE EXTENSION
5 = LIST ALL PERSONS IN A GIVEN ROOM?
6 = EXIT
?1

LAST NAME  FIRST NAME  ROOM  EXTENSION
DUBOIS     AGNES       SEC   301
DUPONT     PETER       BE    100
DUPONT     PAUL        FA    115
DURAND     JOHN        BE    110
LEFEBURE   RICHARD     LABO  310
TALLOW     ARNOLD      COM   300

A TOTAL OF  6 PERSONS FOUND

SELECT DESIRED OPTION
1 = SORT BY LAST NAME
2 = SORT BY LAST AND FIRST NAME
3 = SORT BY FIRST NAME
4 = SORT BY TELEPHONE EXTENSION
5 = LIST ALL PERSONS IN A GIVEN ROOM?
6 = EXIT
?2

LAST NAME  FIRST NAME  ROOM  EXTENSION
DUBOIS     AGNES       SEC   301
DUPONT     PAUL        FA    115
DUPONT     PETER       BE    100
DURAND     JOHN        BE    110
LEFEBURE   RICHARD     LABO  310
TALLOW     ARNOLD      COM   300

A TOTAL OF  6 PERSONS FOUND

SELECT DESIRED OPTION
1 = SORT BY LAST NAME
2 = SORT BY LAST AND FIRST NAME
3 = SORT BY FIRST NAME
4 = SORT BY TELEPHONE EXTENSION
5 = LIST ALL PERSONS IN A GIVEN ROOM?
6 = EXIT
?3
```

Figure 5.22: Dialogue from Telephone Directory Sort Program (continues)

```
LAST NAME  FIRST NAME  ROOM  EXTENSION
DUBOIS     AGNES       SEC   301
TALLOW     ARNOLD      COM   300
DURAND     JOHN        BE    110
DUPONT     PAUL        FA    115
DUPONT     PETER       BE    100
LEFEBURE   RICHARD     LABO  310

A TOTAL OF  6 PERSONS FOUND

SELECT DESIRED OPTION
1 = SORT BY LAST NAME
2 = SORT BY LAST AND FIRST NAME
3 = SORT BY FIRST NAME
4 = SORT BY TELEPHONE EXTENSION
5 = LIST ALL PERSONS IN A GIVEN ROOM?
6 = EXIT
?4

LAST NAME  FIRST NAME  ROOM  EXTENSION
DUPONT     PETER       BE    100
DURAND     JOHN        BE    110
DUPONT     PAUL        FA    115
TALLOW     ARNOLD      COM   300
DUBOIS     AGNES       SEC   301
LEFEBURE   RICHARD     LABO  310

A TOTAL OF  6 PERSONS FOUND

SELECT DESIRED OPTION
1 = SORT BY LAST NAME
2 = SORT BY LAST AND FIRST NAME
3 = SORT BY FIRST NAME
4 = SORT BY TELEPHONE EXTENSION
5 = LIST ALL PERSONS IN A GIVEN ROOM?
6 = EXIT
?5
WHICH ROOM  ?BE

LIST OF ALL OCCUPANTS OF ROOM BE

LAST NAME  FIRST NAME  ROOM  EXTENSION
DUPONT     PETER       BE    100
DURAND     JOHN        BE    110

A TOTAL OF  2 PERSONS FOUND

SELECT DESIRED OPTION
1 = SORT BY LAST NAME
2 = SORT BY LAST AND FIRST NAME
3 = SORT BY FIRST NAME
4 = SORT BY TELEPHONE EXTENSION
5 = LIST ALL PERSONS IN A GIVEN ROOM?
6 = EXIT
?6
```

Figure 5.22: Dialogue from Telephone Directory Sort Program

This technique works well for an alphabetic sort, but in order to perform a numeric sort (e.g., perform a sort on telephone extensions), we must first convert these numbers into character strings, as in the statement below (line 590 of the program):

```
584  Y$ = STR$(T(IP)) . . .
```

Note that this character string-based numeric sort will provide a list of telephone extensions in true numerical order when all the extension numbers have the same number of digits.

The sort code presented here is very similar to the code shown in Exercise 5.1. In this case, however, the exchanges must be done on L$, F$, R$, and T, as well as on B$. Instead of actually swapping the entries, we maintain an array, NA, of indices (pointers) to the entries, and swap them. Since both the sort and output routines access entry number NA(I) when they need entry I, the effect is the same as exchanging the entries, but with much less computational work. Because ATARI BASIC does not allow string arrays, we have packed all the last names into a single string L$, the first names into F$, etc. Since the size of each field is made constant by padding with spaces in lines 335–345 (first and last names allowed 10 each and room name allowed 5), the beginning and finish of a field of an entry can be computed by using simple formulas (lines 355–360 do it for the read and print routines).

Criticism of this program: The major shortcoming of this program is the size limitation imposed on the directory by the inclusion of the data within the text of the program. This text must reside entirely in main memory throughout the program execution. Another version of the program could be written that would work out of an external file, without abandoning the general structure of the program. However, in this situation special attention would have to be given to minimizing the number of times the external storage device is accessed.

Conclusion

The preceding exercises on data processing have been relatively straightforward, because only a limited amount or quantity of data was processed.

Often, however, large files need to be processed and processing these files can present a realm of problems beyond the scope of this text. Even so, the basic techniques remain the same in most cases; data still need to be sorted, merged and printed out in an organized manner. Flowcharts to process input files are not difficult to design. Due to the disparity among BASIC interpreters, however, a programmer must become familiar with the peculiarities of a particular BASIC system, in order to write file access programs.

CHAPTER 6

Mathematical Computations

Introduction

The BASIC language was developed for programming simple mathematical calculations. The flowcharts and programs used to carry out such calculations are generally straightforward and easy to design. In some cases, however, an accumulation of rounding errors can result in imprecise answers.

The calculation of π presented in this chapter will illustrate the problems associated with round-off errors. The method used is that of inscribed and circumscribed polygons.

To avoid the possibility of error accumulation, the following techniques should be considered:

- At the outset, select algorithms that do not lend themselves to round-off errors. In practice, however, this is not always easy to do.
- Program the selected algorithms so that loss of precision is as limited as possible.

It is not possible, in a book of exercises, to cover this important topic in great detail. The interested reader can consult any number of books on numerical analysis.

6.1 Synthetic Division of a Polynomial by (X − S)

Consider a polygon P(X) of degree N with known coefficients:

$$P(X) = A_0X^N + A_1X^{N-1} + A_2X^{N-2} + \ldots + A_{N-1}X + A_N$$

Find a polynomial Q(X) of degree N − 1 such that:

$$P(X) = (X - S)Q(X) + R$$

where the remainder, R, is a constant. If we set:

$$Q(X) = B_0X^{N-1} + B_1X^{N-2} + \ldots + B_{N-2}X + B_{N-1}$$

we will have:

$$\begin{aligned} B_0 &= A_0 \\ B_1 &= A_1 + SB_0 \\ &\vdots \\ B_I &= A_I + SB_{I-1} \\ &\vdots \\ B_{N-1} &= A_{N-1} + SB_{N-2} \end{aligned}$$

and

$$R = A_N + SB_{N-1}$$

Exercise: Write a program that computes the coefficients of Q(X) from the coefficients of P(X) and (X − A1). A1 is the variable in BASIC into which the value of S is read.

Solution: The computational part of this problem is particularly simple. Varying I from 1 to N − 1, we can write:

```
B(I) = A(I) + A1*B(I - 1)
```

- A(I), B(I − 1): Coefficients of P(X)
- B(I): Coefficients of Q(X)

We can even compute B(N) from this formula by making:

R = B(N)

The difficult part of this problem is the input/output (I/O). One solution to this problem is the program shown in Figure 6.1. Obviously, there are also other ways to handle the printout. A sample run of the program is shown in Figure 6.2.

```
20 REM DIVISION OF A
25 REM POLYNOMIAL BY X-A1
30 REM N = THE DEGREE OF
35 REM THE POLYNOMIAL
40 REM THE ARRAY A CONTAINS
45 REM COEFFICIENTS OF P(X)
50 REM THE ARRAY B HOLDS
52 REM THE COMPUTED
55 REM COEFFICIENTS OF Q(X)
70 DIM A(50),B(50)
105 REM READ AN INPUT
110 READ N,A1
115 PRINT "SYNTHETIC DIVISION";
116 PRINT " OF P(X) BY (X - ";
117 PRINT A1;")"
118 PRINT
120 FOR I=0 TO N
130 READ A:A(I)=A
140 NEXT I
145 REM COMPUTATION OF THE
146 REM COEFFICIENTS OF Q(X)
150 B(0)=A(0)
160 FOR I=1 TO N-1
170 B(I)=A(I)+A1*B(I-1)
180 NEXT I
190 R=A(N)+A1*B(N-1)
195 REM PRINTOUT OF RESULTS
200 PRINT "P(X) COEFFICIENTS:";
210 FOR I=0 TO N
220 PRINT " ";A(I);
230 NEXT I
240 PRINT
250 PRINT
260 PRINT "Q(X) COEFFICIENTS:";
270 FOR I=0 TO N-1
280 PRINT " ";B(I);" ";
290 NEXT I
300 PRINT
310 PRINT
320 PRINT "REMAINDER: ";R
330 END
340 DATA 6,1
350 DATA 3,2,-1,5,6,4,1
360 END
```

Figure 6.1: Polynomial Division Program

```
SYNTHETIC DIVISION OF P(X) BY (X - 1)

P(X) COEFFICIENTS: 3 2 -1 5 6 4 1

Q(X) COEFFICIENTS: 3  5  4  9  15  19

REMAINDER: 20
```

Figure 6.2: Output of Coefficients and Remainder

We can easily verify the solution:

$$3X^6 + 2X^5 - X^4 + 5X^3 + 6X^2 + 4X + 1 =$$

$$(X - 1)(3X^5 + 5X^4 + 4X^3 + 9X^2 + 15X + 19) + 20$$

Comments: Note the following observations:

1. In some systems a BASE 0 instruction causes arrays to be indexed from 0. This instruction is not available with all systems. For example, according to the ANSI standard, "BASE 0" would be written as "OPTION BASE 0." (In our program the function is performed automatically when the FOR loop range is specified from 0 to N in line 120.)
2. For a version of BASIC that requires that subscripts begin with 1, simply subtract 1 from the subscripts in the program in Figure 6.1.
3. The format used in printing the output could be modified to produce many types of outputs. Obviously, however, blank lines will be necessary in all cases to set off the results.

6.2 The Calculation of a Definite Integral

Although there are numerous methods available for calculating the definite integral of a continuous and bounded function on a bounded interval, we suggest the following methods:

— Simpson's Rule

— Weddle's Method

These two methods are relatively easy to program. They will serve as the basis for the next two exercises.

Simpson's Rule: To evaluate a definite integral:

$$S = \int_A^B F(X)\,dX$$

First, select an even number, N, then divide the interval [A,B] into N intervals as follows:

$$H = \frac{B - A}{N}$$

After that, calculate:

$$S = \frac{H}{3}[F(X_0) + 4F(X_1) + 2F(X_2) + 4F(X_3) + 2F(X_4) + \ldots + 4F(X_{N-1}) + F(X_N)$$

where:

$$X_0 = A, \ldots, X_I = X_{I-1} + H, \ldots, X_N = B$$

Weddle's Method: In this case we select a number, N, which is a multiple of six, then we calculate H as before. For example, if N = 6, we evaluate:

$$S = \frac{3H}{10}[F(A) + 5F(A + H) + F(A + 2H) + 6F(A + 3H) + F(A + 4H) + 5F(A + 5H) + F(B)]$$

and, if N = 12, 18, etc., we write:

$$S = \frac{3H}{10}[F(A) + 5F(A + H) + F(A + 2H) + 6F(A + 3H) + F(A + 4H) + 5F(A + 5H) + 2F(A + 6H) + \ldots + F(B)]$$

Exercise 1: Using Simpson's rule, write a subroutine that evaluates a definite integral. Then, write a main program that calls this subroutine to evaluate:

$$S = \int_{\frac{-\pi}{2}}^{\frac{\pi}{2}} \cos x \, dx$$

The cosine function was chosen to illustrate the programs because the integral has a simple value:

$$\int_{\frac{-\pi}{2}}^{\frac{\pi}{2}} \cos x \, dx = \sin x \Big|_{\frac{-\pi}{2}}^{\frac{\pi}{2}} = 1 - (-1) = 2$$

Perform the calculation with N = 6, 12, 18, 24, 30; however, do not take into account that S is an "even" function.

Exercise 2: Repeat Exercise 1, but replace Simpson's Rule with Weddle's Method. Compare the results of the two exercises.

Exercise 1 solution: In order to perform the entire computation within a single loop, we add all of the terms that are to be multiplied by four into the variable S1, and all of the terms that are to be multiplied by 2 into the variable S2. We will then have:

$$S1 = F(X_1) + F(X_3) + \ldots + F(X_{N-1})$$
$$S2 = F(X_2) + F(X_4) + \ldots + F(X_{N-2})$$

and

$$S = \frac{H}{3}(4S1 + 2S2 + F(A) + F(B))$$

The flowchart for the computational part of the program is easy to write (see Figure 6.3). Remember that S1 will normally have one more term than S2. Therefore, if both S1 and S2 are to be computed in a common loop, an $F(X_{N-1})$ term will have to be added at the end.

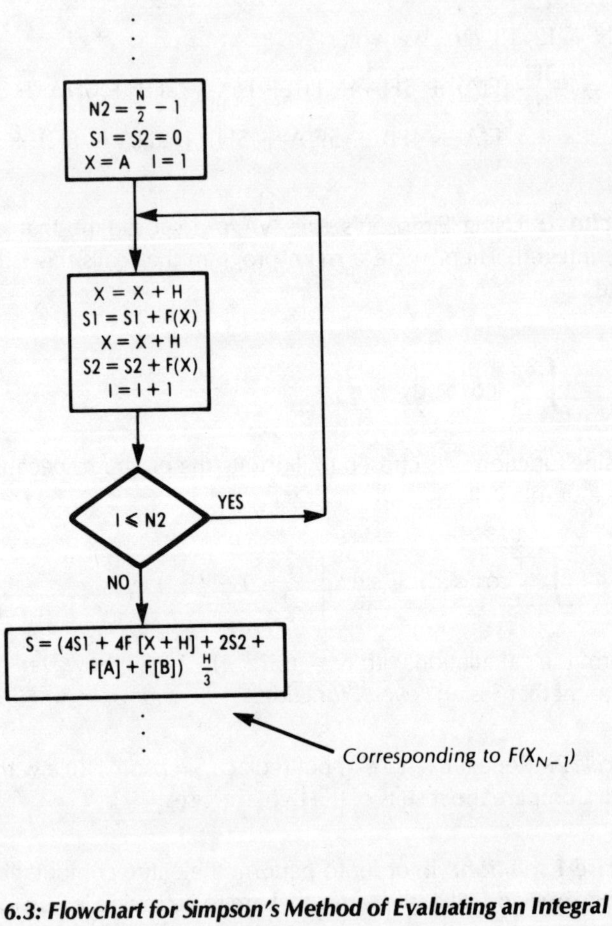

Figure 6.3: Flowchart for Simpson's Method of Evaluating an Integral

Exercise 2 solution: The same method used to obtain the solution for Exercise 1 should be used to obtain the solution for Exercise 2. However, there is a difference. In Exercise 2 we accumulate partial sums in the loop, and make one final sum upon exit from the loop. These additional calculations lengthen the program considerably, but do not make it any more complex. For this reason we have not redrawn the corresponding flowchart for this exercise.

The program and sample run in Figures 6.4 and 6.5 show Simpson's Rule, and the program and sample run in Figures 6.6 and 6.7 show Weddle's Method.

```
10 DIM S$(15),N$(15),P$(40)
15 REM EVALUATION OF AN INTE-
17 REM GRAL BY SIMPSON'S RULE
50 PRINT "APPROXIMATION OF A";
51 PRINT " DEFINITE INTEGRAL"
55 PRINT "BY SIMPSON'S RULE"
60 PRINT
70 PRINT "INTERVALS   INTEGRAL"
80 PRINT
100 PI=3.14159265
102 GOTO 112
105 REM ********FUNCTION TO INTEGRATE
110 Y=COS(X)
111 RETURN
112 A=-PI/2
113 B=PI/2
115 FOR N=6 TO 30 STEP 6
120 GOSUB 3500
130 GOSUB 4000
140 NEXT N
150 END
3400 REM SUBROUTINE TO COMPUTE
3410 REM DEFINITE INTEGRAL BY
3415 REM SIMPSON'S RULE
3420 REM H REPRESENTS THE STEP
3425 REM INTEGRATION SIZE
3500 IF INT(N/2)<>N/2 THEN 3640
3510 N2=N/2-1
3520 H=(B-A)/N
3530 S1=0
3540 S2=0
3550 X=A
3560 FOR I=1 TO N2
3570 X=X+H
3575 GOSUB 105
3580 S1=S1+Y
3590 X=X+H
3595 GOSUB 105
3600 S2=S2+Y
3610 NEXT I
3612 X=X+H:GOSUB 105:YH=Y
```

Figure 6.4: Simpson's Rule Program (continues)

```
3614 X=A:GOSUB 105:YA=Y
3616 X=B:GOSUB 105:YB=Y
3620 S=(4*(S1+YH)+2*S2+YA+YB)*H/3
3630 RETURN
3640 PRINT "ERROR TERMINATION";
3645 PRINT ": ODD # OF ";
3647 PRINT "INTERVALS"
3650 END
3990 REM OUTPUT SUBROUTINE
4000 P$="                              "
4005 N$=STR$(N)
4010 S$=STR$(S)
4020 P$(3-LEN(N$))=N$
4050 P$(13)=S$
4070 PRINT P$
4100 RETURN
9999 END
```

Figure 6.4: Simpson's Rule Program

```
APPROXIMATION OF A DEFINITE INTEGRAL
BY SIMPSON'S RULE

INTERVALS   INTEGRAL

 6          2.0008632
12          2.00005263
18          2.00001035
24          2.00000327
30          2.00000135
```

Figure 6.5: Output of Integral Values

```
10 DIM S$(15),N$(15),P$(40)
15 REM EVALUATION OF AN INTE-
20 REM GRAL BY WEDDLE'S METHOD
80 PRINT "APPROXIMATION OF A ";
81 PRINT "DEFINITE INTEGRAL"
85 PRINT "BY WEDDLE'S METHOD"
90 PRINT
100 PI=3.14159265
102 GOTO 120
105 REM ********FUNCTION TO INTEGRATE
110 Y=COS(Q)
115 RETURN
120 A=-PI/2
130 B=PI/2
140 PRINT "INTERVALS   ";
141 PRINT "INTEGRAL"
145 PRINT
150 FOR N=6 TO 30 STEP 6
160 GOSUB 3500
170 GOSUB 4000
```

Figure 6.6: Weddle's Method Program (continues)

```
175 NEXT N
180 END
3500 IF N-6*INT(N/6)<>0 THEN 3700
3510 P=N/6
3520 X=A
3530 H=(B-A)/N
3540 S1=0
3550 S2=0
3560 S3=0
3570 S6=0
3600 FOR I=1 TO P
3610 Q=X+H:GOSUB 105:S1=S1+Y
3620 Q=X+2*H:GOSUB 105:S2=S2+Y
3630 Q=X+3*H:GOSUB 105:S3=S3+Y
3640 Q=X+4*H:GOSUB 105:S2=S2+Y
3650 Q=X+5*H:GOSUB 105:S1=S1+Y
3660 Q=X+6*H:GOSUB 105:S6=S6+Y
3665 X=X+6*H
3670 NEXT I
3675 Q=A:GOSUB 105:YA=Y
3677 Q=B:GOSUB 105:YB=Y
3680 S=0.3*H*(YA-YB+5*S1+S2+6*S3+2*S6)
3690 RETURN
3700 PRINT "ERROR TERMINATION";
3701 PRINT ": ";N;"  IS NOT ";
3702 PRINT "A MULTIPLE OF SIX."
3720 END
4000 REM OUTPUT SUBROUTINE
4004 P$="                                       "
4005 N$=STR$(N)
4010 S$=STR$(S)
4020 P$(3-LEN(N$))=N$
4050 P$(13)=S$
4070 PRINT P$
4100 RETURN
9999 END
```

Figure 6.6: Weddle's Method Program

```
APPROXIMATION OF A DEFINITE INTEGRAL
BY WEDDLE'S METHOD

INTERVALS    INTEGRAL

 6           1.99994587
12           1.99999922
18           1.99999994
24           1.99999999
30           1.99999999
```

Figure 6.7: Output of Integral Values

Comparison of results: The exact result of the calculation is known from theory to be 2.0. The following table shows how the results are obtained using the two methods.

N	SIMPSON	WEDDLE
6	2.0008632	1.99994587
12	2.00005263	1.99999922
18	2.00001035	1.99999994
24	2.00000327	1.99999999
30	2.00000135	1.99999999

This table shows that (at least for the cosine function) Weddle's method converges much more rapidly than Simpson's, and that round-off errors are not a problem even at 30 intervals.

6.3 Calculation of π Using Regular Polygons

A close approximation of π can be obtained by comparing the perimeter of a regular polygon to the circumference of the inscribed or circumscribed circle. By doubling the sides of the polygons before each iteration, the perimeters of the polygons will eventually approximate (by an upper and lower bound) the perimeter of the circle, which itself can be considered as a polygon with an infinite number of sides.

The first polygon is a square. From the square we can calculate two estimates of values for π; one greater than π, and one less than π. After each iteration, these two values move closer to each other and the two computations are repeated, until the values are no longer moving closer to each other due to round-off errors. These computations are:

1. calculation of the length of the side
2. estimation of π.

Analysis of the exercise: We will now study the two cases of the inscribed and circumscribed polygons separately.

The inscribed polygon: Given a circle of radius 1 (see Figure 6.8), the length of the side, S, of the inscribed square is given by:

$$S^2 = AB^2 = OA^2 + OB^2 = 1 + 1$$

hence,

$$AB = S = \quad 2.$$

We will now calculate the length, AC, of the side of an inscribed octagon:

$$AC^2 = IA^2 + IC^2 \ (*)$$

with

$$IA = S/2$$
$$IC = OC - OI$$

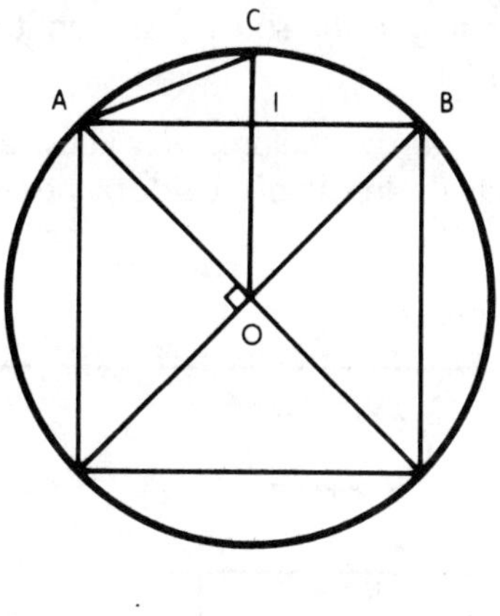

Figure 6.8: Inscribed Square

OI is given by:

$$OI^2 = OA^2 - IA^2 = 1 - \frac{S^2}{4}$$

By substituting the above calculation into the part of the above equation marked by (∗), we have

$$AC^2 = \left(\frac{S}{2}\right)^2 + \left(1 - \sqrt{1 - \frac{S^2}{4}}\right)^2$$

$$= \frac{S^2}{4} + \left(1 - 2\sqrt{1 - \frac{S^2}{4}} + \left(1 - \frac{S^2}{4}\right)\right)$$

$$= \frac{S^2}{4} + \left(2 - 2\sqrt{1 - \frac{S^2}{4}} - \frac{S^2}{4}\right)$$

$$= 2 - 2\sqrt{1 - \frac{S^2}{4}}$$

Now we can estimate π by equating the circumference of the circle to the perimeter of the inscribed octagon:

$$8*AC = 2\pi*OC$$

Thus, the general equation to approximate π, given a circle of radius 1 and a regular inscribed polygon of N sides, is:

$$\pi = \frac{\text{Perimeter}}{2} = \frac{N}{2} * (\text{length of one side})$$

Preliminary flowchart: The flowchart displayed in Figure 6.9 shows the initialization corresponding to the square, and an iterative calculation for polygons of a higher order.

The circumscribed polygon: As before, we will use a circle with a radius 1 (see Figure 6.10). Initially, the length of the side of the circumscribed square is defined as:

$$AB = 2AJ = 2OJ$$

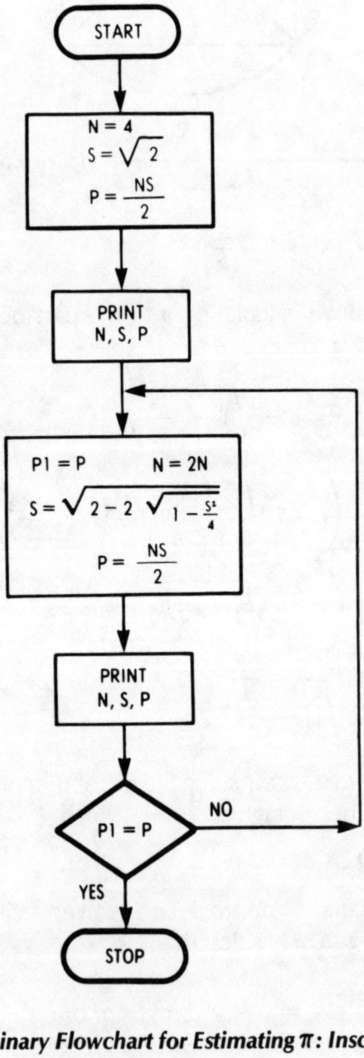

Figure 6.9: Preliminary Flowchart for Estimating π: Inscribed Polygons

and, therefore:

$$AB = S = 2$$

The length, HK, of the circumscribed octagon must now be determined. To do this we note:

$$IK^2 = AK^2 - IA^2 \; (**)$$
with $AK = \frac{S}{2} - IK$ since $IK = KJ$

therefore:

$$AK^2 = \frac{S^2}{4} - S*IK$$

$$OA^2 = \frac{S^2}{4} + 1$$

therefore:

$$IA = \sqrt{1 + \frac{S^2}{4}} - 1$$

$$IA^2 = 2 + \frac{S^2}{4} - 2\sqrt{1 + \frac{S^2}{4}}$$

By substituting the above calculation into the equation noted by (**), we obtain:

$$IK^2 = \frac{S^2}{4} - S*IK + IK^2 - 2 - \frac{S^2}{4} + 2\sqrt{1 + \frac{S^2}{4}}$$

$$S*IK = 2\sqrt{1 + \frac{S^2}{4}} - 2$$

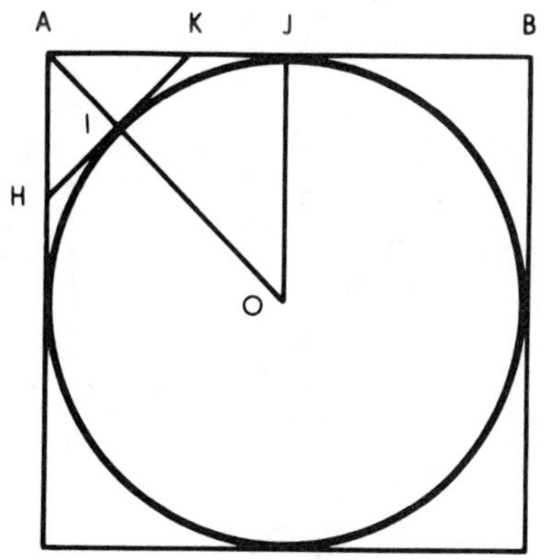

Figure 6.10: Circumscribed Square

Hence, the length of a side of the new circumscribed octagon is:

$$HK = 2IK = \frac{4}{S}\left(\sqrt{1 + \frac{S^2}{4}} - 1\right)$$

We will approximate π by writing NHK = 2π.

Modified flowchart: A new flowchart depicting this method is shown in Figure 6.11. This flowchart closely resembles the flowchart in Figure 6.9. The

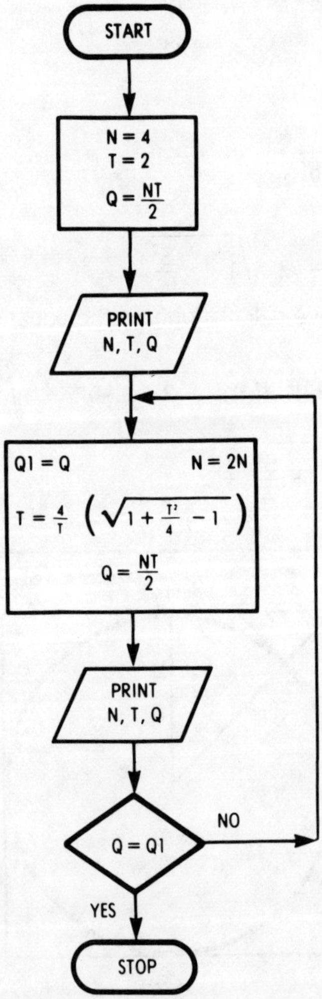

Figure 6.11: Modified Flowchart for Estimating π: Circumscribed Polygons

approach shown in this flowchart yields values greater than π, as opposed to the flowchart in Figure 6.9, where the calculated values are less than π.

Final flowchart: We can combine the two temporary flowcharts to obtain a final flowchart (see Figure 6.12), which, at each iteration, brackets π in a diminishing interval. Writing a program from this flowchart is not very difficult (see Figure 6.13). Experience shows, however, that the effect of round-off errors can be very large, and results can become distorted very quickly. For this reason, we compute the difference between the higher and lower estimates by:

$$E = Q - P$$

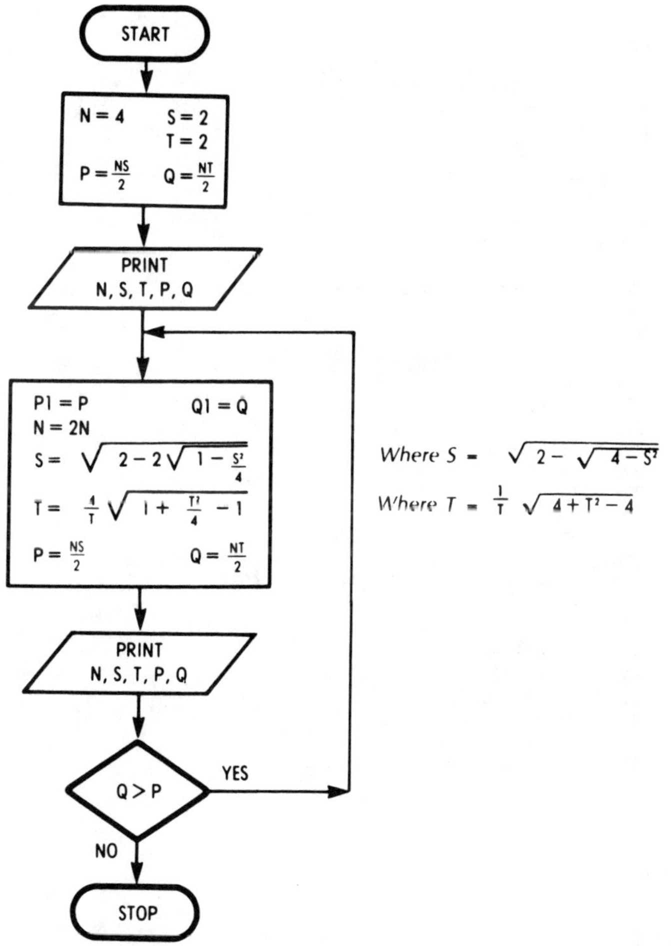

Figure 6.12: Final Flowchart for Estimating π

```
100 REM COMPUTATION OF PI BY THE
101 REM METHOD OF INSCRIBED POLYGON
102 REM AND CIRCUMSCRIBED POLYGON.
105 DIM L$(40),E$(20),ERR(20)
110 I=1:N=4
120 C=SQR(2)
130 D=2
140 P=0.5*N*C
150 Q=0.5*N*D
152 M=0.5*(P+Q)
155 E=Q-P
160 PRINT :PRINT "SIDES LOW-PI";
165 PRINT "    HIGH-PI    MEAN-PI"
167 PRINT
170 GOSUB 400
180 P1=P
190 Q1=Q
200 N=2*N
210 C=SQR(2-2*SQR(1-0.25*C*C))
220 D=4*(SQR(1+0.25*D*D)-1)/D
230 P=0.5*N*C
240 Q=0.5*N*D
242 M=0.5*(P+Q)
245 E=Q-P
250 GOSUB 400
255 IF E<0 THEN E$="E<0":GOTO 280
260 IF P1=P THEN E$="P1=P":GOTO 280
270 IF Q1<>Q THEN 180
280 REM ************PRINT ERROR TABLE
282 S=4
285 PRINT :PRINT "SIDES   ERROR";
290 PRINT "          STOPPED WHEN ";E$
291 PRINT
292 FOR J=2 TO I
293 L$="                                        "
294 L$(1)=STR$(S)
295 L$(5)=STR$(1+ABS(ERR(J)))
296 L$(5,5)=" ":PRINT L$
297 S=2*S
298 NEXT J
300 END
400 REM ****************PRINT RESULTS
405 A=5:B=11
407 L$="                                        "
410 L$(1)=STR$(N)
412 L$(A)=STR$(P)
414 L$(A+B)=STR$(Q)
416 L$(A+2*B)=STR$(M)
420 PRINT L$
425 I=I+1:ERR(I)=M-3.14159265
430 RETURN
```

Figure 6.13: π-Calculation Program

When E becomes negative the iterations are stopped because they are no longer accurate.

We can also calculate a mean estimate for π based on the average of the P and Q results. With this method, the mean converges to π quite rapidly. Although the calculations were done with great precision, the true values beginning with the numbers:

$$\pi = 3.141592653589793\ldots$$

cannot be approximated precisely by using this method because the ninth digit of the mean value of E is not correct. This is due to the computational process, which accumulates round-off errors in a calculation of this type. If this process is continued much further, it will lead to extremely inaccurate results.

A sample run on the ATARI is shown in Figure 6.14. It should be noted that microcomputers can often match the accuracy (but not the speed) of large machines, particularly if their interpreters or compilers permit double precision.

```
SIDES LOW-PI     HIGH-PI     MEAN-PI

4    2.82842712 4           3.41421356
8    3.06146743 3.31370848 3.18758795
16   3.1214451  3.18259749 3.15202129
32   3.13654852 3.15172396 3.14413624
64   3.14033007 3.14411128 3.14222067
128  3.14127882 3.1421878  3.14173331
256  3.14153306 3.1416606  3.14159683
512  3.14161128 3.14114478 3.14137803

SIDES    ERROR          STOPPED WHEN E<0

4      .27262091
8      .0459953
16     .01042864
32     .00254359
64     .00062802
128    .00014066
256    .00000418
512    .00021462
```

Figure 6.14: Output of Estimates of π

6.4 Solving an Equation by Dichotomy

Given an equation F(X) = 0, assume that at least one root is found in the interval (A, B). Assume also that the function is continuous and bounded in that interval, and that F(A) and F(B) are of opposite signs.

Algorithm: Obtain a solution by continually cutting the interval in half and always choosing, for the next iteration, the half in which the function changes sign. For example:

1. Compute: $X = \dfrac{A + B}{2}$

   $Y = F(X)$

2. If F(A) and Y are of the same sign:
   set A = X and go to 3
   If not
   set B = X and go to 3
3. Test for one of the following conditions:
   $|Y| \leqslant E1$
   $|B - A| \leqslant E2$
   E1 and E2 having been specified in advance.

   — If neither condition is met, go to 1 and continue the iteration
   — If either condition occurs, terminate the iteration.

Exercise: Using the algorithm and assumptions given above, write a subroutine that solves an equation.

Solution: The subroutine that is used must be able to operate, regardless of the function defined or input given by the user. In particular, if two points A and B are given such that F(A) and F(B) are of the same sign, the subroutine should be able to detect that fact and display an error message. This leads to the first validity check. In the example given here, we use a variable, L, to which one of three possible values is assigned:

- – 1, if F(A) and F(B) are of the same sign
- 0, if, after one or more iterations, $|F(X)| \leqslant E1$
- 1, if an interval such that $|B - A| \leqslant E2$ is specified, after one or more iterations.

Note that in the solution example we have assumed that the user has assigned positive values to E1 and E2.

So that the values of A and B will not be modified in the subroutine, we use two auxiliary variables, X1 and X2, which represent the end points of the interval. The midpoint is designated as XM, and the values of the function at these points are Y1, Y2 and YM. This is shown in the flowchart in Figure 6.15. The program listing is shown in Figure 6.16.

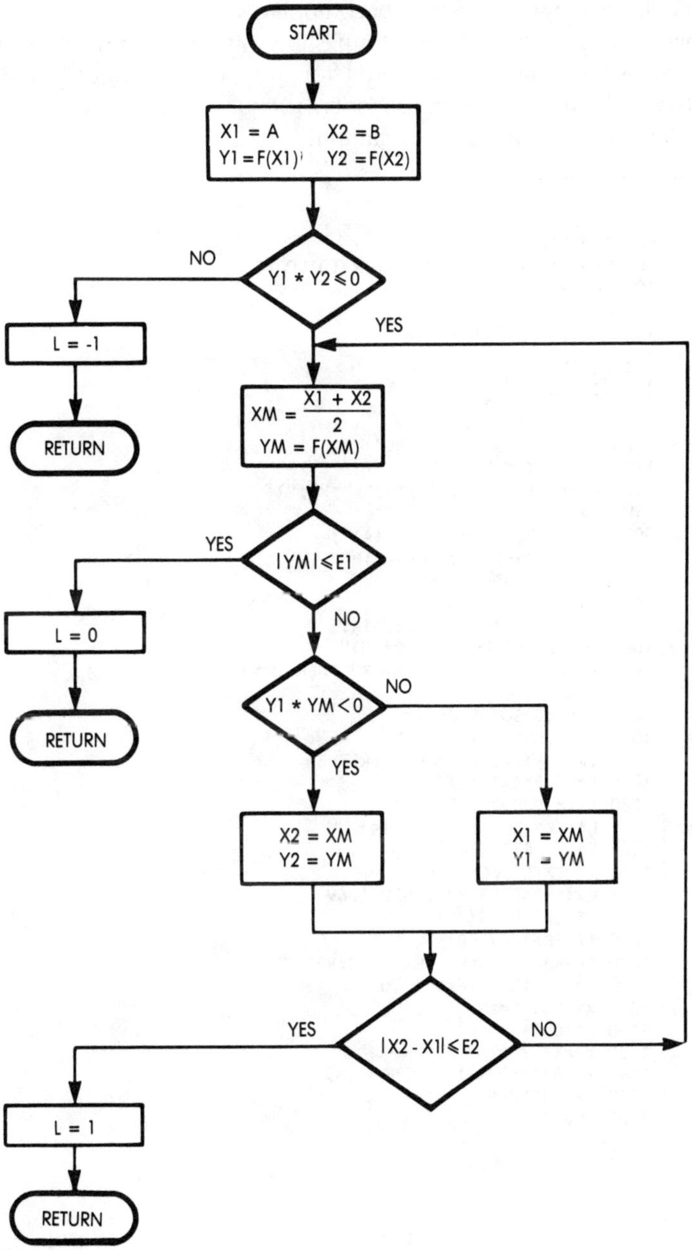

Figure 6.15: Flowchart for Solving an Equation by Dichotomy

On line 1050 in the program in Figure 6.16, the division by 2 was replaced by multiplication by 0.5. This type of computation is faster for ordinary "floating point" computations. In the test run, shown in Figure 6.17, the root value produced by the computation differed from the exact root value by less than .000002%. The root of this transcendental equation is the number which equals ten times its own natural logarithm.

```
80 DIM L$(40),Q$(10)
90 GOTO 110
100 REM ************ FUNCTION TO SOLVE
105 Y=10*LOG(X)-X
108 RETURN
110 E1=1E-08:E2=1E-08
120 A=1:B=4
130 GOSUB 1000
140 IF L=-1 THEN 300
150 PRINT "L =  ";L
160 PRINT "SOLUTION FOUND"
170 PRINT "X = ";XM;"      Y = ";YM
180 PRINT "INTERVAL=(";X1;",";X2;")"
190 END
300 PRINT "NO SOLUTION; F(A)";
301 PRINT " AND F(B) HAVE THE"
305 PRINT " SAME SIGN"
310 END
1000 PRINT "PRINT INTERMEDIATE ";
1002 PRINT "RESULTS (Y OR N)"
1004 PR=0:INPUT Q$:IF Q$="Y" THEN PR=1
1010 X1=A:X2=B
1020 X=X1:GOSUB 100:Y1=Y
1030 X=X2:GOSUB 100:Y2=Y
1040 IF Y1*Y2>0 THEN L=-1:RETURN
1050 XM=0.5*(X1+X2)
1060 X=XM:GOSUB 100:YM=Y
1062 L$="X=               Y=          "
1064 L$(3)=STR$(XM)
1066 IF YM<0 THEN 1068
1067 L$(19)=STR$(YM):GOTO 1069
1068 L$(18)=STR$(YM)
1069 IF PR THEN PRINT L$
1070 IF ABS(YM)<=E1 THEN L=0:RETURN
1080 IF Y1*YM<0 THEN 1120
1090 X1=XM:Y1=YM
1100 GOTO 1140
1120 X2=XM:Y2=YM
1140 IF ABS(X2-X1)>E2 THEN 1050
1150 L=1:RETURN
1200 END
```

Figure 6.16: Program: Solving an Equation by Dichotomy

```
PRINT INTERMEDIATE RESULTS (Y OR N
?Y
X=2.5          Y= 6.66290731
X=1.75         Y= 3.84615787
X=1.375        Y= 1.80953731
X=1.1875       Y= 0.53100257
X=1.09375      Y=-0.19762841
X=1.140625     Y= 0.17513857
X=1.1171875    Y=-9.04384E-03
X=1.12890625   Y= 0.08358618
X=1.12304687   Y= 0.03740724
X=1.12011718   Y= 0.01421586
X=1.11865234   Y= 2.59459E-03
X=1.11791992   Y=-3.22248E-03
X=1.11828613   Y=-3.1341E-04
X=1.11846923   Y= 1.14068E-03
X=1.11837768   Y= 4.1367E-04
X=1.1183319    Y= 5.01E-05
X=1.11830901   Y=-1.3169E-04
X=1.11832045   Y=-4.084E-05
X=1.11832617   Y= 4.59E-06
X=1.11832331   Y=-1.812E-05
X=1.11832474   Y=-6.76E-06
X=1.11832545   Y=-1.13E-06
X=1.11832581   Y= 1.73E-06
X=1.11832563   Y= 3.1E-07
X=1.11832554   Y=-4.1E-07
X=1.11832558   Y=-9E-08
X=1.1183256    Y= 7E-08
X=1.11832559   Y=-2E-08
L =  1
SOLUTION FOUND
X = 1.11832559       Y = -2E-08
INTERVAL=(1.11832559,1.1183256)
```

Figure 6.17: Output of Solution and Interval

6.5 Numerical Evaluations of Polynomials

We wish to calculate the numerical value for a given X of a polynomial P(X) with known coefficients. To do this we use an approach that minimizes the number of operations required. To evaluate the value of P(X), given by:

$$P(X) = A_0X^N + A_1X^{N-1} + \ldots + A_{N-1}X + A_N$$

we compute:

$$P = (\ldots(((A_0X + A_1)X + A_2)X + A_3)X + \ldots + A_{N-1})X + AN$$

Exercise: Write a program that evaluates P(X) in a subroutine using the values of X provided by the main program.

Solution: The formula presented previously entails the following sequence of computations:

$P = A_0$; then $P = PX + A_1$; then $P = PX + A_2$; and so forth, until finally, $P = PX + A_N$.

Based on the calculations presented above, make an iteration like the following:

```
P = A(0)
   FOR I = 1 TO N
P = P * X + A(I)
   NEXT I
```

The complete program is given in Figure 6.18. The subroutine consists of only five instructions (lines 1000 to 1040) including the return command. Figure 6.19 shows a sample run.

```
100 REM NUMERICAL VALUE OF A
102 REM POLYNOMIAL USING
105 REM HORNER'S APPROACH
110 DIM A(100)
115 PRINT "INPUT DEGREE OF ";
117 PRINT "POLYNOMIAL ";
120 INPUT N
130 PRINT "INPUT THE ";N+1;
132 PRINT " COEFFICIENTS IN"
135 PRINT "DESCENDING ORDER"
140 FOR I=0 TO N
150 INPUT A:A(I)=A
160 NEXT I
170 PRINT "INPUT THE VALUE OF";
172 PRINT " X FOR WHICH YOU"
180 PRINT "WOULD LIKE THE ";
182 PRINT "POLYNOMIAL VALUE ";
190 INPUT X
200 IF X=0 THEN END
210 GOSUB 1000
220 PRINT
230 PRINT "POLYNOMIAL VALUE  ";
232 PRINT P
240 PRINT
250 GOTO 170
990 REM POLYNOMIAL EVALUATION
992 REM USING HORNER'S
995 REM APPROACH
1000 P=A(0)
1010 FOR I=1 TO N
1020 P=P*X+A(I)
1030 NEXT I
1040 RETURN
1050 END
```

Figure 6.18: Polynomial Evaluation Program

```
INPUT DEGREE OF POLYNOMIAL ?2
INPUT THE 3 COEFFICIENTS IN
DESCENDING ORDER
?1
?1
?-6
INPUT THE VALUE OF X FOR WHICH YOU
WOULD LIKE THE POLYNOMIAL VALUE ?1

POLYNOMIAL VALUE  -4

INPUT THE VALUE OF X FOR WHICH YOU
WOULD LIKE THE POLYNOMIAL VALUE ?2

POLYNOMIAL VALUE  0

INPUT THE VALUE OF X FOR WHICH YOU
WOULD LIKE THE POLYNOMIAL VALUE ?3

POLYNOMIAL VALUE  6

INPUT THE VALUE OF X FOR WHICH YOU
WOULD LIKE THE POLYNOMIAL VALUE ?0
```

Figure 6.19: Output of Polynomial Values

Conclusion

The exercises presented in this chapter have shown that problems in "the mathematics of the continuous" (the definite integral, solving an equation, etc.) may be solved with few programming difficulties. In fact, the various flowcharts presented in this chapter are actually less complex than those for the integer arithmetic exercises in Chapter 3. It was also noted in this chapter that many iterations are often necessary to obtain an adequate precision for these types of problems. Normally, a computer is well-suited to this type of processing. The programmer must, however, consider the validity of results obtained when certain techniques are used. Round-off errors can have serious effects on the accuracy of the calculation, especially when the calculation is extensive.

Several excellent books have been written on "numerical analysis" for computers. Interested readers can consult these texts for more information on the effect of errors in computation and methods of calculation to use on computers.

CHAPTER 7

Financial Computations

Introduction

This chapter will present several examples of accounting and financial applications. These examples are relatively easy to program but, in the general form presented here, some of them may be difficult to apply to actual situations. They can be useful, however, as a basis from which to derive programs for specific applications.

7.1 Sales Forecasting

In this exercise we want to predict the progress in gross sales, given the rate of growth. Two examples will be considered.

Exercise 1: A company has achieved a given figure, S, of gross sales and is predicting a growth rate, R, for the next N years. Determine future gross sales figures using the following inputs:

Y = Current year
S = Sales for the year Y
R = Rate of growth expressed as a percent
N = Number of years for which we want sales forecasts.

For example:

Y = 1980
S = 20,000
R = 20%
N = 5

Solution: The only difficult part of this problem is arranging the output on the page. We must take into account the fact that a rate expressed as a percent will give rise to a multiplier, R1, of the form:

R1 = 1 + R/100

The program listing is shown in Figure 7.1 and the sample dialogue is shown in Figure 7.2.

```
100 PRINT "SALES FORECAST"
110 PRINT
120 PRINT "CURRENT YEAR AND";
125 PRINT " SALES  ";
130 INPUT Y,S
140 PRINT
150 PRINT "RATE OF GROWTH   ";
160 INPUT R
170 PRINT
180 PRINT "NUMBER OF YEARS TO";
185 PRINT " FORECAST   ";
190 INPUT N
200 PRINT
210 PRINT " YEAR";
215 PRINT "         SALES"
220 PRINT
230 PRINT " ";Y,S
240 R1=1+0.01*R
250 FOR I=1 TO N
260 Y=Y+1
270 S=S*R1
280 PRINT " ";Y,S
290 NEXT I
300 END
```

Figure 7.1: Sales Forecast Program

```
SALES FORECAST

CURRENT YEAR AND SALES  ?1983,1220

RATE OF GROWTH  ?13

NUMBER OF YEARS TO FORECAST  ?6

 YEAR     SALES

 1983     1220
 1984     1378.6
 1985     1557.818
 1986     1760.33434
 1987     1989.177804
 1988     2247.770918
 1989     2539.981137
```

Figure 7.2: Sample Dialogue from the Sales Forecast Program

Exercise 2: In this exercise we are given two basic figures: gross sales and sales volume. We anticipate an increased sales volume of Q percent and an annual inflation rate of I percent. We want to forecast the gross sales and sales volume for the next N years.

The inputs are:

Y = Year from which to start forecasting
V = Volume of sales that year
S = Sales that year
Q = Growth of volume in percent per year
I = Inflation in percent per year
N = Number of years to forecast

Solution: We can use the program presented in Figure 7.1 as a model. For this exercise, however, we must account for two rates of increase (see Figure 7.3). Figure 7.4 shows the sample dialogue.

```
90 DIM L$(40)
100 PRINT "YEAR,VOLUME AND";
105 PRINT " GROSS SALES?"
110 INPUT Y,V,S
120 PRINT "RATES (%) OF INCRE";
125 PRINT "ASE IN VOLUME, AND "
127 PRINT "INFLATION  ";
130 INPUT Q,I
140 PRINT "NUMBER OF YEARS";
145 PRINT " TO FORECAST ";
150 INPUT N
160 Q1=1+0.01*Q
170 I1=Q1*(1+0.01*I)
180 PRINT
190 PRINT " YEAR      VOLUME";
```

Figure 7.3: Expanded Sales Forecast Program (continues)

```
195 PRINT "      GROSS SALES"
200 PRINT
210 GOSUB 400
220 FOR J=1 TO N
230 Y=Y+1
240 V=V*Q1
250 S=S*I1
260 GOSUB 400
270 NEXT J
280 END
400 REM OUTPUT ROUTINE
410 L$="                                  "
420 L$(2)=STR$(Y)
430 L$(12)=STR$(V)
440 L$(24)=STR$(S)
445 PRINT L$
450 RETURN
```

Figure 7.3: Expanded Sales Forecast Program

```
YEAR,VOLUME AND GROSS SALES?
?1983,100,15000
RATES (%) OF INCREASE IN VOLUME, AND
INFLATION  ?5,10
NUMBER OF YEARS TO FORECAST ?6

 YEAR      VOLUME      GROSS SALES

 1983      100         15000
 1984      105         17325
 1985      110.25      20010.375
 1986      115.7625    23111.9831
 1987      121.550625  26694.3404
 1988      127.628156  30831.9631
 1989      134.009563  35610.9173
```

Figure 7.4: Expanded Sales Forecast Output

Note: In an actual situation, we would use a data formatting subroutine to produce more sophisticated output.

7.2 Repayment of Loans

A loan may be repaid in a number of ways. This exercise presents two relatively simple and easily programmed methods for calculating payments.

7.2.1 First Method of Payment: Annuity

A loan, L, is repaid over N years. At the end of each year a fixed fraction of the face value of the note is paid, plus interest on the unpaid balance. For example, if:

L = Loan amount
N = Number of years to pay
R = Rate of interest

then, at the end of the first year the payment is:

$$\frac{L}{N} + L*R$$

At the end of the second year the payment is:

$$\frac{L}{N} + \left(L - \frac{L}{N}\right)*R$$

and so on.

Exercise: Write a program that computes the payments due, and prints out the sum of all the payments to be made.

Solution: We will use the following variables:

R1 = $\frac{L}{N}$, the fraction or portion of the loan payment made each year

I = The amount of interest paid each year

R2 = The total payment made each year (R2 = R1 + I)

To calculate I, we need to know the unpaid balance of the loan. Let U represent the amount of the unpaid balance. Initially, U is equal to L, but each year after the first year, U is diminished by R1 (the amount of the principal repaid). This logic leads us to the following procedure:

Initial values
- R = R/100, since I is given as a percent
- R1 = $\frac{L}{N}$
- U = L

Then, for each year
- I = U * R
- R2 = R1 + I
- U = U − R1

We can calculate the total payments made in one of two ways. We may either:

1. keep a running total of the annual payments; Q = 0 initially, and thereafter, Q = Q + R2, or
2. keep a running total of the principal plus interest expense; Q = L initially, and thereafter, Q = Q + I.

From a theoretical point of view, these two methods are identical. But because the first method is less sensitive to round-off and truncation errors, it is the superior method in this case. The flowchart and resulting program are given in Figures 7.5 and 7.6, respectively. A sample run appears in Figure 7.7.

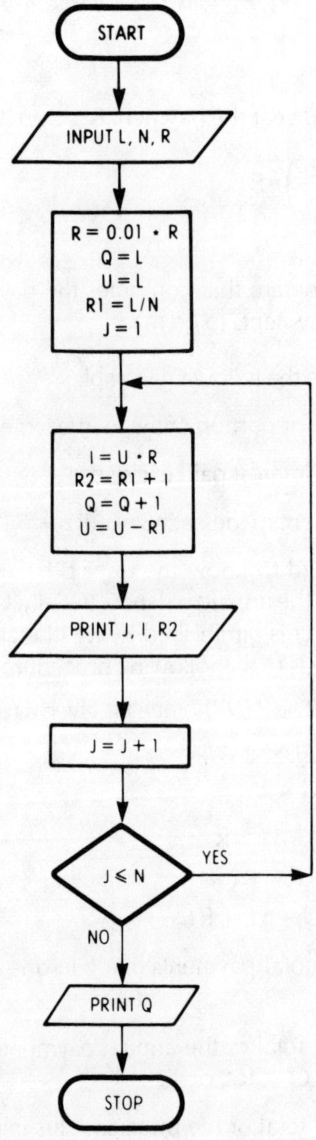

Figure 7.5: Flowchart for Annuity Program

```
100 REM PROGRAM TO COMPUTE AN
103 REM ANNUITY : EACH YEAR THE
105 REM SAME FRACTION OF THE
110 REM PRINCIPAL IS PAID.
115 DIM L$(40)
120 PRINT "AMOUNT OF LOAN, ";
121 PRINT "RATE OF INTEREST &"
122 PRINT "YEARS TO PAY  ";
125 INPUT L,R,N
127 IF L=0 THEN END
130 R=R*0.01
140 Q=L:U=L
150 R1=L/N
160 PRINT
170 PRINT "PAYMENT # INTEREST";
175 PRINT "  TOTAL AMOUNT DUE"
180 FOR J=1 TO N
190 I=U*R
200 R2=R1+I
210 Q=Q+I
220 U=U-R1
222 L$="                                        "
224 L$(4)=STR$(J):L$(11)=STR$(I)
226 L$(24)=STR$(R2)
230 PRINT L$
240 NEXT J
250 PRINT
251 PRINT "SUM TOTAL PAID";
252 PRINT " OUT = ";Q
255 PRINT :GOTO 120
260 END
```

Figure 7.6: Annuity Program

```
AMOUNT OF LOAN, RATE OF INTEREST &
YEARS TO PAY  ?10000,10,10

PAYMENT # INTEREST  TOTAL AMOUNT DUE
   1       1000         2000
   2       900          1900
   3       800          1800
   4       700          1700
   5       600          1600
   6       500          1500
   7       400          1400
   8       300          1300
   9       200          1200
   10      100          1100

SUM TOTAL PAID OUT = 15500
```

Figure 7.7: Sample Output from the Annuity Program (continues)

```
AMOUNT OF LOAN, RATE OF INTEREST &
YEARS TO PAY  ?10000,12,7

PAYMENT # INTEREST   TOTAL AMOUNT DUE
   1      1200          2628.571428
   2      1028.571432   2457.14286
   3      857.14286     2285.714288
   4      685.714289    2114.285717
   5      514.285717    1942.857145
   6      342.857146    1771.428574
   7      171.428575    1600.000003

SUM TOTAL PAID OUT = 14799.9997

AMOUNT OF LOAN, RATE OF INTEREST &
YEARS TO PAY  ?0,0,0
```

Figure 7.7: Sample Output from Annuity Program

7.2.2 Second Method of Payment: Fixed Monthly Payments

A loan, L, is taken at an annual interest rate of I. The loan is to be paid off in N equal monthly payments. Compute the amount of a monthly payment. Also, calculate for a given range of months the amount of each month's payment applied to paying off the principal and the amount paid as interest.

To do this we take the following approach. First, compute the equivalent *monthly* interest rate I1 that corresponds to the *annual* interest rate, I. This is defined by the relation:

$$(1 + I1)^{12} = 1 + I$$

thus:

$$I1 = (1 + I)^{\frac{1}{12}} - 1$$

(If I is given as percent, we will divide it by 100.)

Note that banks often apply a different formula, which is more favorable to them:

$$I1 = \frac{1}{12}$$

Now compute the amount of the monthly payment given by

$$M = L * \frac{I1(1 + I1)^N}{(1 + I1)^N - 1}$$

Finally, upon request, compute a detailed analysis of the payments. The amount of the payment to be applied to the principal is determined by employing a simple line of reasoning:

- On the first payment, the amount of interest is L*I1; thus, the amount used to pay off the principal is M − L*I1. The balance L − (M − L*I1) serves to compute the interest portion of the second payment, and so forth.

Problem: Write a program that:

1. Reads the following data:
   - the loan amount
   - the annual rate of interest expressed as a percent
   - the number of monthly payments.
2. Performs the calculations and prints:
   - the equivalent monthly interest rate
   - the amount of the monthly payment
   - the total amount to be paid out.
3. Inquires if the user wants to see a breakdown of the payments. If yes, asks for the first and last payments the user wants displayed.

Solution: The first part of the program follows directly from the discussion and the formulas given above, provided that:

- I is input as a percent
- I is then set to I/100
- I1 is maintained internally as a decimal value, but is multiplied by 100 on output, so that it will be expressed as a percent.

For the second part of the program, we design a flowchart (Figure 7.8) in which A and B represent the numbers of the first and last monthly payments (respectively) to be analyzed in detail.

In Figure 7.8 the unpaid principal is represented by L1. In the flowchart we provided a loop on K from 1 to N. This was done in case there is a need for future extension. Strictly speaking, in the context of the problem as stated, it would have been sufficient to vary K from 1 to B, which would have allowed the test K>B to be eliminated. The program and sample run appear in Figures 7.9 and 7.10.

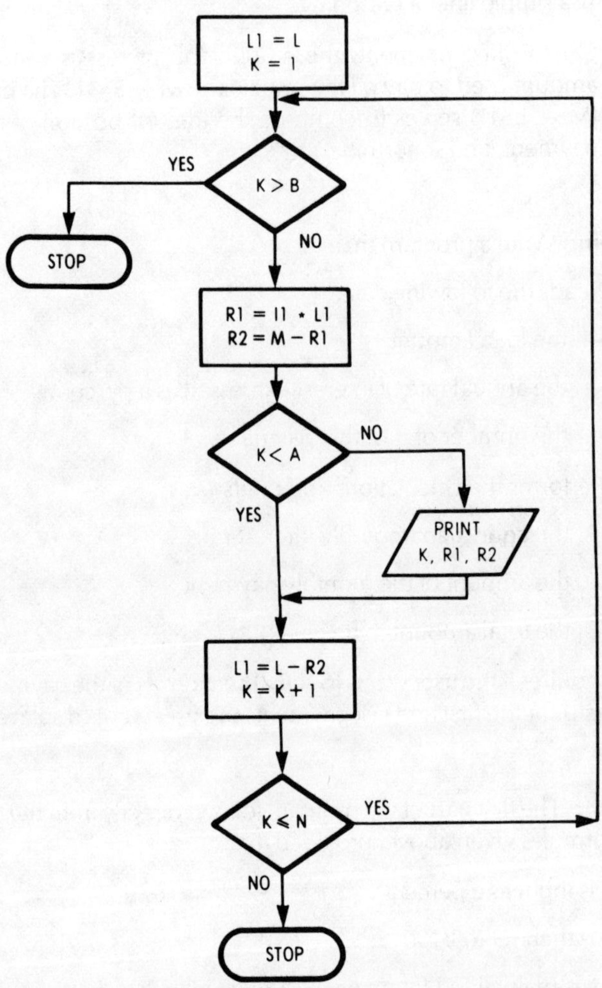

Figure 7.8: Section of Flowchart for Monthly Loan Payments

```
100 REM COMPUTATION OF MONTHLY
105 REM PAYMENTS ON A LOAN
106 DIM R$(10),L$(40)
110 PRINT "AMOUNT OF THE LOAN:  ";
115 INPUT L
120 PRINT "ANNUAL INTEREST IN %:  ";
125 INPUT I
130 PRINT "NUMBER OF MONTHLY ";
```

Figure 7.9: Monthly Loan Payment Program (continues)

```
132 PRINT "PAYMENTS:  ";
135 INPUT N
140 I1=(1+I/100)^(1/12)-1
150 M=L*I1/(1-(1+I1)^(-N))
160 PRINT
170 PRINT "EQUIVALENT MONTHLY"
175 PRINT "INTEREST: ";
177 PRINT 100*I1;"%"
180 PRINT
190 PRINT "MONTHLY PAYMENT: ";M
200 PRINT
210 PRINT "PRINT TOTAL SUM ";
215 PRINT "PAID OUT: ";M*N
220 PRINT
230 PRINT "WOULD YOU LIKE ";
231 PRINT "SOME PAYMENTS "
232 PRINT "DETAILED    "
235 INPUT R$
240 IF R$(1,1)<>"Y" THEN END
250 PRINT "NUMBERS OF THE ";
251 PRINT "FIRST AND LAST "
252 PRINT "PAYMENTS ";
253 PRINT "THAT INTEREST YOU: ";
255 INPUT A,B
260 PRINT
261 PRINT "PAYMENT  ";
262 PRINT "INTEREST    ";
263 PRINT "PRINCIPAL"
270 PRINT :L1=L
280 FOR K=1 TO N
290 IF K>B THEN 350
300 R1=I1*L1:R2=M-R1
310 IF A>K THEN 330
315 L$="                             "
316 L$(2)=STR$(K):L$(10)=STR$(R1)
318 L$(22)=STR$(R2)
320 PRINT L$
330 L1=L1-R2
340 NEXT K
350 END
```

Figure 7.9: Monthly Loan Payment Program

```
AMOUNT OF THE LOAN:  ?33322
ANNUAL INTEREST IN %:  ?6
NUMBER OF MONTHLY PAYMENTS:  ?144

EQUIVALENT MONTHLY
INTEREST: 0.486754%

MONTHLY PAYMENT: 322.438415

PRINT TOTAL SUM PAID OUT: 46431.1317
```

Figure 7.10: Sample Dialogue from Monthly Loan Payment Program (continues)

```
WOULD YOU LIKE SOME PAYMENTS
DETAILED
?YES
NUMBERS OF THE FIRST AND LAST
PAYMENTS THAT INTEREST YOU: ?50,55

PAYMENT  INTEREST    PRINCIPAL

 50      119.151672  203.286743
 51      118.162165  204.27625
 52      117.167843  205.270572
 53      116.16868   206.269735
 54      115.164654  207.273761
 55      114.155741  208.282674
```

Figure 7.10: Sample Dialogue from Monthly Loan Payment Program

7.3 Calculation of the Rate of Growth

A company's annual sales are usually known over a period of several years. The growth of sales generally follows a mathematical law expressed by:

$$C*(1 + R)^{I}$$

where C is a constant, R is the rate of growth, and I is the current year.

The problem is to determine C and R, and then predict the gross sales for the next few years. For our purposes the forecast is limited to a five-year period.

Mathematical analysis: To simplify the problem, we will deviate slightly from a strict mathematical viewpoint. We will try to determine C and R; however, rather than minimizing:

$$\sum_{I}(C(1 + R)^{I} - Y(I))^{2}$$

we will minimize:

$$Q = \sum_{I}(\ln [C(1 + R)^{I}] - \ln Y(I))^{2}$$

$$= \sum_{I}(\ln C + I*\ln (1 + R) - \ln Y(I))^{2}$$

We designate:

$\ln C$ by B
$\ln Y_I$ by Z_I
$\ln (1 + R)$ by A

Now we must minimize the quantity

$$Q = \sum_{I}(B + IA - Z_I)^{2}$$

Note: This exercise should be attempted after the program in Section 10.3 (Chapter 10) on linear regression has been worked through.

Exercise: Based on the program presented in Section 10.3, construct a program that computes the rate of growth R, then produces a five-year sales forecast. In this program, R is represented by the variable R0. We assume that the years are read into an array T and the corresponding gross sales figures are read into an array X.

Solution: This program proceeds in three distinct phases:

1. The reading of the input data N and the arrays T and X, and the computation of:

   $$Y(I) = \ln (X(I))$$

2. The calling of a subroutine to do the linear regression and the computation of the coefficients C and R0. These coefficients are computed from A and B (computed by the subroutine) with the following formulas:

   $$C = e^{B}$$

   and

   $$R0 = e^{A} - 1$$

3. The printing out of R0 and the results:

   — for each known year, the actual and the estimated gross sales
   — for each of the five years to come, the estimated gross sales only.

To avoid printing insignificant decimal places the estimated gross sales, Z, is replaced by:

```
INT (100*Z)/100
```

The high-level flowchart shown in Figure 7.11 is actually quite simple.

The program shown in Figure 7.12 serves as an example of what may be written. This program could be improved by having it print out:

- a correlation coefficient
- a measure of confidence for the forecasted figures. (This would be useful, but it would complicate the program.)

Warning: This type of forecasting should not be used in an actual situation without reservation. In reality, actual sales depend on many things, notably the economic situation and the competition. These and other factors can significantly alter events beyond the predictive power of simple regression.

A sample run is shown in Figure 7.13.

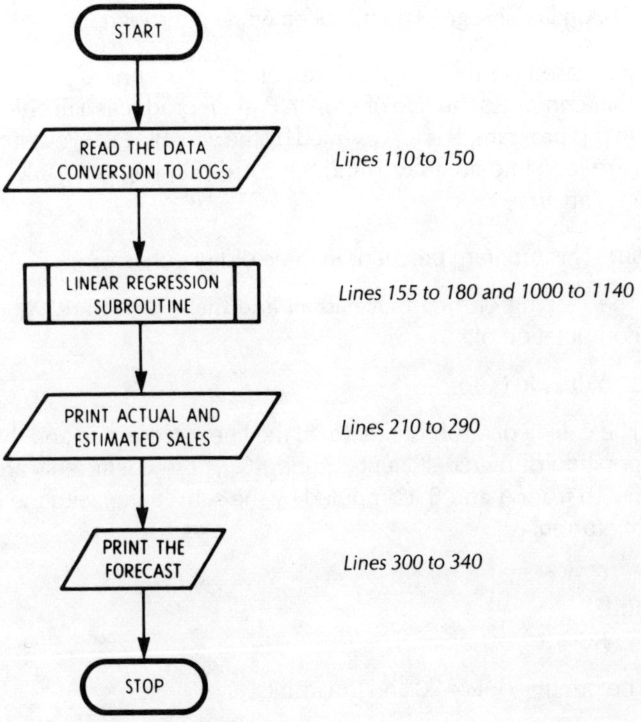

Figure 7.11: High-level Flowchart for Growth Rate Program

```
100 DIM T(15),X(15),Y(15)
110 READ N
120 FOR I=1 TO N
130 READ T,X:T(I)=T:X(I)=X
140 Y(I)=LOG(X(I))
150 NEXT I
155 N0=T(1)
160 GOSUB 1000
170 C=EXP(B)
180 T0=EXP(A)-1
190 PRINT "ESTIMATED GROWTH ";
195 PRINT "RATE:  ";1000*T0
200 PRINT
210 T2=1+T0
220 PRINT " YEAR  ";
221 PRINT "ACTUAL SALES";
223 PRINT " PREDICTED SALES"
230 PRINT
```

Figure 7.12: Growth Rate Program (continues)

```
240 Z=C
260 FOR I=1 TO N
280 PRINT " ";T(I),
281 PRINT X(I),
282 PRINT INT(100*Z)/100
285 Z=Z*T2
290 NEXT I
300 FOR I=1 TO 5
310 T3=T(N)+I
320 Z=Z*T2
330 PRINT " ";T3,,
331 PRINT INT(100*Z)/100
340 NEXT I
400 DATA 6
410 DATA 1975,99.2,1976,110
420 DATA 1977,121.3,1978,133.1
430 DATA 1979,146.3,1980,160
500 END
1000 U1=0
1010 U2=0
1020 V1=0:V2=0
1040 W=0
1050 FOR I=1 TO N
1055 T4=T(I)-N0
1060 U1=U1+T4
1070 V1=V1+Y(I)
1080 U2=U2+T4*T4
1090 V2=V2+Y(I)+Y(I)
1100 W=W+T4*Y(I)
1110 NEXT I
1120 A=(W-U1*V1/N)/(U2-U1*U1/N)
1130 B=(V1-A*U1)/N
1140 RETURN
1150 END
```

Figure 7.12: Growth Rate Program

```
ESTIMATED GROWTH RATE:  100.08464

 YEAR  ACTUAL SALES PREDICTED SALES

 1975      99.2         99.76
 1976      110          109.75
 1977      121.3        120.73
 1978      133.1        132.82
 1979      146.3        146.11
 1980      160          160.73
 1981                   194.52
 1982                   213.99
 1983                   235.4
 1984                   258.96
 1985                   284.88
```

Figure 7.13: Sample Output from the Growth Rate Program

7.4 More on Income Taxes

Using the information from the TAXABLE INCOME program presented in Chapter 1, we will now compute the actual tax due, using various tables. We will limit our discussion to the case of married persons filing a joint return. Additional cases, though, could be readily added to the program.

The table shown in Figure 7.14, taken from an Internal Revenue Service Form 1040, will be used to compute the tax for this case.

Tax-Rate Schedules
SCHEDULE Y
MARRIED INDIVIDUALS, SURVIVING SPOUSES

Taxable Income Over	Not Over	Pay	+	Tax Over	On Excess Over
....	$ 3,400	....		....	....
$ 3,400	5,500	....		14%	$ 3,400
5,500	7,600	294		16%	5,500
7,600	11,900	630		18%	7,600
11,900	16,000	1,404		21%	11,900
16,000	20,200	2,265		24%	16,000
20,200	24,600	3,273		28%	20,200
24,600	29,900	4,505		32%	24,600
29,900	35,200	6,201		37%	29,900
35,200	45,800	8,162		43%	35,200
45,800	60,000	12,720		49%	45,800
60,000	85,600	19,678		54%	60,000
85,600	109,400	33,502		59%	85,600
109,400	162,400	47,544		64%	109,400
162,400	215,400	81,464		68%	162,400
215,400	....	117,504		70%	215,400

Figure 7.14: Tax Table from IRS Form 1040

Exercise: Construct a program that computes tax due using the table given previously.

Solution: The initial input is a figure specifying the amount of TAXABLE INCOME. This figure may be either input directly or calculated by means of the program developed in Chapter 1. Next a table is needed that gives the base tax and the tax rate for each tax bracket. Since this same table is used for all the necessary calculations, it is read only once. A tax computation subroutine is then used. This leads us to the conceptual flowchart shown in Figure 7.15.

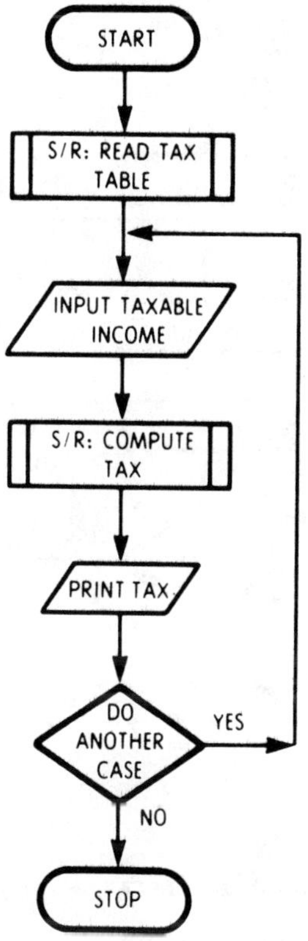

Figure 7.15: Conceptual Flowchart for Income Tax Calculation

A READ-DATA subroutine should be provided with the program, so that the tax table will not have to be entered from the keyboard each time the program is run. Since this table is valid for an entire year, it is appropriate to incorporate the table into the program source. This could be done using DATA instructions (see the flowchart in Figure 7.16).

This leads to the subroutine that appears as lines 500 to 710 of the program shown in Figure 7.18.

We are now ready to calculate the tax. We must first define the arrays that

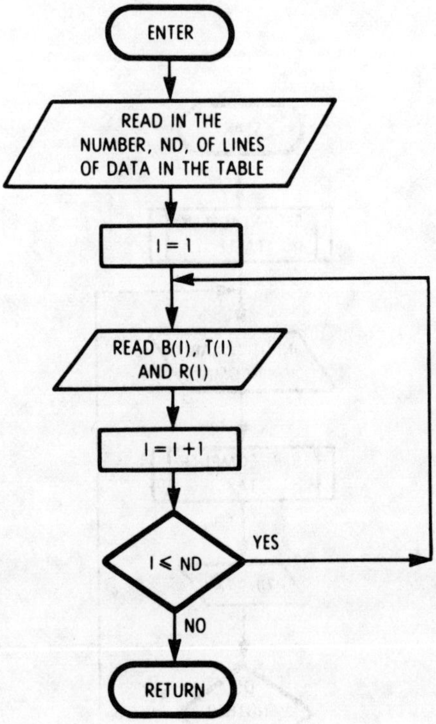

Figure 7.16: Flowchart for READ-DATA Subroutine

are indexed by the tax brackets:

B(I) = The lowest (base) income in tax bracket I
T(I) = The tax corresponding to B(I)
R(I) = The tax rate for this bracket.

If a TAXABLE INCOME, TI, is in bracket I, that is:

$$B(I) \leq TI < B(I + 1)$$

then the tax, T, is given by:

$$T = B(I) + (TI - B(I)) * R(I)$$

To determine the proper tax bracket, we perform a series of tests until we find TI < B(I). At this point we know that I now exceeds the actual bracket by one. This is incorporated into the flowchart displayed in Figure 7.17.

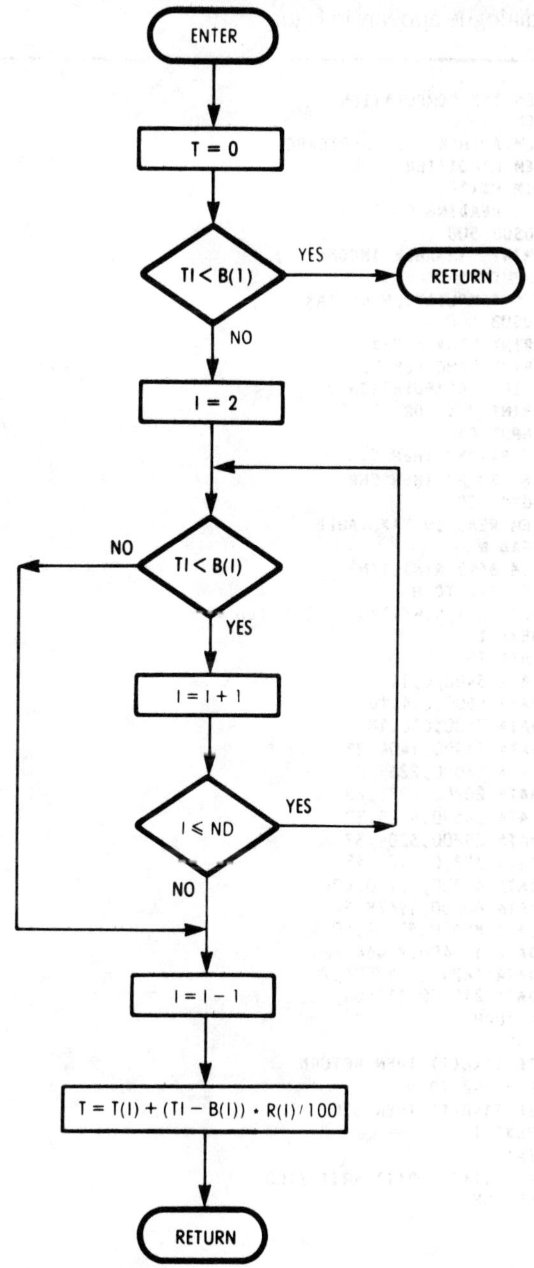

Figure 7.17: Flowchart for Income Tax Program

This flowchart is realized in lines 800 to 870 of the program shown in Figure 7.18. Sample dialogue appears in Figure 7.19.

```
100 REM TAX COMPUTATION
110 REM
120 REM AUTHOR : JEAN-PIERRE
125 REM LAMOITIER
127 DIM R$(10)
130 REM READING OF DATA
140 GOSUB 500
145 PRINT "TAXABLE INCOME  ";
150 INPUT T1
160 REM COMPUTATION OF TAX
170 GOSUB 800
190 PRINT "TAX = ";X
200 PRINT "ANOTHER ";
201 PRINT "COMPUTATION";
202 PRINT " (Y OR N)  ";
205 INPUT R$
210 IF R$="Y" THEN 145
220 IF R$="N" THEN END
230 GOTO 200
490 REM READ IN TAX TABLE
500 READ N
510 DIM B(N),R(N),T(N)
520 FOR I=2 TO N
530 READ B,T,R:B(I)=B:T(I)=T:R(I)=R
540 NEXT I
550 DATA 15
560 DATA 3400,0,14
570 DATA 5500,294,16
580 DATA 7600,630,18
590 DATA 11900,1404,21
600 DATA 16000,2265,24
610 DATA 20200,3273,28
620 DATA 24600,4505,32
630 DATA 29900,6201,37
640 DATA 35200,8162,43
650 DATA 45800,12720,49
660 DATA 60000,19678,54
670 DATA 85600,33502,59
680 DATA 109400,81464,68
690 DATA 162400,117504,70
700 DATA 215400,117504,70
710 RETURN
800 X=0
810 IF T1<B(1) THEN RETURN
820 FOR I=2 TO N
830 IF T1<B(I) THEN 850
840 NEXT I
850 I=I-1
860 X=T(I)+(T1-B(I))*R(I)/100
870 RETURN
```

Figure 7.18: Income Tax Calculation Program

By changing only a few instructions, we can merge the program presented in Chapter 1 with the program shown in Figure 7.18. The outcome of this union—a single, more complete tax program—is shown in Figure 7.20.

```
TAXABLE INCOME  ?100000
TAX = 41998
ANOTHER COMPUTATION (Y OR N)  ?Y
TAXABLE INCOME  ?50000
TAX = 14778
ANOTHER COMPUTATION (Y OR N)  ?Y
TAXABLE INCOME  ?18000
TAX = 2745
ANOTHER COMPUTATION (Y OR N)  ?N
```

Figure 7.19: Sample Dialogue from the Income Tax Program

```
100 REM TAX COMPUTATION
110 REM
120 REM AUTHOR : JEAN-PIERRE
125 REM LAMOITIER
127 DIM R$(9)
130 REM READING OF DATA
140 GOSUB 500
150 GOSUB 900
160 REM COMPUTATION OF TAX
170 GOSUB 800
190 PRINT "TAX = ";TX
200 PRINT "ANOTHER ";
201 PRINT "COMPUTATION";
202 PRINT " (Y OR N)  ";
205 INPUT R$
210 IF R$="Y" THEN 150
220 IF R$="N" THEN END
230 GOTO 200
490 REM READ IN TAX TABLE
500 READ ND
510 DIM B(ND),R(ND),T(ND)
520 FOR I=1 TO ND
530 READ B,T,R:B(I)=B:T(I)=T:R(I)=R
540 NEXT I
550 DATA 15
560 DATA 3400,0,14
570 DATA 5500,294,16
580 DATA 7600,630,18
590 DATA 11900,1404,21
600 DATA 16000,2265,24
610 DATA 20200,3273,28
620 DATA 24600,4505,32
630 DATA 29900,6201,37
640 DATA 35200,8162,43
650 DATA 45800,12720,49
660 DATA 60000,19678,54
670 DATA 85600,33502,59
```

Figure 7.20: A More Complete Tax Program (continues)

```
680 DATA 109400,81464,68
690 DATA 162400,117504,70
700 DATA 215400,117504,70
710 RETURN
800 TX=0
810 IF TI<B(1) THEN RETURN
820 FOR I=2 TO ND
830 IF TI<B(I) THEN 850
840 NEXT I
850 I=I-1
860 TX=T(I)+(TI-B(I))*R(I)/100
870 RETURN
900 PRINT "TOTAL INCOME  ";
905 INPUT I
910 PRINT "TOTAL ADJUSTMENTS  ";
915 INPUT A
920 G=I-A
930 PRINT "TOTAL DEDUCTIONS  ";
935 INPUT D
940 PRINT "NUMBER OF ";
942 PRINT "DEPENDENTS  ";
945 INPUT N
950 TI=G-D-N*1000
960 PRINT "THE TAXABLE ";
965 PRINT "INCOME IS ";TI
970 RETURN
```

Figure 7.20: A More Complete Tax Program

This program was derived from Figure 7.18 by replacing

150 INPUT "TAXABLE INCOME? ";T1

with

150 GOSUB 900

and adding lines 900 to 970 from Chapter 1. Figure 7.21 shows the sample dialogue.

```
TOTAL INCOME  ?27624
TOTAL ADJUSTMENTS  ?1737
TOTAL DEDUCTIONS  ?4727
NUMBER OF DEPENDENTS  ?5
THE TAXABLE INCOME IS 16160
TAX = 2303.4
ANOTHER COMPUTATION (Y OR N)  ?N
```

Figure 7.21: Dialogue from the Complete Tax Program

7.5 The Effect of Additional Income on Purchasing Power

An individual does extra work to earn additional income. The following question arises: given the additional expenses associated with doing the work and the additional tax resulting from the extra income, what has been the actual increase in purchasing power?

Problem: Modify the program in Figure 7.20 to request the following information:

ADDITIONAL INCOME (AI)

and

ADDITIONAL ADJUSTMENTS (AA)

after the original tax computation has been completed. After this new data has been added, add the computation of true increase in purchasing power, which is given by:

AI – (AA + (new tax – old tax)

Solution: After completing line 190 of the program shown in Figure 7.20, input the new data to AI and AA, then compute the new tax. To do this we insert as line 195 a call to a subroutine by writing:

```
195  GOSUB 1000
```

Starting with line 1000 we write a subroutine that:

- inputs AI and AA
- computes a new TAXABLE INCOME
- saves the old tax in a variable T1
- calls the tax computation subroutine on line 800
- outputs the information relevant to true purchasing power

This all translates into the lines of BASIC displayed in Figure 7.22.

```
100 REM TAX COMPUTATION
110 REM
120 REM AUTHOR : JEAN-PIERRE
125 REM LAMOITIER
127 DIM R$(9)
130 REM READING OF DATA
140 GOSUB 500
150 GOSUB 900
160 REM COMPUTATION OF TAX
170 GOSUB 800
180 PRINT
190 PRINT "TAX = ";TX
```

Figure 7.22: Program Calculating the Effect of Additional Income on Purchasing Power (continues)

```
195 GOSUB 1000
200 PRINT "ANOTHER ";
201 PRINT "COMPUTATION";
202 PRINT " (Y OR N)  ";
205 INPUT R$
210 IF R$="Y" THEN 150
220 IF R$="N" THEN END
230 GOTO 200
490 REM READ IN TAX TABLE
500 READ ND
510 DIM B(ND),R(ND),T(ND)
520 FOR I=1 TO ND
530 READ B,T,R:B(I)=B:T(I)=T:R(I)=R
540 NEXT I
550 DATA 15
560 DATA 3400,0,14
570 DATA 5500,294,16
580 DATA 7600,630,18
590 DATA 11900,1404,21
600 DATA 16000,2265,24
610 DATA 20200,3273,28
620 DATA 24600,4505,32
630 DATA 29900,6201,37
640 DATA 35200,8162,43
650 DATA 45800,12720,49
660 DATA 60000,19678,54
670 DATA 85600,33502,59
680 DATA 109400,47544,64
690 DATA 162400,81464,68
700 DATA 215400,117504,70
710 RETURN
800 TX=0
810 IF TI<B(1) THEN RETURN
820 FOR I=2 TO ND
830 IF TI<B(I) THEN 850
840 NEXT I
850 I=I-1
860 TX=T(I)+(TI-B(I))*R(I)/100
870 RETURN
900 PRINT "TOTAL INCOME  ";
905 INPUT I
910 PRINT "TOTAL ADJUSTMENTS  ";
915 INPUT A
920 G=I-A
930 PRINT "TOTAL DEDUCTIONS  ";
935 INPUT D
940 PRINT "NUMBER OF ";
942 PRINT "DEPENDENTS  ";
945 INPUT N
950 TI=G-D-N*1000
960 PRINT "THE TAXABLE ";
965 PRINT "INCOME IS ";TI
970 RETURN
990 REM COMPUTATION OF NEW TAX
1000 PRINT "ADDITIONAL ";
1002 PRINT "INCOME  ";
```

Figure 7.22: Program Calculating the Effect of Additional Income on Purchasing Power (continues)

```
1005 INPUT AI
1010 PRINT "ADDITIONAL ";
1012 PRINT "ADJUSTMENTS  ";
1015 INPUT AA
1020 TI=TI+AI-AA
1030 PRINT
1032 PRINT "NEW TAXABLE ";
1035 PRINT "INCOME: ";TI
1040 T1=TX
1050 GOSUB 800
1060 PRINT "NEW TAX: ";TX
1070 PRINT
1080 PRINT "INCREASE IN PURCH";
1082 PRINT "ASING POWER: ";
1085 PRINT AI-AA-TX+T1
1090 PRINT
1100 RETURN
```

Figure 7.22: Program Calculating the Effect of Additional Income on Purchasing Power

A sample dialogue with this final enhanced version of the program shown in Figure 7.20 appears in Figure 7.23.

```
TOTAL INCOME  ?18000
TOTAL ADJUSTMENTS  ?2000
TOTAL DEDUCTIONS  ?1500
NUMBER OF DEPENDENTS  ?2
THE TAXABLE INCOME IS 12500

TAX = 1530
ADDITIONAL INCOME  ?4000
ADDITIONAL ADJUSTMENTS  ?500

NEW TAXABLE INCOME: 16000
NEW TAX: 2265

INCREASE IN PURCHASING POWER: 2765

ANOTHER COMPUTATION (Y OR N)  ?Y
TOTAL INCOME  ?150000
TOTAL ADJUSTMENTS  ?5000
TOTAL DEDUCTIONS  ?10000
NUMBER OF DEPENDENTS  ?4
THE TAXABLE INCOME IS 131000

TAX = 61368
ADDITIONAL INCOME  ?25000
ADDITIONAL ADJUSTMENTS  ?4000

NEW TAXABLE INCOME: 152000
NEW TAX: 74808

INCREASE IN PURCHASING POWER: 7560

ANOTHER COMPUTATION (Y OR N)  ?N
```

Figure 7.23: Sample Dialogue on Purchasing Power

This program demonstrates that:

1. the increase in purchasing power is less than the amount of ADDITIONAL INCOME;
2. the higher the income tax bracket, the greater the discrepancy between ADDITIONAL INCOME and actual increase in purchasing power.

Conclusion

This chapter has presented exercises on the following topics: predicting the progress in gross sales, calculating loan payments, calculating rate of growth and computing income tax payments. These exercises may be useful for designing programs for similar applications.

CHAPTER 8

Games

Introduction

Experience has shown that the writing of game programs is a long and difficult process that, in most cases, is beyond the abilities of a beginning programmer. This is obviously the case with a game like chess. Programming a computer to play chess would be a difficult task for even the most experienced programmer. Trying to computerize even simple games can result in long programs that do not play well and run very slowly. This, in itself, removes an important aspect from the enjoyment of the game.

Some games, however, can be programmed easily because either (1) there is a minimum of strategy involved in the program (for example, the game "TOO LOW/TOO HIGH"), or (2) the strategy can be expressed as a simple algorithm (for example, NIM). It should be noted that as soon as the strategy becomes even a little more complex, the size of the program will increase significantly.

The four programs presented in this chapter qualify in one of these two categories.

8.1 The Game: Too Low/Too High

First part: The object of the game TOO LOW/TOO HIGH is to guess an integer, N, between 0 and A, that has been randomly selected by the computer. The player inputs a guess, X, and the computer determines whether or not the player's guess is correct. This is done by comparing X to the random number, N, in the following manner:

If X = N, the computer prints:

"YOU GOT IT IN I TRIES."

where I is the number of guesses input by the player.

If X < N, the computer prints:

"TOO LOW . . ."

If X > N, the computer prints:

"TOO HIGH . . ."

Analysis: Four variables are needed for this program:

A = The largest legal number that can be chosen
N = The number to be guessed
X = The number currently guessed
I = The number of guesses made

The variable A is not indispensable, but it offers an effective means to vary the units of the game with minimal change to the program.

The variable I is actually a "counter" that is incremented by one at each new guess. This variable keeps track of the number of tries made by the player.

Flowchart: There are many ways to approach this problem. The flowchart displayed in Figure 8.1 shows one of the simplest approaches.

The program (shown in Figure 8.2) must select a random integer, N, in the interval [0,A]. To do this, we write:

```
N = INT((A + 1) * RND(X))
```

since 0 < RND(X) < 1. Note that the exact form of this statement may vary from one system to another.

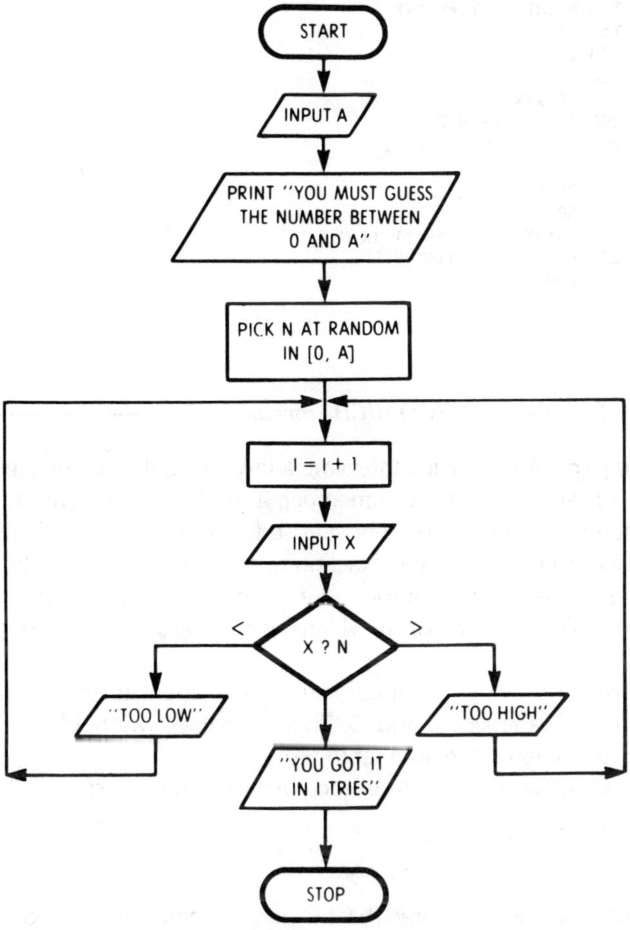

Figure 8.1: Flowchart for TOO LOW/TOO HIGH Game

```
100 PRINT "THE HIGHEST NUMBER";
102 PRINT " TO USE  ";
105 INPUT A
110 PRINT
120 PRINT "GUESS THE NUMBER ";
125 PRINT "BETWEEN 0 AND ";A
130 PRINT
140 PRINT "WHAT DO YOU GUESS"
```

Figure 8.2: TOO LOW/TOO HIGH Program (continues)

```
150 N=INT((A+1)*RND(X))
160 I=0
170 I=I+1
180 INPUT X
190 IF X=N THEN GOTO 220
200 IF X<N THEN 203
201 PRINT "TOO HIGH..."
202 GOTO 170
203 PRINT "TOO LOW..."
210 GOTO 170
220 PRINT "YOU GOT IT IN ";
225 PRINT I;" TRIES."
230 END
```

Figure 8.2: TOO LOW/TOO HIGH Program

Second part: After playing the game a few times, the player usually realizes that it is advantageous to remember, at each turn, the current interval from which the number should be guessed. The game is usually played by narrowing the interval until the exact number is found. To make this process easier, the program could output after each unsuccessful guess the most recently established interval from which the number should now be guessed.

Analysis: To provide this additional enhancement to the program, we need two new variables, C and D. These variables will hold the currently known boundaries for the number to be guessed.

Initially, C = 0 and D = A. After each unsuccessful guess:

If X < N, set C = MAX(C,X)
If X > N, set D = MIN(D,X)

If the program could be assured that the player (being rational and incapable of error) would never guess a number outside the currently known boundary for N, we could simply write C = X and D = X.

The PRINT statement is the same after any unsuccessful guess, since both upper and lower boundary values will always be printed.

Flowchart: The new flowchart (shown in Figure 8.3) can be easily derived from the flowchart in Figure 8.1.

Third part: One way to find the desired number quickly is to guess, at each stage, a number in the middle of the currently known range. In fact, the program can be modified to do the calculation and then print the number. This would reduce the number of guesses.

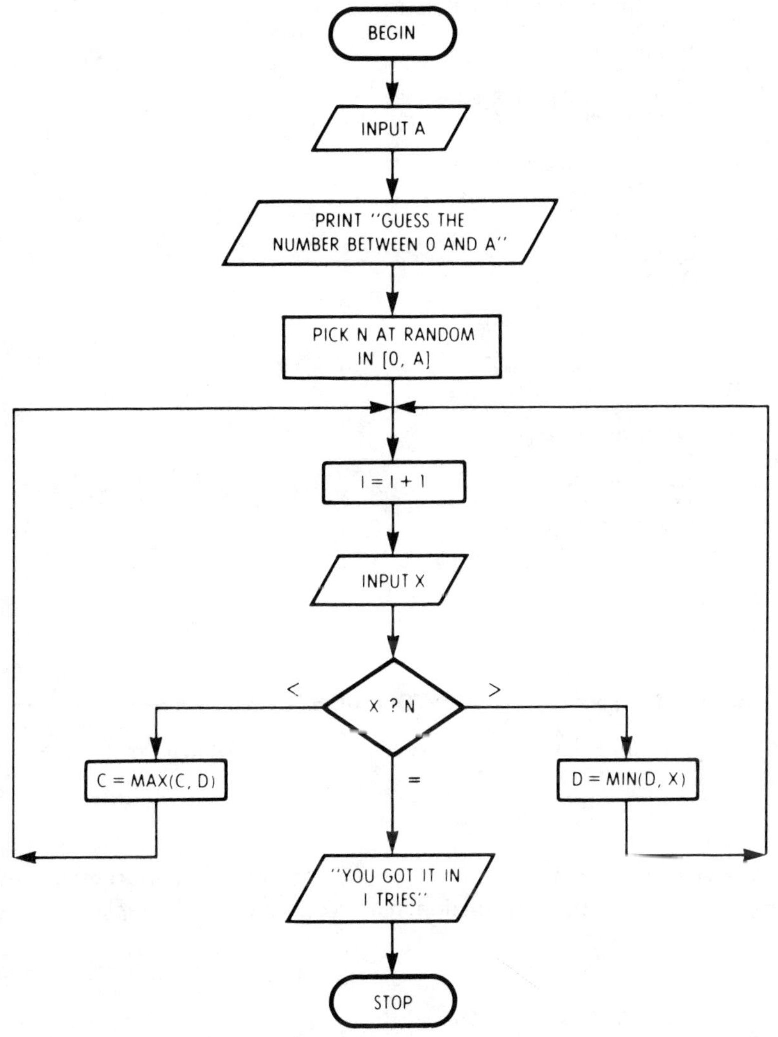

Figure 8.3: Flowchart for Expanded TOO LOW/TOO HIGH Game

Analysis: All that is necessary to do this is to add the expression (C + D)/2 to the PRINT instruction. Figure 8.4 shows this version of the program.

Fourth part: The program could also be modified so that when the player uses the number suggested by the computer, the computer takes

```
10 PRINT "THE HIGHEST NUMBER";
12 PRINT " TO USE  ";
15 INPUT A
20 PRINT
30 PRINT "GUESS THE NUMBER ";
35 PRINT "BETWEEN 0 AND ";A
40 PRINT
50 PRINT "WHAT DO YOU GUESS"
60 N=INT((A+1)*RND(X))
70 I=0:C=0:D=A
80 I=I+1
90 INPUT X
100 IF X=N THEN GOTO 130
110 IF X>=N THEN GOTO 116
112 IF X<=C THEN 116
114 C=X:GOTO 118
116 IF X<D THEN D=X
118 PRINT "BETWEEN ";C;
119 PRINT "  AND ";D;
120 PRINT "  AVERAGE = ";
121 PRINT (C+D)/2
122 GOTO 80
130 PRINT "YOU GOT IT IN ";I;
135 PRINT "  TRIES."
```

Figure 8.4: Expanded TOO LOW/TOO HIGH Program

over the game and plays it out. However, the player would then become only a spectator.

Analysis: Few changes would be needed to the flowchart to modify the program in this way. The instruction that accepts X would be replaced by:

X = INT((C + D)/2

or

X = INT((C + D + 1)/2)

and the instruction that prints out the new boundaries could be eliminated. On the other hand, if the player wants to see the "moves" made by the computer, then an instruction must be added to print out X at each cycle.

Note: A program that is operating in an automatic output mode (such as the one proposed above) will produce output at great speed, especially if a CRT screen is used. In some BASIC systems, we could add a "SLEEP 5" instruction, which would give the user the time necessary to read each line. The "SLEEP 5" instruction suspends the execution of the program for five seconds after each move. This feature is not available on all systems, but generally the same result can be obtained on other BASICs by:

- using a "WAIT" instruction, if available
- inserting a compute-bound "delay loop" that must execute a certain number of times before proceeding to the next move. For example, in ATARI BASIC:

  FOR T = 1 TO 500:NEXT T

as in line 85 in the program in Figure 8.5. Each five hundred iterations of this simple loop provides approximately one second of delay.

One version of this program is shown in Figure 8.5.

```
10 PRINT "THE HIGHEST NUMBER";
12 PRINT " TO USE  ";
15 INPUT A
20 PRINT
30 PRINT "GUESS THE NUMBER ";
35 PRINT "BETWEEN 0 AND ";A
40 PRINT
50 PRINT "WHAT DO YOU GUESS"
60 N=INT((A+1)*RND(1))
70 I=0:C=0:D=A
80 I=I+1
85 FOR T=1 TO 500:NEXT T
90 X=INT((C+D)/2)
100 IF X=N THEN GOTO 130
110 IF X>N THEN GOTO 116
112 IF X<=C THEN 116
114 C=X:GOTO 118
116 IF X<D THEN D=X
118 PRINT "BETWEEN ";C;
119 PRINT "  AND ";D;
120 PRINT "  AVERAGE = ";
121 PRINT (C+D)/2
122 GOTO 80
130 PRINT "YOU GOT IT IN ";I;
132 PRINT "  TRIES."
135 GOTO 50
140 END
```

Figure 8.5: TOO LOW/TOO HIGH Program in Automatic Output Mode

8.2 Finding an Unknown Number by Bracketing

This game, which is a variation on the previous game, consists of finding an unknown, randomly chosen number by bracketing it between two numbers supplied by the player. On receiving the two numbers the program will indicate:

— if the number has been bracketed

— if the interval is too low

— if the interval is too high.

For example, if the random number is 55, and the player inputs 18 and 24, then the program should respond "TOO LOW . . ."

Exercise 1: Design a simple program that implements this game and keeps track of the number of tries made by the player.

Exercise 2: Propose a more sophisticated program that determines whether or not the player has made a reasonable guess.

Exercise 1 solution: For this program we will need the following variables:

A = The largest legal number that can be chosen
N = The computer's selected number
X,Y = The limits of the bracket guessed by the player
I = The number of guesses made by the player.

Flowchart: Let us study the flowchart shown in Figure 8.6. This flowchart leads to the program in Figure 8.7. As before, the program could be enhanced to provide suggestions to the player or even carry out the rest of the play. A sample round appears in Figure 8.8.

Note: The best way to determine a number within the framework of this game is to subdivide the total range of numbers into three equal intervals and then guess the middle interval. For example, with [0,1000] try [333,666]. If the computer's response is "TOO LOW . . . [667,1000]" then try [778,889] next. With this strategy the player can obtain the maximum amount of information possible with each attempt, thereby providing the best path to the solution.

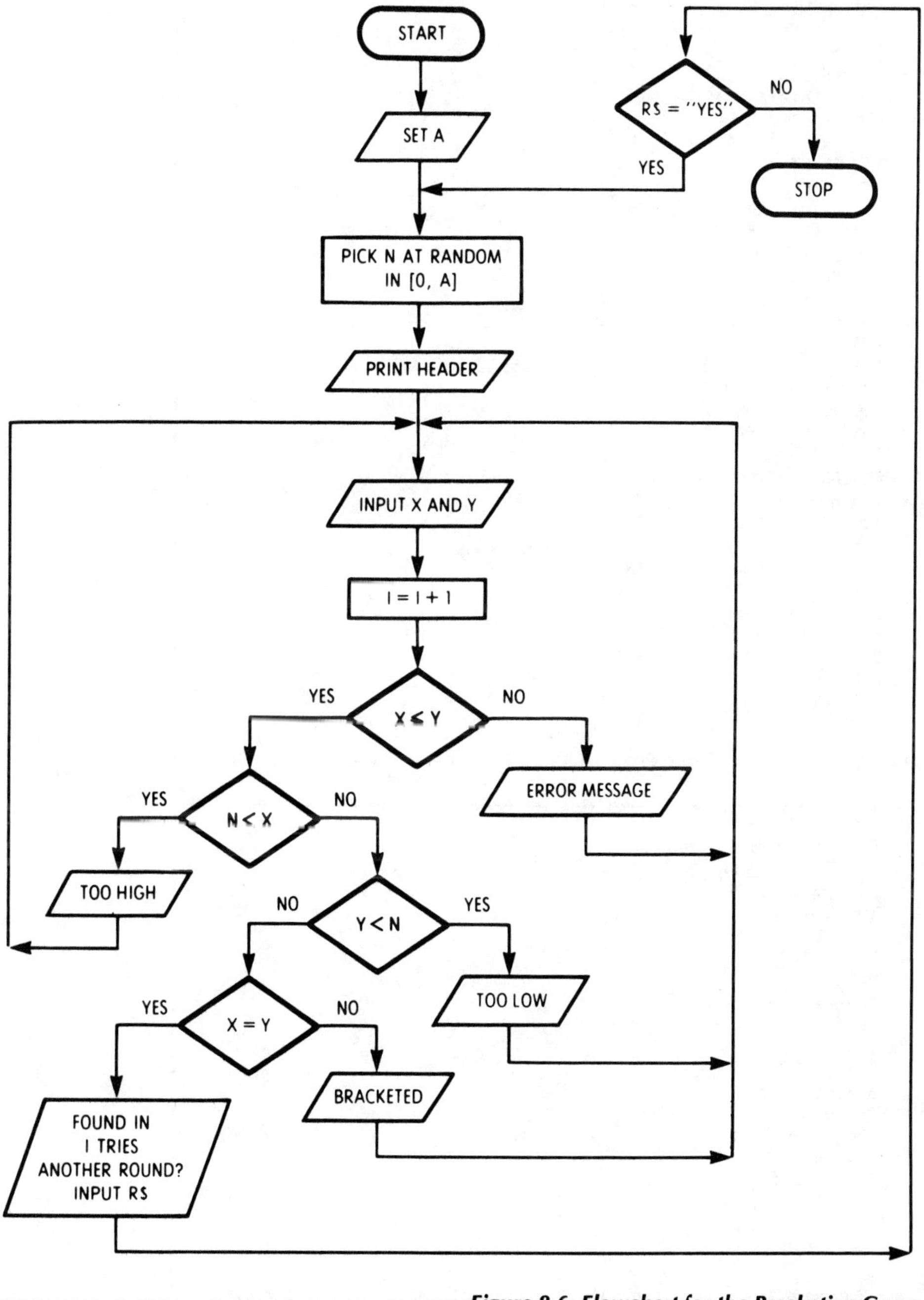

Figure 8.6: Flowchart for the Bracketing Game

```
100 REM A GAME TO FIND A
105 REM NUMBER BY BRACKETING
108 DIM R$(9)
110 A=1000
115 N=INT((A+1)*RND(1))
120 I=0
130 PRINT "FIND THE NUMBER ";
132 PRINT "BETWEEN 0 AND"
135 PRINT " ";A;"  BY ";
137 PRINT "BRACKETING (X,Y)?"
140 INPUT X,Y
145 I=I+1
150 IF X<=Y THEN 180
160 PRINT "X MUST BE LESS ";
165 PRINT "THAN OR EQUAL TO Y."
170 GOTO 140
180 IF N<X THEN 210
190 IF N>Y THEN 220
200 IF X=Y THEN 230
205 PRINT "BRACKETED"
207 GOTO 140
210 PRINT "TOO HIGH..."
215 GOTO 140
220 PRINT "TOO LOW..."
225 GOTO 140
230 PRINT "YOU GOT IT IN ";I;
235 PRINT " TRIES.":PRINT
240 PRINT "ANOTHER ROUND  ";
245 INPUT R$
250 IF R$(1,1)="Y" THEN 115
260 END
```

Figure 8.7: Bracketing Game Program

```
FIND THE NUMBER BETWEEN 0 AND
 1000  BY BRACKETING (X,Y)?
?0,500
TOO LOW...
?500,800
TOO LOW...
?850,950
TOO HIGH...
?825,830
TOO HIGH...
?810,825
BRACKETED
?8915,815
X MUST BE LESS THAN OR EQUAL TO Y.
?815,815
TOO LOW...
?820,823
```

Figure 8.8: Sample Dialogue from the Bracketing Game Program (continues)

```
TOO HIGH...
?815,819
BRACKETED
?816,816
YOU GOT IT IN 10 TRIES.

ANOTHER ROUND  ?NO
```

Figure 8.8: Sample Dialogue from the Bracketing Game Program

8.3 The Matchstick Game

This simple game provides the knowledgeable player with a sure win if he or she is playing second. Let us look at the rules of the game.

The game begins with two players and a pile of 21 matches. The players alternate turns and at each turn each player may remove from one to four matches from the pile. The player to pick up the last match loses the game.

The winning strategy for player 2 is to pick up just enough matches to obtain a sum of five by adding the number of matches picked up by player 1 to the number of matches player 2 plans to remove. Thus, no matter what player 1 does, he or she will be faced with a pile of 21, 16, 11, 6 and 1 matches and will eventually be forced to remove the last match. For example:

FIRST PLAYER	**SECOND PLAYER**	**PILE**
Removes	*Removes*	*Contains*
-	-	21
3	2	16
2	3	11
4	1	6
1	4	1
1 *and loses*		

Exercise: Construct a program in which the computer always plays second, and apply the winning strategy to that program. The program must be able to detect any cheating attempted by the first player.

Solution: The algorithm can be represented by the conceptual flowchart shown in Figure 8.9.

To check for possible cheating we add two tests that will:

— insure that I is an integer
— insure that I is a number from one to four, inclusive.

If either of these tests fails, the program should display an error message and go back to input I, so that the player can make a legal move.

The program displayed in Figure 8.10 was derived from the flowchart in Figure 8.9. This program incorporates two "cheat" tests at lines 200 and 210. The corresponding error messages are listed at lines 400 and 430, along with a return control to the input-move instruction in line 190.

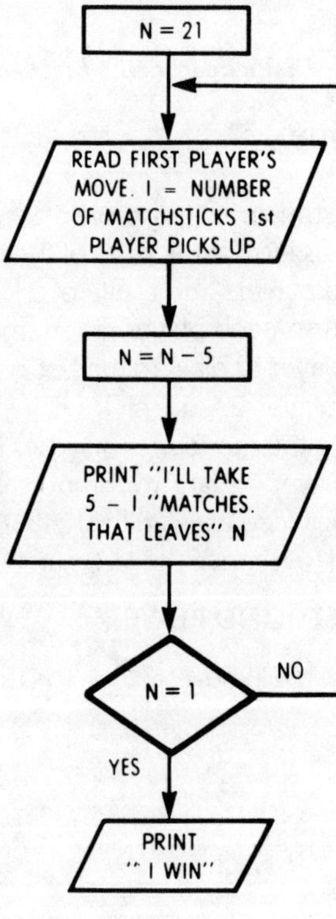

Figure 8.9: Conceptual Flowchart for the Matchstick Game

```
100 REM THE GAME FROM THE LAST
105 REM YEAR AT MARIENBAD
110 REM
120 DIM R$(9)
160 PRINT "WE START WITH 21 ";
165 PRINT "MATCHES. WE WILL"
170 PRINT "ALTERNATE TURNS ";
175 PRINT "REMOVING MATCHES:"
180 PRINT "UP TO FOUR PER ";
181 PRINT "TURN. IF YOU HAVE"
182 PRINT "TO PICK UP THE ";
```

Figure 8.10: Matchstick Game Program (continues)

```
183 PRINT "LAST MATCH YOU ";
184 PRINT "LOSE."
185 PRINT :N=21
190 PRINT "HOW MANY WILL YOU TAKE  ";
195 INPUT I
200 IF I<>INT(I) THEN 400
210 IF I<1 OR I>4 THEN 430
220 N=N-5
230 PRINT " I TAKE ";5-I;
235 PRINT " THAT LEAVES ";N
240 IF N>1 THEN 190
250 PRINT "AND PICK UP ";
255 PRINT "THE LAST ONE"
260 PRINT
270 PRINT "I WIN.":PRINT
280 PRINT "ANOTHER ROUND ";
285 INPUT R$
290 IF R$(1,1)="Y" THEN 185
300 END
400 PRINT "WHOLE NUMBERS ONLY."
410 GOTO 190
430 PRINT "DO NOT TRY TO ";
432 PRINT "CHEAT. YOU MUST"
435 PRINT "TAKE 1,2,3, OR 4!"
440 GOTO 190
```

Figure 8.10: Matchstick Game Program

Figure 8.11 displays a sample game.

```
WE START WITH 21 MATCHES. WE WILL
ALTERNATE TURNS REMOVING MATCHES:
UP TO FOUR PER TURN. IF YOU HAVE
TO PICK UP THE LAST MATCH YOU LOSE.

HOW MANY WILL YOU TAKE  ?3
 I TAKE 2 THAT LEAVES 16
HOW MANY WILL YOU TAKE  ?4
 I TAKE 1 THAT LEAVES 11
HOW MANY WILL YOU TAKE  ?6
DO NOT TRY TO CHEAT. YOU MUST
TAKE 1,2,3, OR 4!
HOW MANY WILL YOU TAKE  ?4
 I TAKE 1 THAT LEAVES 6
HOW MANY WILL YOU TAKE  ?4
 I TAKE 1 THAT LEAVES 1
AND PICK UP THE LAST ONE

I WIN.

ANOTHER ROUND ?NO
```

Figure 8.11: Sample Dialogue from the Matchstick Game Program

8.4 The Game of Craps

The game of Craps is played with a pair of dice and has the following rules:

> The dice are thrown. If the numbers showing on the dice add up to 7 or 11, the player wins. If the numbers add up to 2, 3, or 12, the player loses. If they add up to some number other than 7, 11, 2, 3 or 12, this number becomes the "point" and the player continues throwing until either:
>
> — The dice total 7, and the player loses
> — The point comes up, and the player wins.

Exercise 1: Construct a program that will play the game of Craps N times and then compute the proportion of games won to the total games played.

Exercise 2: Extend the program to compute the average number of throws per point.

Solution: First, we want to simulate a throw of the dice. To do this we use the random number generating function, RND, which normally returns a random number uniformly distributed in the interval [0,1]. To obtain a random integer in the interval [1,6] we must write:

```
INT(6*RND(X)) + 1
```

In some BASICs, such as Microsoft's MBASIC, RND does not need a parameter and we can write:

```
INT(6*RND) + 1
```

Note: In ATARI BASIC, the parameter X has no effect on the random number.

To simulate the throwing of two dice, we might be tempted to write:

```
2*(INT(6*RND(1)) + 1)
```

but the computer would then be acting as if both dice always had the same value. The correct simulation requires the instruction:

```
(INT(6*RND(1)) + 1) + (INT(6*RND(1)) + 1)
```

or the instruction:

```
INT(6*RND(1)) + INT(6*RND(1)) + 2
```

Let us now look at the flowchart presented in Figure 8.12.

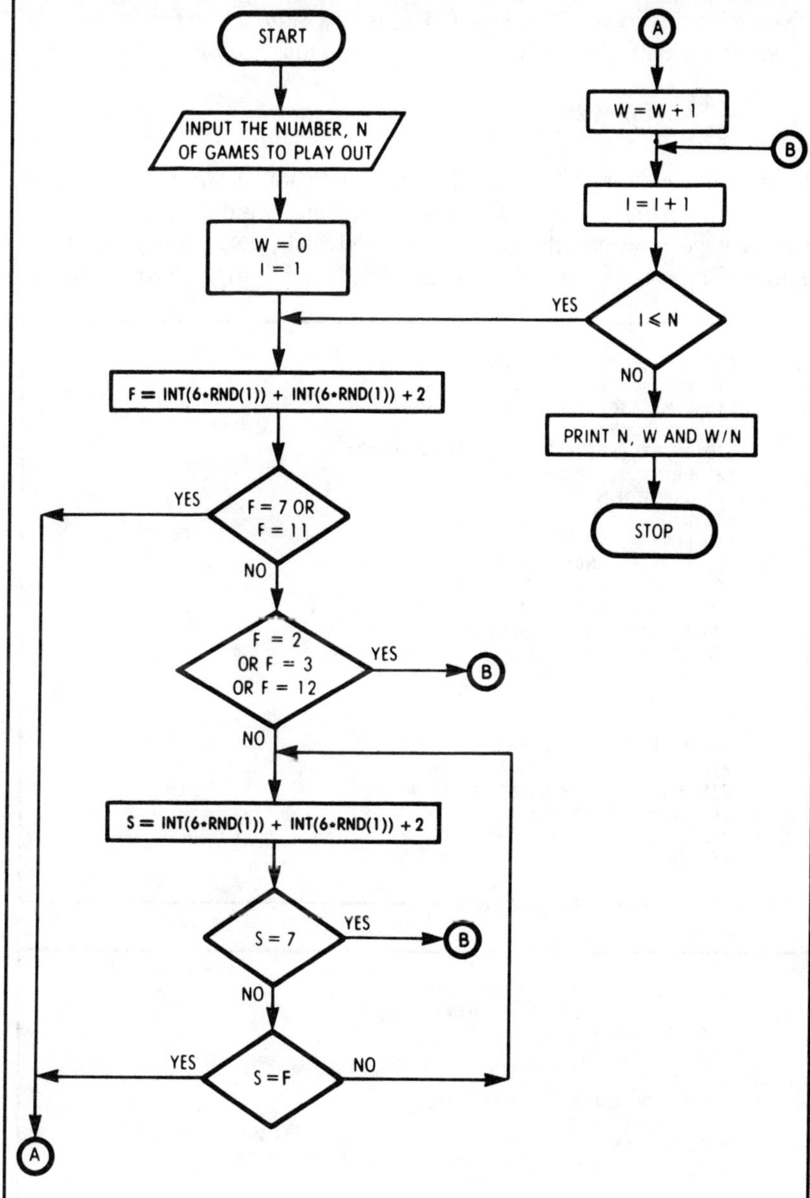

Figure 8.12: Flowchart for the Game of Craps Program

Programming this exercise presents no particular problems. The program derived from the flowchart in Figure 8.12 is very simple (see Figure 8.13). It can be shown mathematically that the true probability of winning is:

$$\frac{244}{495} = 0.4929$$

If the average of the result obtained varies significantly from this figure (in a large number of trials), the random number generator is defective.

The average number of throws per game is given by J/N, where J is the total number of throws. We can solve Exercise 2 by extending the program shown

```
100 REM CRAPS SIMULATOR
110 REM AUTHOR: J. P.
115 REM LAMOITIER
118 DIM R$(9)
120 PRINT :PRINT "NUMBER OF GAMES ";
122 PRINT "TO PLAY  ";
125 INPUT N
130 W=0
140 FOR I=1 TO N
150 F=INT(6*RND(1))+INT(6*RND(1))+2
160 IF F=7 OR F=11 THEN 210
170 IF F=2 OR F=3 OR F=12 THEN 220
180 S=INT(6*RND(1))+INT(6*RND(1))+2
190 IF S=7 THEN 220
200 IF S<>F THEN 180
210 W=W+1
220 NEXT I
230 PRINT "      GAMES = ";N;
232 PRINT "       WINS = ";W
235 PRINT " PROPORTION = ";W/N
240 PRINT "PLAY AGAIN  ";:INPUT R$
250 IF R$(1,1)="Y" THEN 120
260 END
```

Figure 8.13: Game of Craps Program

```
NUMBER OF GAMES TO PLAY  ?50
      GAMES = 50          WINS = 24
 PROPORTION = 0.48
PLAY AGAIN  ?Y

NUMBER OF GAMES TO PLAY  ?100
      GAMES = 100         WINS = 51
 PROPORTION = 0.51
PLAY AGAIN  ?Y

NUMBER OF GAMES TO PLAY  ?200
      GAMES = 200         WINS = 95
 PROPORTION = 0.475
PLAY AGAIN  ?N
```

Figure 8.14: Sample Rounds from the Craps Program

in Figure 8.13 and adding:

J = O

D = J + 1 (twice)

and a corresponding output statement. This leads to the program shown in Figure 8.15, which, when executed, yields the results given in Figure 8.16.

```
100 REM CRAPS SIMULATOR
110 REM AUTHOR: J. P.
115 REM LAMOITIER
118 DIM R$(9)
120 PRINT :PRINT "NUMBER OF GAMES ";
122 PRINT "TO PLAY  ";
125 INPUT N
130 W=0:J=0
140 FOR I=1 TO N
150 F=INT(6*RND(1))+INT(6*RND(1))+2
160 IF F=7 OR F=11 THEN 210
170 IF F=2 OR F=3 OR F=12 THEN 220
180 S=INT(6*RND(1))+INT(6*RND(1))+2
185 J=J+1
190 IF S=7 THEN 220
200 IF S<>F THEN 180
210 W=W+1
220 NEXT I
230 PRINT "GAMES = ";N;
232 PRINT "      WINS = ";W
235 PRINT "PROPORTION = ";W/N
240 PRINT
250 PRINT "AVERAGE NUMBER OF THROWS"
255 PRINT "PER GAME = ";
260 PRINT J/N
270 PRINT "PLAY AGAIN  ";:INPUT R$
280 IF R$(1,1)="Y" THEN 120
290 END
```

Figure 8.15: Modified Craps Program

```
NUMBER OF GAMES TO PLAY  ?100
GAMES = 100      WINS = 51
PROPORTION = 0.51

AVERAGE NUMBER OF THROWS
PER GAME = 1.98
PLAY AGAIN  ?Y

NUMBER OF GAMES TO PLAY  ?200
GAMES = 200      WINS = 89
PROPORTION = 0.445

AVERAGE NUMBER OF THROWS
PER GAME = 2.26
PLAY AGAIN  ?N
```

Figure 8.16: Sample Rounds from Modified Craps Program

Conclusion

The four games presented in this chapter were particularly easy to program for two reasons. There was either:

1. an absence of strategy, or a very elementary strategy

or

2. no strategic position to evaluate.

For any game that is played on a board (e.g., Othello, Checkers, Chess) the manipulation of position coordinates will add still another layer of complexity to any strategy program.

We would advise anyone who is interested in programming games to begin with simple games and then gradually build on this experience before attempting a task such as a Chess program.

The following suggestions should give the game enthusiast a good basis in game programming:

— the game of NIM (like the Matchstick game but with several piles of matches)

— the game of MasterMind

— the game of Othello (beginning with a simple strategy, and then refining the strategy, progressively).

CHAPTER 9

Operations Research

Introduction

Problems in operations research often involve the manipulations of graphs. The Traveling Salesman Problem, PERT, and the topological sort all involve the use of graphs in one way or another.

When working with graphs, the management of subscripts (coordinates) is quite subtle and can be difficult for even the most experienced programmer. Since subscripts usually have integer values, BASIC interpreters that support integer variables in addition to "floating point" variables (such as MICRO-SOFT BASIC and XY BASIC) perform well in this type of application, since the arrays occupy less memory.

Because of their subtlety, the following exercises should not be attempted until the previous exercises have been thoroughly understood.

9.1 Topological Sort

Let $T_1, T_2, \ldots T_N$ represent tasks that must be carried out in an order subject to precedence constraints. These constraints are entered as pairs (I,J), which indicate that task T_J cannot be started until task T_I has been completed. The pair (0,0) will terminate the list of precedence constraints.

Exercise: Given the following data—a set of tasks and a list of precedence constraints (I,J)—find an order for executing the tasks that satisfies the constraints.

Analysis: The following approach should be taken:

— Initialize an array T to zero. As the list of pairs (I,J) is read, place a 1 in the corresponding array element T(I,J)

— After T is set up, search for a task that either has no constraints or has constraints that have been previously satisfied. Such a task, K, is characterized by:

T(I,K) = 0 for all I

The execution of this task satisfies, in turn, some constraints. To denote this, set:

T(K,J) = 0 for all J

The task (K) should now be "checked off" and its number should be output to indicate that it has been completed. Now set:

T(K,K) = 1

so that the same task will not be considered again. Continue the process for unconstrained tasks until all tasks have been completed. At this point one of the following situations must be the case:

Case 1: After counting the number of completed tasks, we find that all N tasks have been processed. In this case, we have a solution to the problem.

Case 2: After counting the number of completed tasks, we find that the number is less than N. In this case, the problem has no solution and an appropriate message should be output.

Now apply the program to the example given by the directed graph presented in Figure 9.1. In this graph we can see that an arrow goes (for example) from node 8 to node 5. This arrow signifies that task 5 cannot be started until task 8 is completed. This graph is represented in the program by the DATA statements listed in Figure 9.2.

Solution: Break the problem into three parts as suggested in the analysis:

1. Initialize the array T to zero.
2. Read the data and set up the array T.
3. Execute the algorithm.

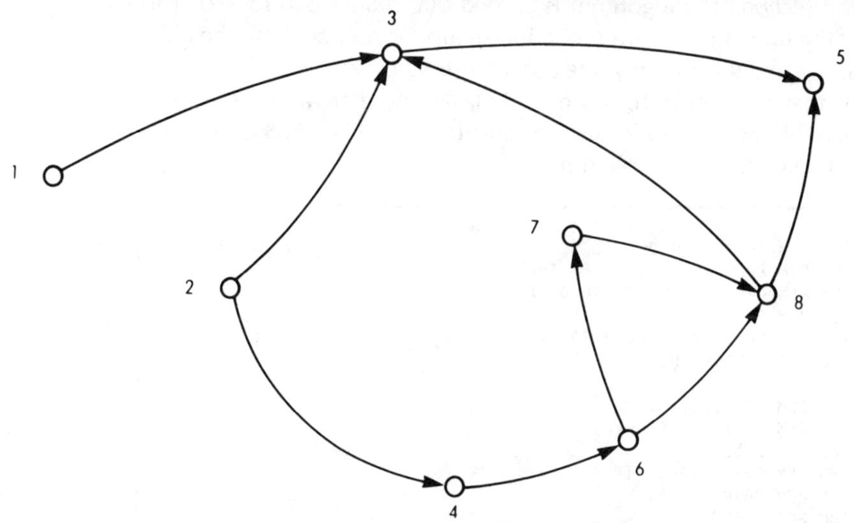

Figure 9.1: Directed Graph Illustrating Precedence Constraints

```
1000 DATA 8
1010 DATA 1,3
1020 DATA 2,3
1030 DATA 8,3
1040 DATA 3,5
1050 DATA 4,6
1060 DATA 6,7
1070 DATA 6,8
1080 DATA 2,4
1090 DATA 8,5
1100 DATA 7,8
1110 DATA 0,0
```

Figure 9.2: Data Statements for Precedence Constraints

These three parts correspond to the subroutines illustrated in Figure 9.3. Let us take a closer look at each part:

Initialization section: Some BASIC interpreters automatically initialize all variables to zero, but, since this should never be relied on, it should be done explicitly as in lines 500 to 540 of the program.

Set-up section: As the input data are read, the task numbers are checked, and constraints are verified to consist of distinct components (otherwise, a task would have to be preceded by itself). If an error is detected, a message is output. If a constraint (K,L) is accepted we set:

T(K,L) = 1

This is done in lines 600 to 730 of the program.

Execution section: The algorithm is carried out in lines 800 to 960. This portion of the program is shorter than the set-up section, because the algorithm is simple and there is only one output instruction.

We note that for a graph consisting of N tasks, there are at most $\frac{N(N-1)}{2}$ constraints. This fact is used in the FOR instruction on line 605 of the program. Figure 9.4 shows a sample run.

```
100 REM THIS TOPOLOGICAL SORT
102 REM PROGRAM DETERMINES THE
105 REM ORDER IN WHICH TO DO A
107 REM SET OF TASKS TO CERTAIN
110 REM PRECEDENCE CONSTRAINTS
120 PRINT "TOPOLOGICAL SORT"
125 PRINT
150 DIM T(20,20):N9=20
170 REM INITIALIZE ARRAY T
180 GOSUB 500
190 REM READ, VALIDATE AND
195 REM PRINT DATA.
200 GOSUB 600
210 REM INVOKE ALGORITHM
220 GOSUB 800
225 PRINT
230 END
500 FOR I=1 TO N9
510 FOR J=1 TO N9
520 T(I,J)=0
530 NEXT J
540 NEXT I:RETURN
600 READ N
601 PRINT "NUMBER OF TASKS = ";
602 PRINT N:PRINT
603 PRINT "LIST OF PRECEDENCE";
604 PRINT " CONSTRAINTS":PRINT
605 FOR I=1 TO N*(N-1)/2
610 READ K,L
620 IF K=0 AND L=0 THEN 720
630 IF K<>L THEN 650
640 PRINT "ERROR: TWO TASKS ";
642 PRINT "HAVE THE SAME ";
644 PRINT "NUMBER: ";K:STOP
650 IF K>0 AND K<N9 THEN 670
660 PRINT "ILLEGAL FIRST TASK";
665 PRINT " NUMBER: ";K:STOP
670 IF L>0 AND L<N9 THEN 690
680 PRINT "ILLEGAL LAST TASK";
685 PRINT " NUMBER: ";L:STOP
690 T(K,L)=1
695 PRINT " ";K;"    ";L
700 NEXT I
710 PRINT "ERROR IN THE DATA."
715 STOP
720 C=I-1:PRINT
730 PRINT "NUMBER OF ";
```

Figure 9.3: Topological Sort Program (continues)

```
732 PRINT "CONSTRAINTS: ";C
734 RETURN
800 PRINT
802 PRINT "THE ORDER OF THE ";
804 PRINT "TASKS IS:":I=0
810 K=1
820 FOR J=1 TO N
830 IF T(J,K)=1 THEN 920
840 NEXT J
850 I=I+1
855 PRINT K;"   ";
860 FOR J=1 TO N
870 T(K,J)=0
880 NEXT J
890 T(K,K)=1:GOTO 810
920 K=K+1
922 IF K<=N THEN 820
930 IF I=N THEN RETURN
940 PRINT "NO SOLUTION. ";
942 PRINT N-I;"  TASKS ";
944 PRINT "CANNOT BE"
946 PRINT "CARRIED OUT."
960 STOP
```

Figure 9.3: Topological Sort Program

```
TOPOLOGICAL SORT

NUMBER OF TASKS = 8

LIST OF PRECEDENCE CONSTRAINTS

 1    3
 2    3
 8    3
 3    5
 4    6
 6    7
 6    8
 2    4
 8    5
 7    8

NUMBER OF CONSTRAINTS: 10

THE ORDER OF THE TASKS IS:
1   2   4   6   7   8   3   5
```

Figure 9.4: Output of Ordered Tasks

9.2 The Critical Path in a Graph

The program presented here handles the ordering of a sequence of tasks of known duration. The tasks have been numbered in ascending order to simplify the programming and to allow reasonably good output even on a microcomputer-based system.

In view of the complexity of the problem, we will not formally state it as an exercise; instead, we will proceed directly to the implementation of a solution.

Representation of the data: The set of tasks may be represented as a directed graph having one entry node and, in principle, one exit. This directed graph must not contain any cycles. An example of a legal graph appears in Figure 9.5.

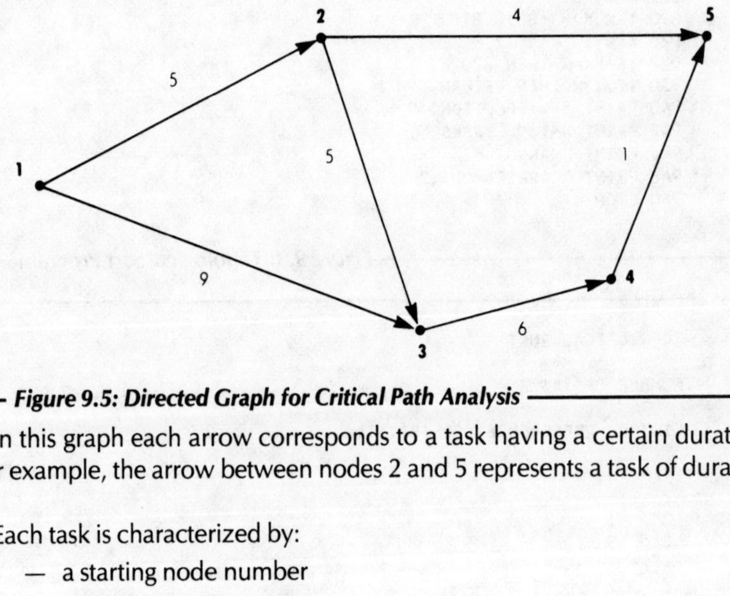

Figure 9.5: Directed Graph for Critical Path Analysis

In this graph each arrow corresponds to a task having a certain duration. For example, the arrow between nodes 2 and 5 represents a task of duration 4.

Each task is characterized by:

- a starting node number
- an ending node number
- a duration (in arbitrary units)
- a caption.

Thus, the graph shown in Figure 9.5 corresponds to the task list displayed in Figure 9.6.

```
2010 DATA 1,2,5,JACK UP
2020 DATA 1,3,9,REMOVE WHEEL
2030 DATA 2,3,5,WHEEL EXCHANGE
2040 DATA 2,5,4,BOLT ON WHEEL
2050 DATA 3,4,6,LET DOWN
2060 DATA 4,5,1,TIGHTEN UP
```

Figure 9.6: Data Statements for Critical Path Analysis

We will read the data into three arrays:

1. Array S will contain the start nodes for each task.
2. Array F will contain the finish nodes for each task.
3. Array D will contain a duration for each task.

A character string of C$ will hold the captions. We limit the program to problems involving a maximum of twenty tasks. To simplify the input of data, a string variable D$ (with a maximum length of twenty characters) will be used to receive the caption field of each task. Thus, all the captions will be limited to twenty characters. The string C$ will have a length of $20 \times 20 = 400$ characters.

The read subroutine will:

- Read the input data.
- Detect end-of-data coded by N1 = N2 = 0.
- Verify that N1 < N2.
- Initialize certain arrays.
- Accumulate the number of tasks. The total is stored in the variable N.
- Print out the input data.

In this subroutine, which is listed in Figure 9.7, the variables will have the following significance:

- N9: a variable that is set to the maximum number of tasks at the beginning of the main program.
- N1 and N2: the variables into which the numbers of the starting and finishing nodes are read. N1 and N2 are ultimately transferred to the arrays S and F.
- Array E: the earliest possible starting time for each task. E is initialized to zero.
- Array L: the latest possible starting time for a task without delaying project completion. L is initialized to zero.

After calling the read subroutine displayed above, the main program will compute the earliest possible starting time for each task.

Consider the example from the graph shown in Figure 9.5. The task going from node 3 to node 4 cannot start unless the tasks that terminate at node 3 have been completed. This time E(3) is characterized by

$$\left.\begin{array}{l} 9 \leqslant E(3) \\ 5 + 5 \leqslant E(3) \end{array}\right\} \text{which implies } E(3) = 10$$

For the general case, we start with E(1) = 0 and make the following computation:

E(F(I)) = MAX [E(F(I)),(E(S(I)) + D(I)]

```
950 REM SUBROUTINE TO READ AND
960 REM PRINT DATA AND
970 REM INITIALIZE
980 PRINT "FROM TO  ";
985 PRINT "DURATION    TASK "
990 PRINT
1000 FOR I=1 TO N9
1010 READ N1,N2,D,D$:D(I)=D
1020 IF N1=0 AND N2=0 THEN 1100
1025 IF N1<N2 THEN 1050
1030 PRINT "TASKS MUST BE IN ";
1035 PRINT "ASCENDING ORDER"
1040 STOP
1050 E(N1)=0:E(N2)=0
1055 L(N1)=0:L(N2)=0
1060 S(I)=N1:F(I)=N2
1062 L$="                    "
1063 L$(1,LEN(D$))=D$
1065 C$(20*I-19)=L$
1070 PRINT " ";S(I);"     ";
1072 PRINT F(I);"     ";
1074 PRINT D(I);"     ";D$
1080 NEXT I
1090 N=N9:GOTO 1110
1100 N=I-1
1110 PRINT
1120 PRINT "NUMBER OF TASKS";
1125 PRINT " = ";N
1130 RETURN
```

Figure 9.7: Read Subroutine for Critical Path Analysis

which is implemented in lines 270 to 300 of the program given in Figure 9.9.

To compute the latest acceptable time for finishing a task, we work in the opposite direction. For the exit node we have:

L(F(N)) = E(F(N))

where L is the array of latest acceptable finishing times. Working backwards:

L(S(I)) = MIN[L(S(I)),(L(F(I)) – D(I))]

This calculation is realized in lines 320 to 360 of the program shown in Figure 9.9.

As soon as we know the following information for each task:

— E(S(I)), the earliest starting time
— L(F(I)), the latest finishing time
— D(I), the normal duration

we can obtain the maximum delay permitted for each task. This time is given by:

F1(I) = L(F(I)) – E(S(I) – D(I))

If F1(I) = 0, then any delay in the completion of this task will delay the entire project. The variable C1 is used to count these "critical" tasks. This count is carried out in lines 410 to 440 of the program in Figure 9.9.

We can now print out the following information for each task:

Number of the starting node Number of the finishing node Duration	Input Data
Earliest starting time Latest finishing time Maximum admissible delay	Results of the Computation

This output is done in lines 495 to 550 of the program shown in Figure 9.9.

The calculation of the total duration of the critical path is defined by the variable C3 (which was initialized to zero) in lines 570 to 590:

```
C3 = MAX(C3,L(F(I)))
```

Since the critical path consists of only those tasks with admissible delays of zero, the path can be output starting from the entry node (lines 595 to 720) as follows:

- Find the initial task (lines 640 to 660).
- Print the task (lines 670 and 675).
- Find the next task (lines 700 to 720), print the task, and continue until the end is reached.

The flowchart for this example is displayed in Figure 9.8. The program listing is shown in Figure 9.9.

When the program is executed its output consists of three parts (see Figure 9.10):

1. the display of the inputs and the total number of tasks
2. the critical path analysis; i.e., for each task:
   - the start task node number
   - the finish task node number
   - the earliest possible start date
   - the latest possible completion date without delaying project completion
   - the time available for "slippage"
3. the critical path.

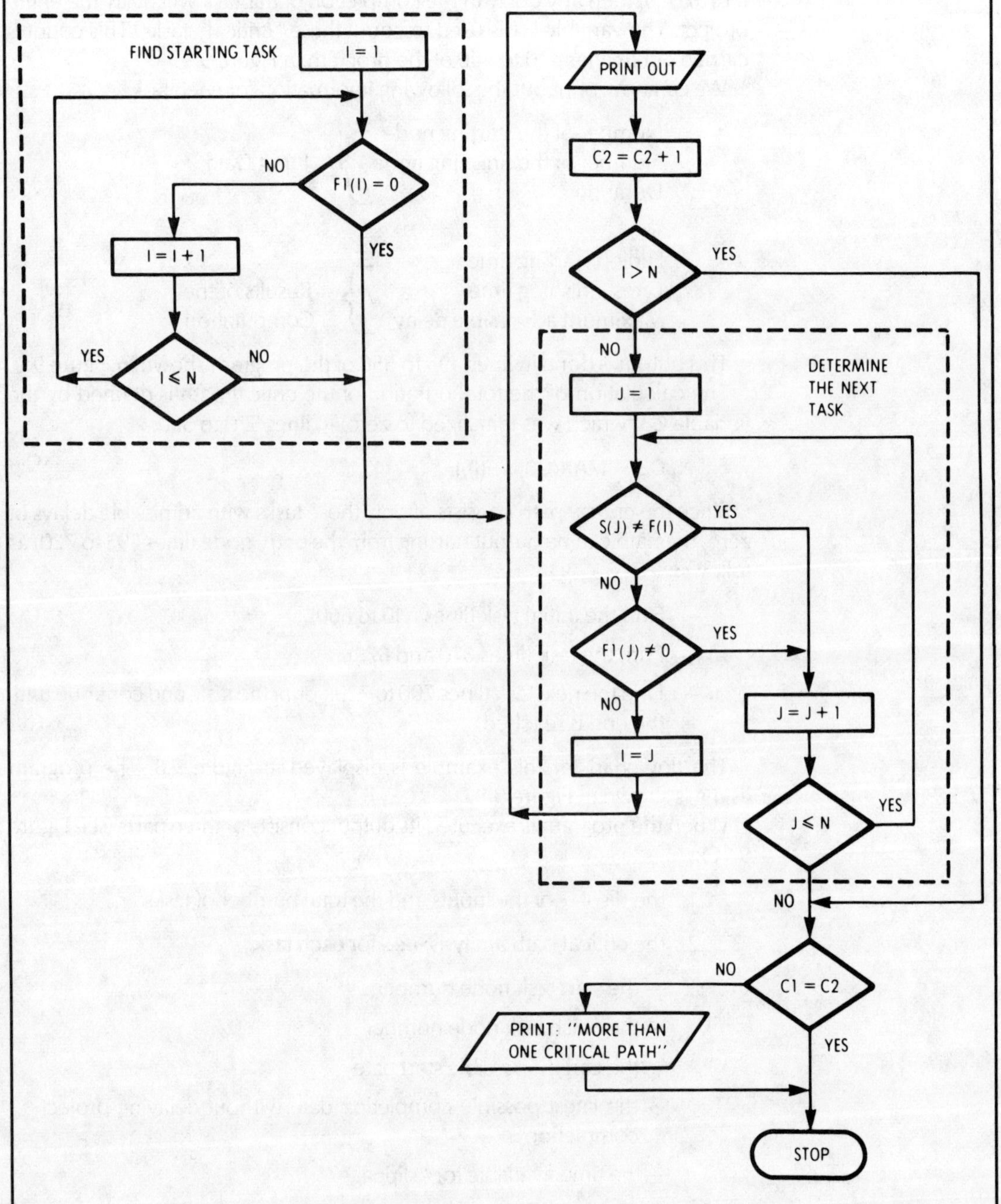

Figure 9.8: Flowchart for the Critical Path Program

```
100 REM THE CRITICAL PATH IN
105 REM A GRAPH
110 DIM S(20),F(20),E(20),L(20),L$(40)
112 DIM F1(20),C$(400),D$(20),D(20)
115 N9=6
120 REM
130 REM READ AND PRINT DATA
150 GOSUB 980
250 REM INITIALIZE AND COMPUTE
255 REM EARLIEST START DATE
260 C1=0:C2=0:C3=0
270 FOR I=1 TO N
280 M1=E(S(I))+D(I)
290 IF E(F(I))<=M1 THEN E(F(I))=M1
300 NEXT I
310 REM
320 L(F(N))=E(F(N))
330 FOR I=N TO 1 STEP -1
340 L1=S(I)
345 M2=L(F(I))-D(I)
350 IF L(L1)>=M2 OR L(L1)=0 THEN L(L1)=M2
360 NEXT I
400 REM
410 FOR I=1 TO N
420 F1(I)=L(F(I))-E(S(I))-D(I)
430 IF F1(I)=0 THEN C1=C1+1
440 NEXT I
495 PRINT
500 PRINT "CRITICAL PATH ";
510 PRINT "ANALYSIS":PRINT
520 PRINT "FROM TO START ";
525 PRINT "DONE STOP  TASK":PRINT
530 FOR I=1 TO N
532 L$="                                      "
535 L$(2)=STR$(S(I))
536 L$(6)=STR$(F(I))
540 L$(11)=STR$(E(S(I)))
542 L$(16)=STR$(L(F(I)))
544 L$(21)=STR$(F1(I))
546 L$(24,37)=C$(20*I-19,20*I)
548 PRINT L$
550 NEXT I
560 REM
570 FOR I=1 TO N
580 IF L(F(I))>C3 THEN C3=L(F(I))
590 NEXT I
595 PRINT
600 PRINT "THE LENGTH OF THE ";
602 PRINT "CRITICAL PATH IS ";
604 PRINT C3
610 PRINT
620 PRINT "IT GOES FROM  TO"
630 PRINT
640 FOR I=1 TO N
650 IF F1(I)=0 THEN 670
660 NEXT I
```

Figure 9.9: Critical Path Program (continues)

```
670 PRINT "            ";S(I);
675 PRINT "    ";F(I)
680 C2=C2+1
690 IF I>N THEN 730
700 FOR J=1 TO N
710 IF S(J)<>F(I) OR F1(J)<>0 THEN 720
715 I=J:GOTO 670
720 NEXT J
730 IF C1=C2 THEN 740
732 PRINT "MORE THAN ONE ";
734 PRINT "CRITICAL PATH."
740 PRINT
800 END
```

Figure 9.9: Critical Path Program

```
FROM TO  DURATION   TASK

 1    2      5    JACK UP
 1    3      9    REMOVE WHEEL
 2    3      5    WHEEL EXCHANGE
 2    5      4    BOLT ON WHEEL
 3    4      6    LET DOWN
 4    5      1    TIGHTEN UP

NUMBER OF TASKS = 6

CRITICAL PATH ANALYSIS

FROM TO START DONE STOP  TASK

 1   2    0     5    0  JACK UP
 1   3    0    10    1  REMOVE WHEEL
 2   3    5    10    0  WHEEL EXCHANGE
 2   5    5    17    8  BOLT ON WHEEL
 3   4   10    16    0  LET DOWN
 4   5   16    17    0  TIGHTEN UP

THE LENGTH OF THE CRITICAL PATH IS 17

IT GOES FROM  TO

             1  2
             2  3
             3  4
             4  5
```

Figure 9.10: Output from the Critical Path Program

9.3 The Traveling Salesman Problem

A salesman must visit customers living in N cities. He must decide in which order he should visit his customers, so that he can minimize the total cost of the trip. In this version of the problem the salesman must return to his original starting point. A graph showing the locations of the cities that must be visited is shown in Figure 9.11.

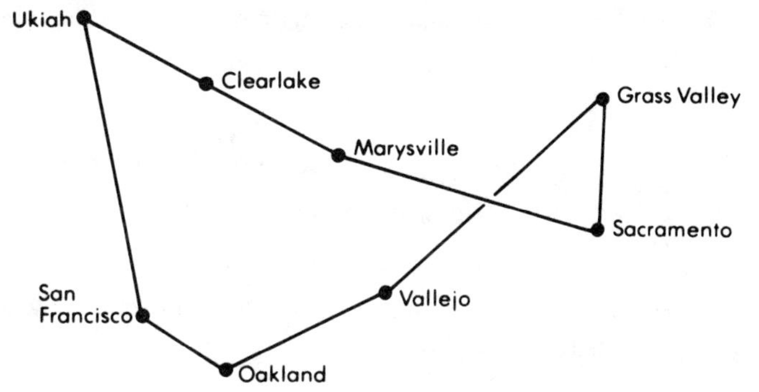

Figure 9.11: Cities for the Traveling Salesman Program

Note: The costs, D(I,J) of traveling from city I to city J are known for this problem. These costs can be expressed as distances in miles or in other units.

Suggested method: For this problem we will not use the general solution, which is complex and slow to run. Instead, we will use the following heuristic method:

1. Select a city as the starting point.
2. Go to the next closest city.
3. Go from that city to the next closest city not yet visited and so on until all of the cities have been visited. Then return to the starting city.
4. Note the cost of this route. Repeat the process, using each of the other cities in turn as the starting city.

Exercise: There are four steps to this problem:

1. Analyze the problem by breaking it up into small sections.
2. Construct a concise flowchart, detailed to the level of subroutine calls.
3. Construct detailed flowcharts for each subroutine.
4. Write the program.

For this problem we will use the following variables:

V$ = an array of character strings containing the names of the cities to be visited.

D = a two-dimensional array containing the costs (distances):

D(I,J) is the cost of going from city I to city J

D(I,I) = 0.

T = an array containing the route currently being constructed.

T1 = an array containing the best route yet found.

S = a variable containing the cost of the best route yet found.

C = a variable containing the cost of the route currently being constructed.

Solution: As usual, this problem is not difficult provided it is attacked methodically. The complete program will contain several parts:

- Read the data.
- Print the data.
- Find the best itinerary (the computational part).
- Print this itinerary.

As an aid in evaluating an algorithm, we might want to see the provisional itineraries displayed. For this reason it is desirable to use a subroutine to print the output. Thus, we could insert a GOSUB instruction when a display of the output is desired.

The "cost matrix," D, may be either symmetrical or asymmetrical. We will address both cases in the section that reads the data. The user's data preparation can be simplified when the cost matrix is symmetrical. This line of attack leads to the conceptual flowchart shown in Figure 9.12.

The output display of a cost matrix is the same whether or not the matrix is symmetrical, but the length of the lines must be taken into account.

To obtain a suitable printout we use the string array, V$, which contains the names of the cities visited. The cost matrix is represented by a square array containing rows and columns captioned with the names of the cities.

In the flowchart shown in Figure 9.12, the structure of the algorithm was not revealed. Let us try to fill it in progressively. First, we must put together an itinerary, and then compare the cost of that itinerary to the cost of a different itinerary. To do this, we will use the following variables:

- an array, T, that contains the sequence of city numbers in the order that they were visited on the itinerary.

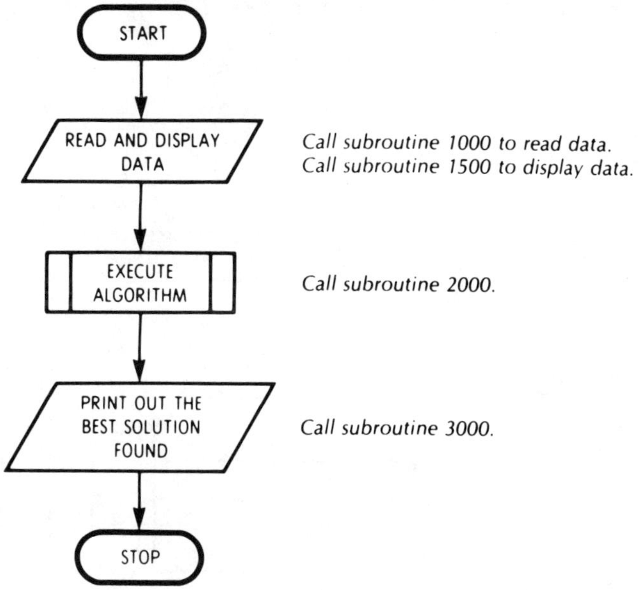

Figure 9.12: Conceptual Flowchart for the Traveling Salesman Program

— a constant, C, that represents the cost of an itinerary. The constant C is given by:

$$C = \sum_{I=1}^{N-1} D(T(I),T(I+1)) + D(T(N),T(1))$$

We are now at the point where we can construct a more detailed flowchart (see Figure 9.13). This flowchart will not, however, indicate the method used to select the next city. To determine this final detail, let us consider what happens in the course of working out an itinerary. We will assume that L − 1 cities have been selected, and their numbers have been moved into (T)1 through T(L − 1). We then successively examine all cities, J, such that

$$J \neq T(K) \text{ for } K = 1, 2, \ldots, L-1$$

and retain the city for which the cost D(T(L−1),J) is the least. This J is then stored in T(L). This leads us, finally, to the flowchart shown in Figure 9.14, which is now detailed enough to be used for programming.

The program, shown in Figure 9.15, has been divided into subroutines to

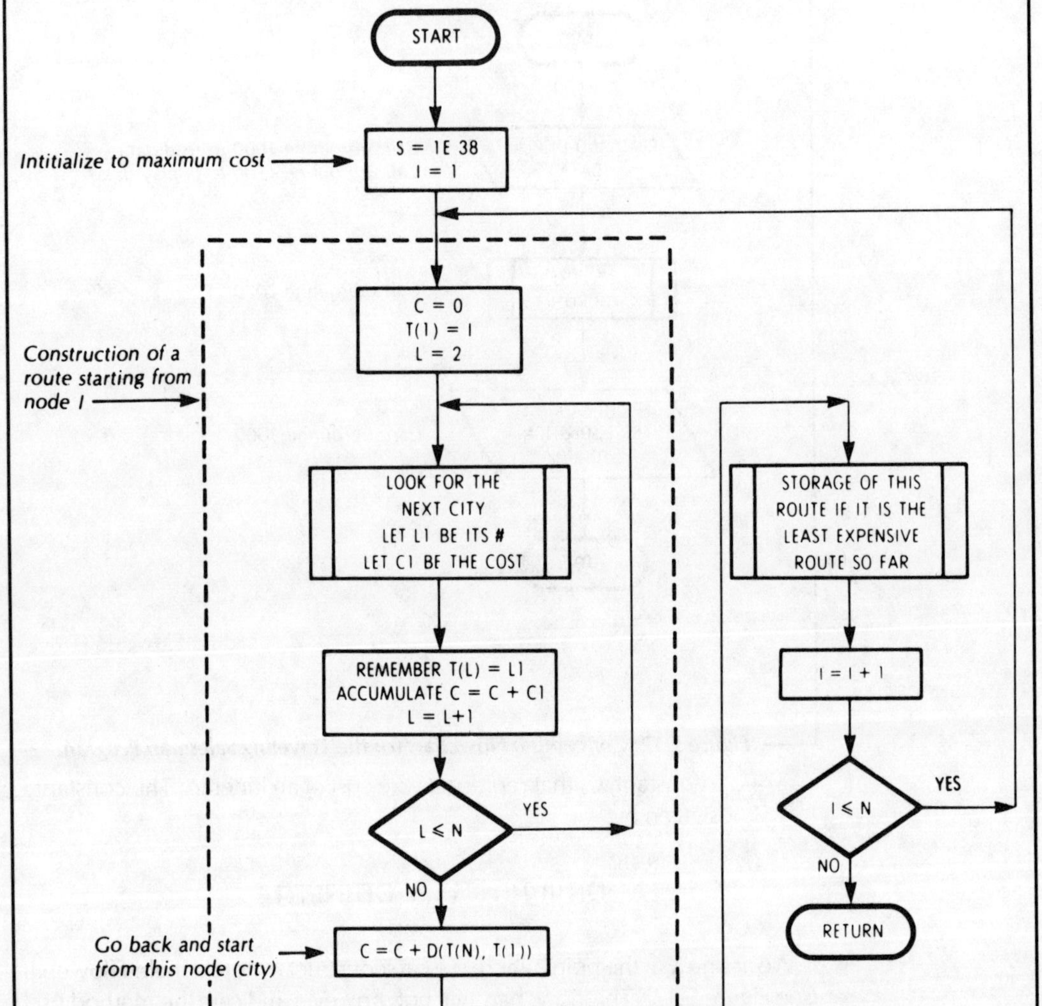

Figure 9.13: More Detailed Flowchart for the Traveling Salesman Program

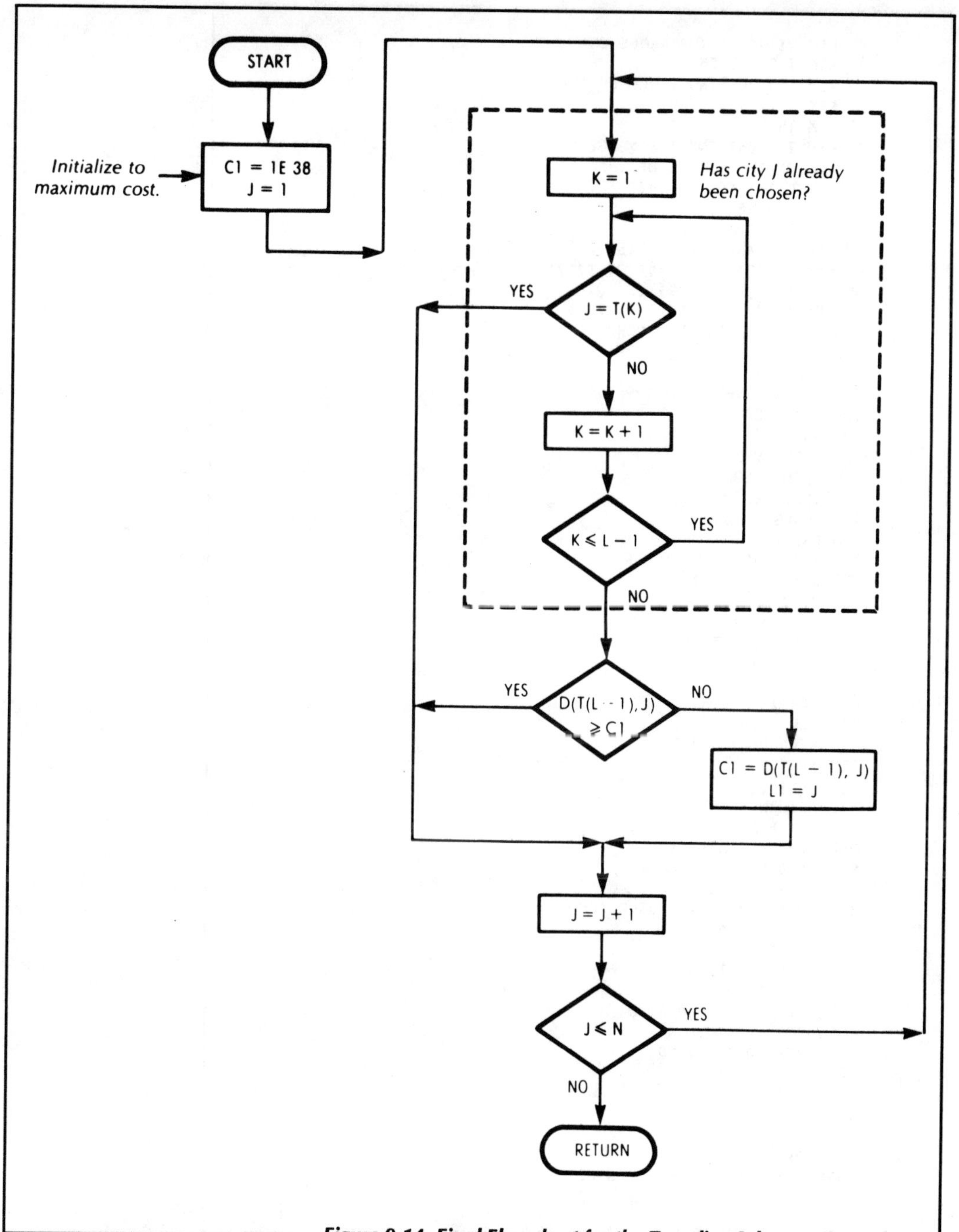

Figure 9.14: Final Flowchart for the Traveling Salesman Program

```
20 REM V$ HOLDS THE NAMES OF
22 REM THE CITIES
25 REM T = WORKING TABLE OF THE
30 REM CITIES ALREADY ON
32 REM THE ROUTE
35 REM T1 CONTAINS THE NUMBERS
37 REM OF THE CITIES OF THE
40 REM LEAST COSTLY TRIP YET
42 REM DEVISED
45 REM D = THE MATRIX OF
47 REM DISTANCES OR COSTS
90 DIM V$(60),T(20),T1(20),S$(9)
95 DIM D(20,20),N$(9),L$(40)
100 PRINT "THE TRAVELING ";
105 PRINT "SALESMAN PROGRAM"
110 PRINT
120 READ S$
125 IF S$="SYM" THEN 129
126 GOSUB 800
127 GOTO 130
129 GOSUB 995
130 GOSUB 1500
140 GOSUB 2000
150 GOSUB 3000
780 END
790 REM READ AN UNSYMETRIC
795 REM COST MATRIX
800 READ N
810 FOR I=1 TO N
820 READ N$:CIT=I:GOSUB 4000
822 V$(B,E)=N$
825 NEXT I
827 FOR I=1 TO N
830 FOR J=1 TO N
840 READ D:D(I,J)=D
850 NEXT J
860 NEXT I
870 RETURN
990 REM READ A SYMETRIC
992 REM COST MATRIX
995 READ N
1000 FOR I=1 TO N
1010 READ N$:CIT=I:GOSUB 4000
1015 V$(B,E)=N$
1020 NEXT I
1030 FOR I=1 TO N
1040 D(I,I)=0
1050 IF I+1>N THEN 1090
1055 FOR J=I+1 TO N
1060 READ D:D(I,J)=D
1070 D(J,I)=D(I,J)
1080 NEXT J
1090 NEXT I
1100 RETURN
1480 REM
1490 REM SUBROUTINE TO PRINT
```

Figure 9.15: Traveling Salesman Program (continues)

```
1495 REM COST MATRIX
1500 PRINT "THE COST OF TRAV";
1505 PRINT "EL BETWEEN CITIES:"
1510 PRINT :PRINT "    ";
1520 FOR I=1 TO N
1530 CIT=I:GOSUB 4000
1535 PRINT V$(B,E);" ";
1540 NEXT I
1550 PRINT
1555 PRINT
1560 FOR I=1 TO N
1562 L$="
1565 CIT=I:GOSUB 4000
1570 L$(1)=V$(B,E)
1580 FOR J=1 TO N
1595 L$(4*J+2)=STR$(D(I,J))
1600 NEXT J
1605 PRINT L$
1608 PRINT
1610 NEXT I
1620 RETURN
1970 REM
1980 REM BEGIN ALGORITHM TO
1985 REM FIND THE BEST ROUTE
1990 REM
2000 S=1E+38
2002 FOR I=1 TO N
2005 C=0
2010 T(1)=I
2020 FOR L=2 TO N
2030 GOSUB 2500
2040 T(L)=L1
2050 C=C+C1
2060 NEXT L
2065 C=C+D(T(N),T(1))
2070 GOSUB 2700
2090 NEXT I
2470 REM
2480 REM SELECT THE NEXT
2485 REM CITY TO VISIT
2490 REM
2500 C1=1E+38
2510 FOR J=1 TO N
2515 FOR K=1 TO L-1
2520 IF T(K)=J THEN 2560
2525 NEXT K
2530 IF D(T(L-1),J)>=C1 THEN 2560
2540 C1=D(T(L-1),J)
2550 L1=J
2560 NEXT J
2570 RETURN
2670 REM
2680 REM IS SOLUTION THE BEST
2685 REM SO FAR? IF SO,SAVE
2690 REM T IN T1 AND C IN S.
2700 IF S<=C THEN 2750
```

Figure 9.15: Traveling Salesman Program (continues)

```
2710 S=C
2720 FOR K=1 TO N
2730 T1(K)=T(K)
2740 NEXT K
2750 RETURN
3000 PRINT
3010 PRINT "           RECOM";
3012 PRINT "MENDED ITINERARY:"
3015 PRINT
3020 FOR L=1 TO N-1
3025 CIT=T1(L):GOSUB 4000
3030 PRINT V$(B,E);
3031 CIT=T1(L+1):GOSUB 4000
3032 PRINT " TO ";V$(B,E);
3034 PRINT "      ";
3036 PRINT D(T1(L),T1(L+1))
3040 PRINT
3050 NEXT L
3051 CIT=T1(N):GOSUB 4000
3052 PRINT V$(B,E);
3054 CIT=T1(1):GOSUB 4000
3056 PRINT " TO ";V$(B,E);
3057 PRINT "      ";
3058 PRINT D(T1(N),T1(1))
3060 PRINT
3070 PRINT "TOTAL COST:";
3075 PRINT "                 ";S
3080 RETURN
4000 REM STRING INDEXING SUBROUTINE
4010 B=3*(CIT-1)+1
4020 E=3*CIT
4030 RETURN
5000 END
```

Figure 9.15: Traveling Salesman Program

make it easier to understand. The main program does little more than call the four subroutines:

800 or 995	Read the cost matrix.
1500	Display the cost matrix.
2000	Perform the computation.
3000	Display the solution found.

The computation subroutine then calls two other subroutines:

2500	Select the next city
2700	Check to see if the itinerary just constructed is better than the previous itineraries. If so, store it.

Let us now look at two sample runs in Figures 9.16 and 9.17.

```
THE TRAVELING SALESMAN PROGRAM

THE COST OF TRAVEL BETWEEN CITIES:

     SAC  MVL  OAK  GVL  VAL  CLK  SF   UKH

SAC   0   45   67   13   40   68   89   81

MVL  47    0   29   37   22   23   41   36

OAK  68   30    0   73   21   24   12   37

GVL  13   36   74    0   42   60   95   73

VAL  40   24   22   43    0   36   33   49

CLK  67   23   25   60   35    0   36   13

SF   89   40   13   98   35   36    0   47

UKH  81   36   37   75   48   15   46    0

           RECOMMENDED ITINERARY:

GVL  TO  SAC          13

SAC  TO  VAL          40

VAL  TO  OAK          22

OAK  TO  SF           12

SF   TO  CLK          36

CLK  TO  UKH          13

UKH  TO  MVL          36

MVL  TO  GVL          37

TOTAL  COST:                    209
```

```
6155 DATA NON,8
6160 DATA SAC,MVL,OAK,GVL,VAL
6165 DATA CLK,SF ,UKH
6170 DATA 0,45,67,13,40,68,89,81
6180 DATA 47,0,29,37,22,23,41,36
6190 DATA 68,30,0,73,21,24,12,37
6200 DATA 13,36,74,0,42,60,95,73
6210 DATA 40,24,22,43,0,36,33,49
6220 DATA 67,23,25,60,35,0,36,13
6230 DATA 89,40,13,98,35,36,0,47
6240 DATA 81,36,37,75,48,15,46,0
```

Figure 9.16: First Run of the Traveling Salesman Program

```
THE TRAVELING SALESMAN PROGRAM

THE COST OF TRAVEL BETWEEN CITIES:

     SAC MVL OAK GVL VAL CLK SF  UKH

SAC  0   45  67  13  40  68  89  81

MVL  45  0   29  37  22  23  41  36

OAK  67  29  0   73  21  24  12  37

GVL  13  37  73  0   42  60  95  73

VAL  40  22  21  42  0   36  33  49

CLK  68  23  24  60  36  0   36  13

SF   89  41  12  95  33  36  0   47

UKH  81  36  37  73  49  13  47  0

           RECOMMENDED ITINERARY:

GVL TO SAC        13

SAC TO VAL        40

VAL TO OAK        21

OAK TO SF         12

SF  TO CLK        36

CLK TO UKH        13

UKH TO MVL        36

MVL TO GVL        37

TOTAL COST:                 208
```

```
6155 DATA SYM,8
6160 DATA SAC,MVL,OAK,GVL,VAL,CLK
6165 DATA SF ,UKH
6170 DATA 45,67,13,40,68,89,81
6180 DATA 29,37,22,23,41,36
6190 DATA 73,21,24,12,37
6200 DATA 42,60,95,73
6210 DATA 36,33,49
6220 DATA 36,13
6230 DATA 47
```

Figure 9.17: Second Run of the Traveling Salesman Program

Figure 9.18 shows the route that corresponds to the sample run in Figure 9.17.

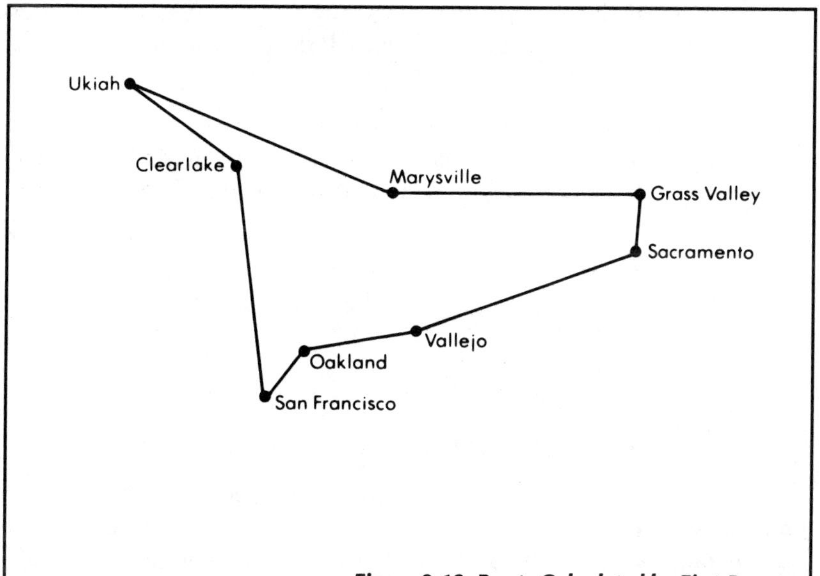

Figure 9.18: Route Calculated by First Run

This result is not actually the trip that would be the least expensive. More elaborate methods would have to be used to find the least expensive trip. This trip is shown in Figure 9.19. The cost associated with this itinerary is 206.

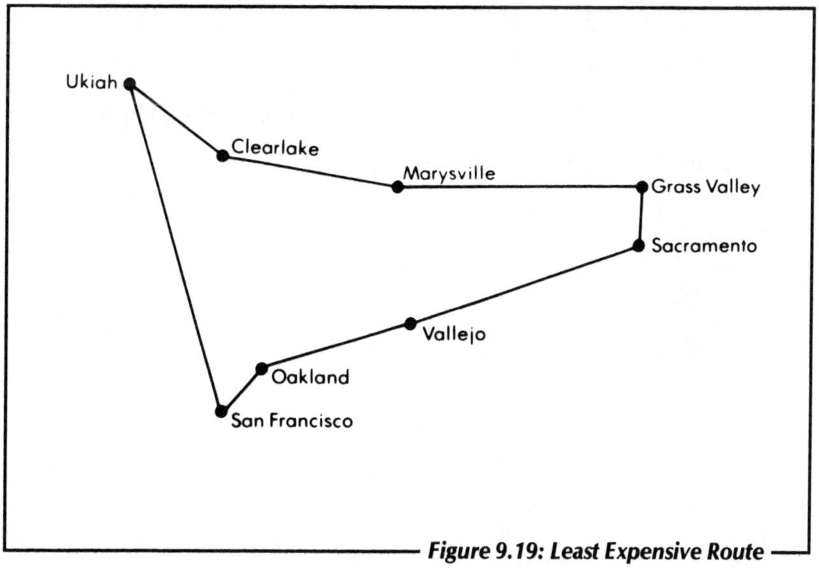

Figure 9.19: Least Expensive Route

Note: The following information should be considered:

- If one city is "equidistant" from two other cities and if the costs are minimal, the algorithm we programmed does not perform successive attempts with each city in turn. Instead, it systematically selects the city that comes first, in the order of subscripting.
- To force the program to attempt a route from the second city, the cost of the transit to the first city must be increased artificially by a small amount. The program must then be run a second time.
- To increase the algorithm's execution speed, the program could be made more elaborate; this would involve forcing the program to consider the byways required to make up a truly minimal cost itinerary.

Conclusion

We have studied three simple programs in operations research. You have probably seen that, although the problems seemed simple, the corresponding programs were lengthy and sometimes quite complicated. Generally speaking, each time we had to "walk a graph" we ended up with a subtle subscript-handling operation that made the programming a challenge.

If you find this subject interesting, we recommend studying the following problems:

1. Kruskal's algorithm
2. the Transportation Problem
3. flow optimization in a graph (the Ford-Fulkerson algorithm)
4. linear programming (the simplex method).

CHAPTER 10

Statistics

Introduction

The computer is a prime tool for handling problems that involve statistics and statistical applications because it can provide high-speed computations and rapid access to large amounts of data.

This chapter will present simple, but extremely useful, statistics programs. As an example of their usefulness, note that the linear regression subroutine explained in this chapter has already been applied to the rate of growth computation studied in Chapter 7.

The number of exercises presented here has been limited to maintain a balance with the rest of the book. It should be realized, however, that a large number of programs have been written in this domain.

10.1 The Average of a Sequence of Measurements

We want to compute the arithmetic mean, M, of a sequence of measurements. In this exercise all the data are assumed to be incorporated into the program. A numerical value of −999 signals the end of the data.

Exercise: First, analyze the problem. Then, draw a flowchart, and, finally, write the program.

Solution: Each sample measurement is used only once in the course of computing the sum M. Therefore, there is no need to use an array. The total number of samples will be tallied in a variable, N, which will be available later for the division. So that the dummy value −999 is not added to M, the following test for end-of-data must be carried out:

If $A \neq -999$, then continue the accumulation:

$$M = M + A$$
$$N = N + 1$$

If $A = -999$, then all the data have been read and we must complete the computation with the division:

$$M = M/N$$

This leads to the flowchart shown in Figure 10.1.

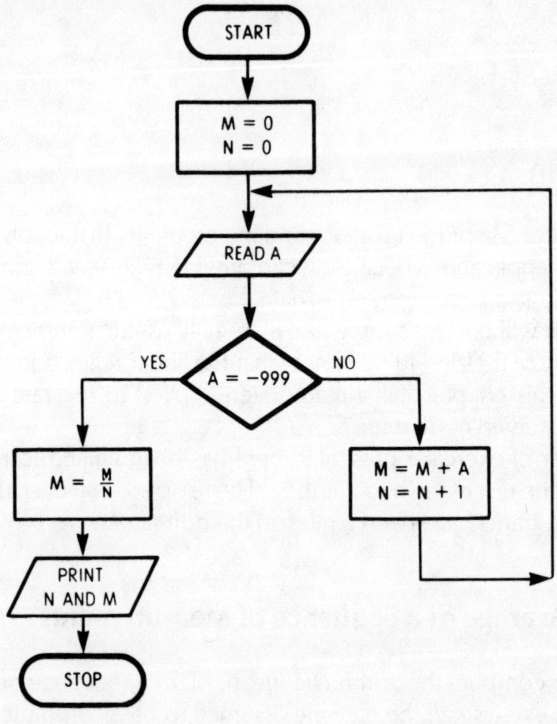

Figure 10.1: Flowchart for Calculating Arithmetic Mean

Programming this flowchart is easy (see Figure 10.2). The only complication lies in seeing that the results are presented clearly (as in Figure 10.3).

```
10 M=0:N=0
110 READ A
120 IF A=-999 THEN 170
130 N=N+1
140 M=M+A
150 GOTO 110
170 M=M/N
180 PRINT "NUMBER OF ";
185 PRINT "SAMPLES = ";N
190 PRINT
200 PRINT "MEAN                 ";
205 PRINT "= ";M
210 DATA 12,25,15,0,-999
220 END
```

Figure 10.2: Arithmetic Mean Program

```
NUMBER OF SAMPLES = 4

MEAN              = 13
```

Figure 10.3: Output from Arithmetic Mean Program

10.2 Mean, Variance and Standard Deviation

We can use the following formulas to calculate the mean, variance, and standard deviation of a series of N measurements:

$$\text{Mean } M = \frac{1}{N} \sum_{I=1}^{N} A(I)$$

$$\text{Variance } V = \frac{1}{N-1} \sum_{I=1}^{N} (A(I) - M)^2$$

$$\text{Standard Deviation } S = \sqrt{V}$$

As was done in the preceding program, the data is incorporated into the program, and the value −999 signals the end of the data (similar to an end-of-file indicator).

Exercise 1: Given a series of measurements (assumed to be contained in the program), compute the mean, variance, and standard deviation, using the preceding formulas. Consider the exercise in three phases:

Phase A: Draw a flowchart that describes the computation of the three quantities.

Phase B: Modify the formula for V, so that the flowchart will contain only one loop.

Phase C: Write a program that corresponds to the second flowchart.

Solution: Let us look at the three phases in detail.

Phase A: It seems natural to construct the flowchart in two parts:

1. to compute the mean
2. to compute the variance and standard deviation.

This yields the flowchart shown in Figure 10.4 that incorporates two loops and two passes over the data.

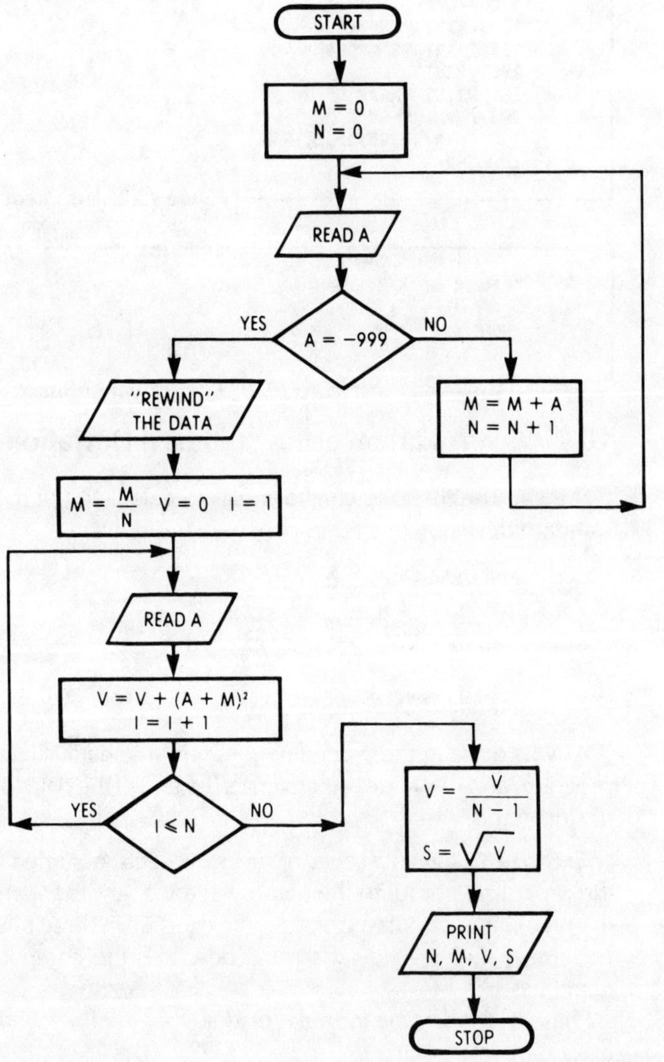

Figure 10.4: Flowchart with Two Loops for Mean, Variance and Standard Deviation

When the amount of data is small, reading the data twice is not a problem. Quite the contrary is true, however, in practical applications when large files of data are being handled: two passes over the data would approximately double the execution time in a multiprogramming environment.

More importantly, though, in a time-sharing environment, other programs would be much slower in their response time. For this reason, we attempt to minimize the number of file accesses.

Phase B: Expanding the formula for V we obtain:

$$V = \frac{1}{N-1}\left[\sum_{I=1}^{N} A(I)^2 - 2M\sum_{I=1}^{N} A(I) + NM^2\right]$$

and since:

$$\sum_{I=1}^{N} A(I) = NM$$

we can simplify the equation, giving:

$$V = \frac{1}{N-1}\left[\sum_{I=1}^{N} A(I)^2 - NM^2\right]$$

This formula allows M and V to be computed within a single loop. This is illustrated by the flowchart in Figure 10.5.

Phase C: This flowchart is simple and straightforward to program. As usual, an effort should be made to obtain a careful and clear display of the results. The program is shown in Figure 10.6. The sample run is shown in Figure 10.7.

Exercise 2: Modify the program in Figure 10.6 to compute the numeric value of the following indicators of sample dispersion:

$$\text{Skewness: } S = \frac{1}{N(S_1)^3}\sum_{I=1}^{N}\Big(A(I) - M\Big)^3$$

$$\text{Kurtosis: } K = \frac{1}{N(S_1)^4}\sum_{I=1}^{N}\Big(A(I) - M\Big)^4$$

where S_1 equals standard deviation.

Solution: We note that the second-order moment is written:

$$M_2 = \frac{1}{N}\sum_{I=1}^{N}(A(I) - M)^2$$

It corresponds to a "biased" estimator of variance.

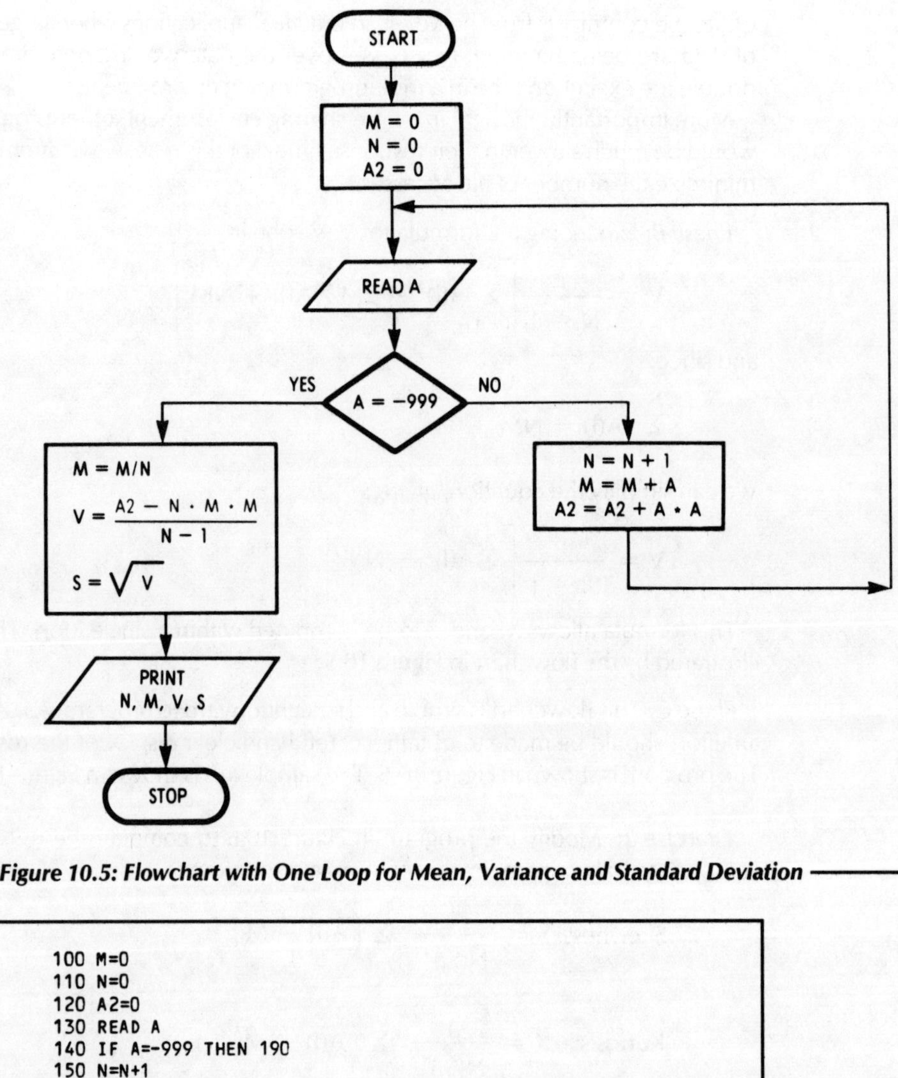

Figure 10.5: Flowchart with One Loop for Mean, Variance and Standard Deviation

```
100 M=0
110 N=0
120 A2=0
130 READ A
140 IF A=-999 THEN 190
150 N=N+1
160 M=M+A
170 A2=A2+A*A
180 GOTO 130
190 M=M/N
200 V=(A2-N*M*M)/(N-1)
210 S=SQR(V)
220 PRINT "NUMBER OF ";
225 PRINT "SAMPLES = ";N
```

Figure 10.6: Mean, Variance and Standard Deviation Program (continues)

```
230 PRINT "                ";
235 PRINT "MEAN = ";M
240 PRINT "            ";
245 PRINT "VARIANCE = ";V
250 PRINT "STANDARD ";
255 PRINT "DEVIATION = ";S
260 END
300 DATA 9,9.9,10,8.5,9,10.1
310 DATA 10,9.8,10.2
320 DATA -999
330 END
```

Figure 10.6: Mean, Variance and Standard Deviation Program

```
NUMBER OF SAMPLES = 9
             MEAN = 9.61111111
         VARIANCE = 0.37361125
STANDARD DEVIATION = 0.6112374743
```

Figure 10.7: Statistical Output

Let us define:

$$V_1 = \sum_{I=1}^{N} (A(I) - M)^2$$

We have:

$$V = \frac{1}{N-1} V_1$$

$$M_2 = \frac{1}{N} V_1$$

We can now expand the two formulas for S and K:

$$S = \frac{1}{N\left(\frac{V_1}{N}\right)^{\frac{3}{2}}} \left(\Sigma\, A(I)^3 - 3M\, \Sigma\, A(I)^2 + 3M^2\, \Sigma\, A(I) - NM^3\right)$$

$$= \frac{1}{N\left(\frac{V_1}{N}\right)^{\frac{3}{2}}} \left(\Sigma\, A(I)^3 - 3M\, \Sigma\, A(I)^2 + 2NM^3\right)$$

$$K = \frac{1}{N\left(\frac{V_1}{N}\right)^{2}} \left(\Sigma\, A(I)^4 - 4M\, \Sigma\, A(I)^3 + 6M^2\, \Sigma\, A(I)^2 - 4M^3\, \Sigma\, A(I) + NM^4\right)$$

$$= \frac{N}{V_1^2} \left(\Sigma\, A(I)^4 - 4M\, \Sigma\, A(I)^3 + 6M^2\, \Sigma\, A(I)^2 - 3NM^4\right)$$

Now we need to insert the calculations $\Sigma A(I)^3$ and $\Sigma A(I)^4$ into the loop. If we accumulate them in variables A3 and A4, respectively, we can obtain S and K by:

$$S = \frac{1}{N\left(\frac{V_1}{N}\right)^{\frac{3}{2}}}\left(A3 - 3M\,A2 + 2NM^2\right)$$

$$K = \frac{N}{V_1^{\,2}}\left(A4 - 4M\,A3 + 6M^2\,A2 - 3NM_4\right)$$

The program shown in Figure 10.8 can now be written with no further difficulty. A sample run of that program is shown in Figure 10.9a. Figure 10.9b shows another set of data with the corresponding printout.

```
100 N=0
110 A1=0
120 A2=0
125 A3=0
127 A4=0
130 READ A
140 IF A=-999 THEN 190
150 N=N+1
155 A1=A1+A
160 X=A*A
162 A2=A2+X
165 A3=A3+X*A
167 A4=A4+X*X
180 GOTO 130
190 M=A1/N
200 V=(A2-N*M*M)/(N-1)
210 S=SQR(V)
220 PRINT "NUMBER OF ";
225 PRINT "SAMPLES = ";N
230 PRINT "             ";
235 PRINT "MEAN = ";M
240 PRINT "          ";
245 PRINT "VARIANCE = ";V
250 PRINT "STANDARD ";
252 PRINT "DEVIATION = ";S
253 M2=M*M
255 S1=(A3-3*M*A2+2*M2*A1)/(N*V*S)
260 K=(A4-4*M*A3+6*M2*A2-3*N*M2*M2)/(N*V*V)
270 PRINT "SKEWNESS = ";S1
280 PRINT "KURTOSIS = ";K
285 END
300 DATA 1,2,3,4,5
310 DATA -999
330 END
```

Figure 10.8: Program for Skewness and Kurtosis

```
NUMBER OF SAMPLES = 5
             MEAN = 3
         VARIANCE = 2.5
STANDARD DEVIATION = 1.58113883
SKEWNESS = 0
KURTOSIS = 1.088
```

Figure 10.9a: Skewness and Kurtosis Output

```
300 DATA 2,2.5,3,3.5,4
NUMBER OF SAMPLES = 5
             MEAN = 3
         VARIANCE = 0.625
STANDARD DEVIATION = 0.790569415
SKEWNESS = 0
KURTOSIS = 1.088
```

Figure 10.9b: Another Run and the Data Analyzed

Notes:

- Skewness and kurtosis should be used with caution as they are not valid estimators for all populations.
- The skewness is zero if the distribution is symmetrical.
- The kurtosis increases in magnitude with the flatness of the density function.

10.3 Linear Regression

Find the straight line that "best" fits through a set of experimental points (X,Y). The criterion generally used is that of "least squares," which consists of determining coefficients A and B, such that

$$\sum_{I=1}^{N} (A * X(I) + B - Y(I))^2$$

is minimized.

To minimize this sum, we must compute A and B so that:

$$A = \frac{N \Sigma X(I) * Y(I) - (\Sigma X(I))(\Sigma Y(I))}{N \Sigma X(I) - (\Sigma X(I))^2}$$

$$B = \frac{N \Sigma X(I) - A \Sigma X(I)}{N \Sigma X(I)^2 - (\Sigma X(I))^2}$$

To assess the "statistical validity" of the computation, we can compute the coefficient R given by:

$$R = (\text{sign of } B)\sqrt{I - \frac{\Sigma (Y(I) - \hat{Y}(I))^2}{\Sigma (\hat{Y}(I) - \bar{Y})^2}}$$

If R is close to one, then the regression is statistically valid; if it is not, then linear regression is not well suited to the distribution of data points.

A variance may be calculated and confidence limits established on A and B.

Exercise: Write a subroutine that fits a regression line to the data in arrays T(100) and Y(100) and computes the coefficient R.

The computation of the coefficients A and B is done in the subroutine starting at line 1000. The coefficient R is to be computed in a subroutine starting at line 600 (Figure 10.14).

Solution: The part of the program that computes A and B follows from the formulas developed above. In a single program loop

$$\Sigma\, T(I),\ \Sigma\, Y(I),\ \Sigma\, X(I)^2 \text{ and } \Sigma\, X(I) * Y(I)$$

are computed, and the values of A and B can be determined from the results. This is expressed in the flowchart in Figure 10.10.

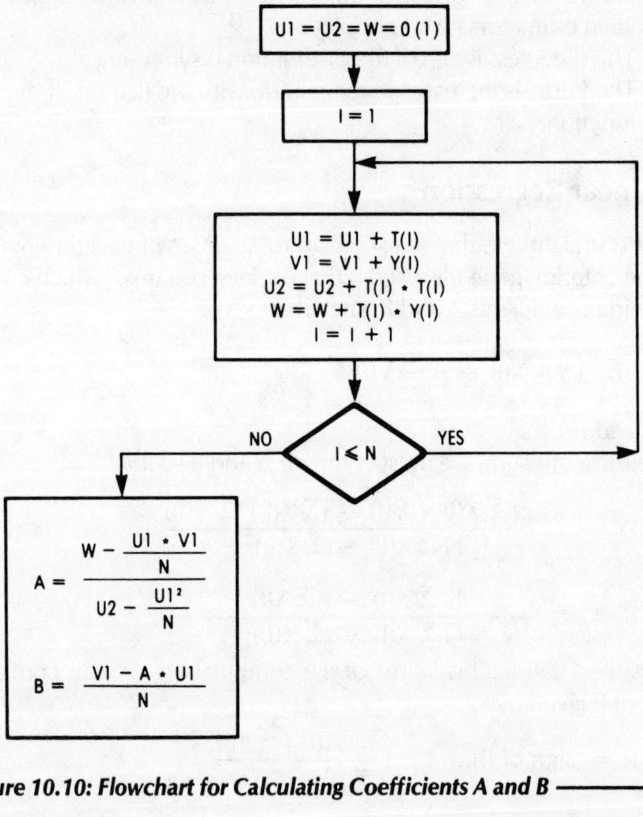

Figure 10.10: Flowchart for Calculating Coefficients A and B

R is computed on another loop, which is shown in Figure 10.11, appearing below.

A program written from the flowchart in Figure 10.10 is presented in Figure 10.12. This program was written as a linear regression without the coefficient R. The sample run appears in Figure 10.13.

The program shown in Figure 10.14 combines the information from both Figures 10.10 and 10.11 and includes the calculation for R. This program is the complete computation of the coefficients A and B and the coefficient R. Sample runs using different sets of data are shown in Figure 10.15. The results of the sample runs show the sensitivity of the correlation coefficient R.

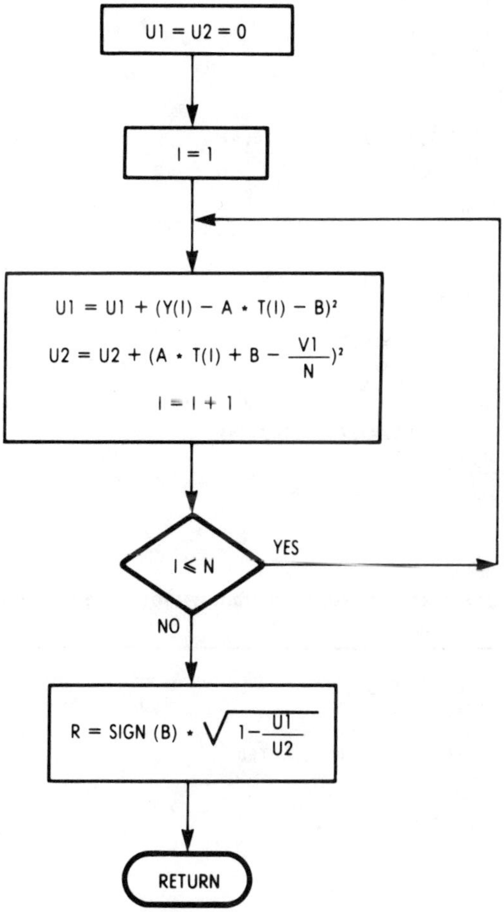

Figure 10.11: Flowchart for Calculating Coefficient R

```
100 DIM T(100),Y(100)
110 READ N
120 FOR I=1 TO N
130 READ T,Y:T(I)=T:Y(I)=Y
140 NEXT I
150 GOSUB 1000
160 PRINT "      SLOPE = ";A
170 PRINT "Y INTERCEPT = ";B
180 PRINT
190 PRINT " T   Y";
192 PRINT "MEASURED  ";
194 PRINT "Y CALCULATED"
200 PRINT
210 FOR I=1 TO N
220 Y1=A*T(I)+B
230 PRINT " ";T(I),
232 PRINT Y(I),
234 PRINT Y1
240 NEXT I
245 END
250 DATA 5
260 DATA 0,1,1,1.5,2,2,4,3,6,4
1000 U1=0
1010 U2=0
1020 V1=0
1030 V2=0
1040 W=0
1050 FOR I=1 TO N
1060 U1=U1+T(I)
1070 V1=V1+Y(I)
1080 U2=U2+T(I)*T(I)
1090 V2=V2+Y(I)*Y(I)
1100 W=W+T(I)*Y(I)
1110 NEXT I
1120 A=(W-U1*V1/N)/(U2-U1*U1/N)
1130 B=(V1-A*U1)/N
1140 RETURN
1200 END
```

Figure 10.12: Linear Regression Program without Coefficient R

```
      SLOPE = 0.5
Y INTERCEPT = 1

 T   Y MEASURED  Y CALCULATED

 0       1           1
 1       1.5         1.5
 2       2           2
 4       3           3
 6       4           4
```

Figure 10.13: Sample Run without Coefficient R

```
100 DIM T(100),Y(100)
110 READ N
120 FOR I=1 TO N
130 READ T,Y:T(I)=T:Y(I)=Y
140 NEXT I
150 GOSUB 1000
155 GOSUB 600
160 PRINT "       SLOPE = ";A
170 PRINT "Y INTERCEPT = ";B
175 PRINT "COEFFICIENT R = ";R
180 PRINT
190 PRINT " T   Y ";
192 PRINT "MEASURED  ";
194 PRINT "Y CALCULATED"
200 PRINT
210 FOR I=1 TO N
220 Y1=A*T(I)+B
230 PRINT " ";T(I),
232 PRINT Y(I),
234 PRINT Y1
240 NEXT I
245 END
600 U1=0
605 U2=0
610 FOR I=1 TO N
620 U1=U1+(Y(I)-A*T(I)-B)^2
630 U2=U2+(A*T(I)+B-V1/N)^2
640 NEXT I
650 R=SGN(B)*SQR(1-U1/U2)
660 RETURN
1000 U1=0
1010 U2=0
1020 V1=0
1030 V2=0
1040 W=0
1050 FOR I=1 TO N
1060 U1=U1+T(I)
1070 V1=V1+Y(I)
1080 U2=U2+T(I)*T(I)
1090 V2=V2+Y(I)*Y(I)
1100 W=W+T(I)*Y(I)
1110 NEXT I
1120 A=(W-U1*V1/N)/(U2-U1*U1/N)
1130 B=(V1-A*U1)/N
1140 RETURN
1200 END
2000 DATA 5
2010 DATA 0,1,1,1.5,2,2,4,3,6,4
2020 REM DATA 0,.95,1,1.55,2,2.05,4,2.95,4,3.05
2030 REM DATA 0,.95,1,1.55,2,2.95,4,3.05,6,4
```

Figure 10.14: Linear Regression Program with Coefficient R

```
        SLOPE = 0.5
  Y INTERCEPT = 1
  COEFFICIENT R = 1

   T    Y MEASURED   Y CALCULATED

   0         1            1
   1         1.5          1.5
   2         2            2
   4         3            3
   6         4            4
```

```
        SLOPE = 0.503125
  Y INTERCEPT = 1.003125
  COEFFICIENT R = 0.9981658279

   T    Y MEASURED   Y CALCULATED

   0         0.95         1.003125
   1         1.55         1.50625
   2         2.05         2.009375
   4         2.95         3.015625
   4         3.05         3.015625
```

```
        SLOPE = 0.4806034482
  Y INTERCEPT = 1.25043103
  COEFFICIENT R = 0.9322739458

   T    Y MEASURED   Y CALCULATED

   0         0.95         1.25043103
   1         1.55         1.73103447
   2         2.95         2.21163792
   4         3.05         3.17284482
   6         4            4.13405171
```

Figure 10.14: Linear Regression Program with Coefficient R

10.4 The Distribution of Random Numbers Obtained From the Function RND

The random number generating function, RND, is very useful in some applications. However, before we use any source of random numbers, it is important to assess the quality of that source. Since this is not a statistics book, we will merely construct a program that will reveal how the numbers produced are actually distributed.

Specification: The BASIC function RND normally provides a random number uniformly distributed in the open interval (0,1). The problem is to divide this interval into C classes of the same length. After that we want to generate a specified number, N, of random numbers and, finally, print a list showing the number of random numbers that fit into each class. Figure 10.16 shows examples of the type of output we want to obtain.

```
NUMBER OF CLASSES  ?10
NUMBER OF RANDOM NUMBERS TO
PRODUCE  ?10
 1        1
 2        0
 3        3
 4        2
 5        0
 6        1
 7        1
 8        0
 9        1
 10       1
```

```
NUMBER OF CLASSES  ?10
NUMBER OF RANDOM NUMBERS TO
PRODUCE  ?100
 1        12
 2        12
 3        8
 4        11
 5        9
 6        11
 7        11
 8        10
 9        7
 10       9
```

```
NUMBER OF CLASSES  ?10
NUMBER OF RANDOM NUMBERS TO
PRODUCE  ?1000
 1        102
 2        104
 3        98
 4        96
 5        96
 6        102
 7        102
 8        106
 9        106
 10       88
```

Figure 10.16: Desired Output from Analysis of Function RND

Solution: One method that we might use involves making a series of tests on each random number to determine the class to which it belongs. This method, however, is too slow.

Another method might be to derive, from each random number, an integer that corresponds to the class to which the number belongs.

With C classes we need a number that runs from 1 to C. This number can be obtained by using:

$$X = \underbrace{\text{INT}(C*\overbrace{\text{RND}(1))}^{\textit{between 0 and 1}}}_{\textit{between 0 and } C - 1} + 1$$

Then we simply write:

A(X) = A(X) + 1

where A is an array of counts, one element for each class. A is initialized to zero when the number of classes is specified by the user. This leads to the flowchart shown in Figure 10.17.

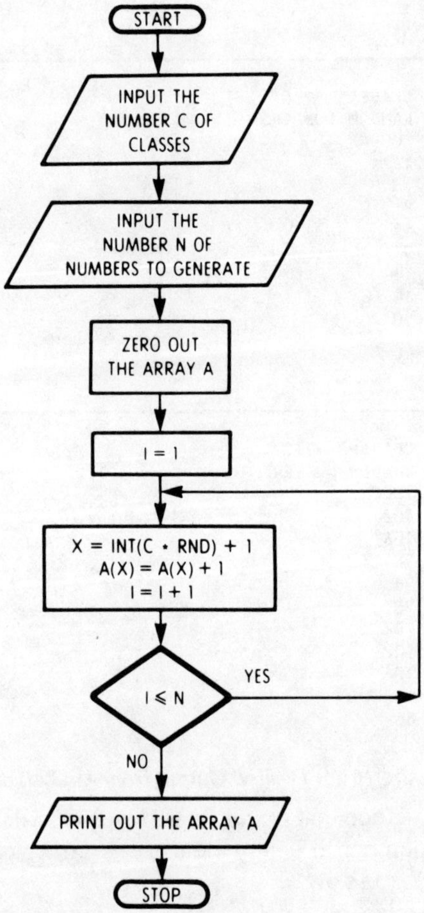

Figure 10.17: Flowchart for the Analysis of Function RND

The program displayed in Figure 10.18 is written in ATARI BASIC, which allows the size in a dimension statement to be expressed as a variable (line 130).

```
100 REM TEST OF THE DISTRIBU-
102 REM TION OF THE RANDOM
105 REM NUMBER GENERATOR
110 REM AUTHOR : J. P.
115 REM LAMOITIER
120 PRINT "NUMBER OF CLASSES  ";
125 INPUT C
130 DIM A(C)
140 FOR I=1 TO C
150 A(I)=0
160 NEXT I
170 PRINT "NUMBER OF RANDOM";
172 PRINT " NUMBERS TO"
173 PRINT "PRODUCE  ";
175 INPUT N
180 FOR I=1 TO N
190 X=INT(RND(1)*C)+1
200 A(X)=A(X)+1
210 NEXT I
220 FOR I=1 TO C
230 PRINT " ";I,
235 PRINT A(I)
240 NEXT I
```

Figure 10.18: Function RND Program

If you are using a BASIC that does not allow this syntax, you can simply dimension A statically, for example:

```
100 DIM A(100)
    .
    .
    .
    INPUT . . . C
    (must not exceed 100)
```

Conclusion

The exercises in this chapter demonstrate that programming elementary computations like mean, variance, etc., offers few if any problems. It was noted that the exercise involving the computation of a linear regression is particularly useful. In fact, the calculation is used in Chapter 7 for estimating rate of growth.

The random number generating function, RND, is also useful in many applications. It is used, for example, to simulate the throwing of dice in the Craps implementation developed in Chapter 8.

On the other hand, when more sophisticated computations are used (for example, statistical tests, multiple regression, polynomial regression, etc.), the programs will become longer and subject to problems of round-off.

CHAPTER 11

Miscellaneous

Introduction

This chapter consists of exercises that are of interest from an information-processing point of view, but do not fit under any of the previous chapter headings. These exercises are of particular interest because they either involve clever programming techniques or because the development of the flowchart is not obvious.

11.1 The Signs of the Zodiac

Given a month and day of birth, determine the corresponding sign of the zodiac. The table shown in Figure 11.1 gives birth dates and the corresponding signs of the zodiac.

SIGN	PERIOD
CAPRICORN	DECEMBER 23 TO JANUARY 19
AQUARIUS	JANUARY 20 TO FEBRUARY 19
PISCES	FEBRUARY 20 TO MARCH 20
ARIES	MARCH 21 TO APRIL 19
TAURUS	APRIL 20 TO MAY 20
GEMINI	MAY 21 TO JUNE 20
CANCER	JUNE 21 TO JULY 21
LEO	JULY 22 TO AUGUST 22
VIRGO	AUGUST 23 TO SEPTEMBER 22
LIBRA	SEPTEMBER 23 TO OCTOBER 22
SCORPIO	OCTOBER 23 TO NOVEMBER 21
SAGITTARIUS	NOVEMBER 22 TO DECEMBER 22

Figure 11.1: Signs of the Zodiac

Exercise 1: Write a program that determines the sign of the zodiac that corresponds to an input day and month of birth. Assume that we are using a BASIC that allows arrays of character strings.

Exercise 2: Repeat Exercise 1, but this time assume that we are using ATARI BASIC. It does not allow arrays of character strings.

Exercise 1 solution: To complete Exercise 1, we must compare the day of the month, D, with a limit, L, that varies between 20 and 23, depending on the month:

— If D < L, use I = M

— If D ≥ L, use I = M + 1, except in the case where M + 1 = 13; in this case we must set I = 1. This will be the case for a person born between the 23rd and the 31st of December.

To obtain the correct value for L, we first set L to 20. Then, we use an ON GOTO instruction to jump into a cascade of increment L instructions, which will establish the correct value for L. This method avoids numerous tests and GOTO instructions.

Figure 11.2 shows a flowchart of this method.

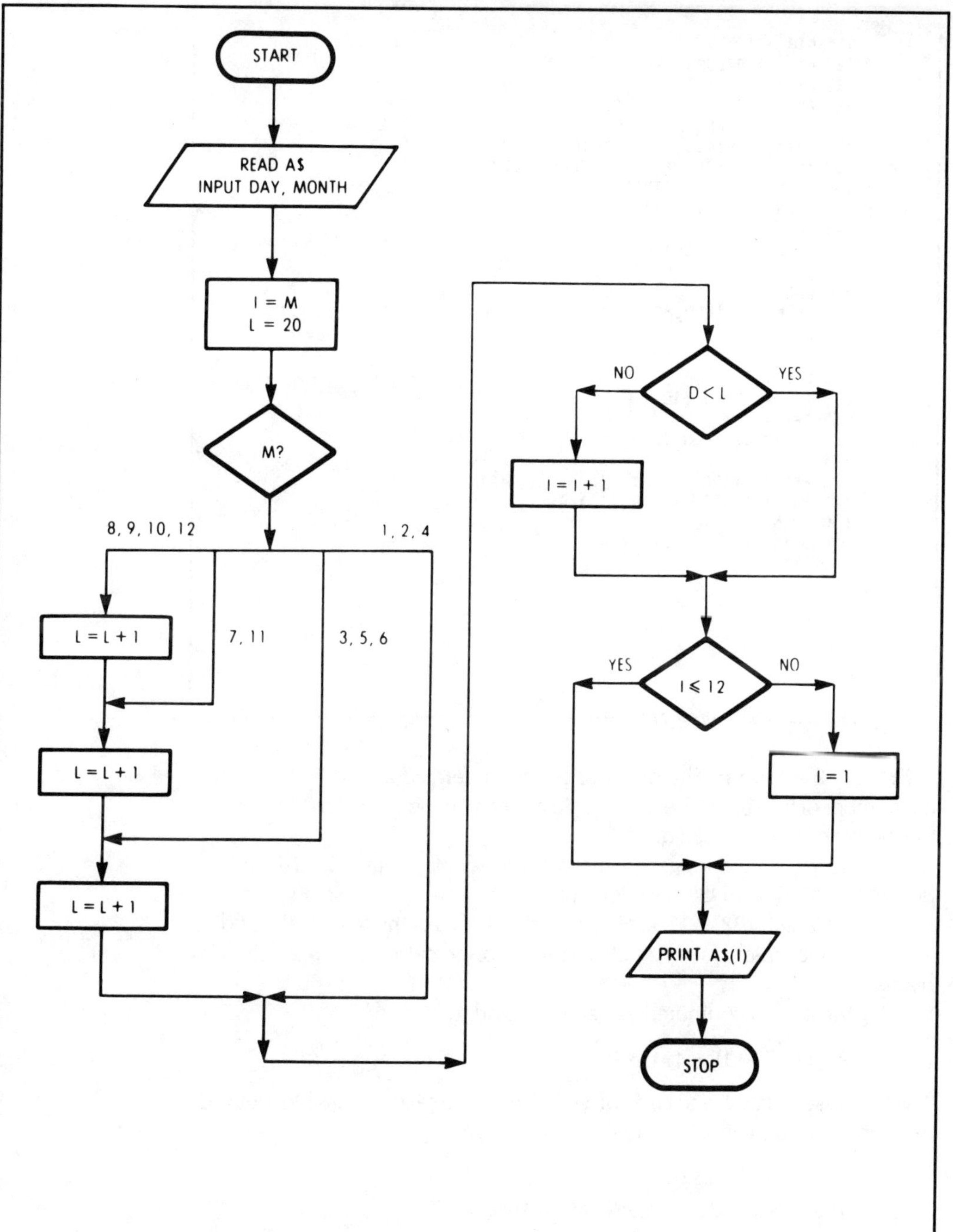

Figure 11.2: Flowchart for Determining the Signs of the Zodiac

```
115 DIM A$(132)
120 A$="CAPRICORN  AQUARIUS   "
122 A$(23)="PISCES     ARIES      "
124 A$(45)="TAURUS     GEMINI     "
126 A$(67)="CANCER     LEO        "
128 A$(89)="VIRGO      LIBRA      "
130 A$(111)="SCORPIO    SAGITTARIUS"
140 PRINT "YOUR BIRTHDAY ";
142 PRINT "(MONTH,DAY)  ";
145 INPUT M,D
150 IF M=0 THEN END
180 I=M
190 L=20
200 ON M GOTO 600,600,500,600,500,500,400,300,300,300,400,300
300 L=L+1
400 L=L+1
500 L=L+1
600 IF D<L THEN 610
605 I=I+1
610 IF I<=12 THEN 620
615 I=1
620 PRINT "YOUR SIGN IS ";
625 PRINT A$(11*(I-1)+1,11*I)
630 PRINT
650 GOTO 140
990 END
```

Figure 11.3: Zodiac Program

Exercise 2 solution: The previous program derived an index, I, which is the number of the sign of the zodiac. However, with no string array capability, the index I cannot be used directly.

We observe that the longest name we will have to write is SAGITTARIUS. Because "SAGITTARIUS" has eleven characters, we must use a string variable, A$, of length 132 = 11 * 12 to hold the names of the signs of the zodiac in twelve, eleven-character "fields" (the shorter names are padded with blanks).

Using the index I computed as before, we print:

```
A$(11*(I - 1) + 1, 11*I)
```

We must see that A$ is set up correctly. There are several possible methods that can be used to do this. One such method is:

```
115  DIM A$(132)
120  A$ = "CAPRICORN  AQUARIUS   "
122  A$(23) = "PISCES     ARIES      "
```

```
124  A$(45) = "TAURUS       GEMINI      "
126  A$(67) = "CANCER       LEO         "
128  A$(89) = "VIRGO        LIBRA       "
130  A$(111) = "SCORPIO     SAGITTARIUS "
```

By filling out each name with the correct number of blanks, we assure that the name of each sign will begin in a regular position (1, 12, 23, 34, 45, . . . etc.) and, thus, can be easily selected for printout. Figure 11.4 shows sample dialogue.

The program, shown in Figure 11.3, stops when the given month equals 0.

```
YOUR BIRTHDAY (MONTH,DAY)  ?2,27
YOUR SIGN IS PISCES

YOUR BIRTHDAY (MONTH,DAY)  ?1,8
YOUR SIGN IS CAPRICORN

YOUR BIRTHDAY (MONTH,DAY)  ?3,20
YOUR SIGN IS PISCES

YOUR BIRTHDAY (MONTH,DAY)  ?4,21
YOUR SIGN IS TAURUS

YOUR BIRTHDAY (MONTH,DAY)  ?10,11
YOUR SIGN IS LIBRA

YOUR BIRTHDAY (MONTH,DAY)  ?0,0
```

Figure 11.4: Sample Output from the Zodiac Program

11.2 The Eight Queens Problem

By now the Eight Queens problem is a classical problem for computer science students as well chess players. This problem entails finding all of the possible ways to arrange eight queens on a chess board so that no two queens are *"en prise"* (threatening to take one another).

Exercise: Find all possible solutions to the general N queen problem; arrange N queens on an "N by N" board so that no two queens are *en prise.* Let N vary from two to eight.

We will eliminate solutions that can be deduced from other solutions by arguments of symmetry.

Proposed method: One possible solution is shown in Figure 11.5.

An array, Q, will hold the position of the queens while a solution is being worked out. For example, the solution illustrated in Figure 11.5 would be

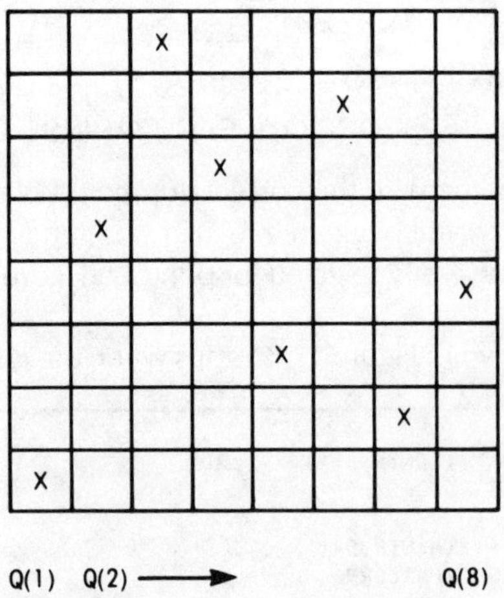

Figure 11.5: One Solution for the Eight Queens Problem

represented by:

$Q(1) = 1$ $Q(5) = 3$

$Q(2) = 5$ $Q(6) = 7$

$Q(3) = 8$ $Q(7) = 2$

$Q(4) = 6$ $Q(8) = 4$

Using this representation of board positions, the following conditions must be met in order that no two queens should be *en prise:*

— Not more than one queen may occupy a column. This is inherent in our representation: only one queen can be specified per column.

— Not more than one queen may occupy a given row, which means:

$Q(I) \neq Q(J)$ for any I, J

— Not more than one queen may occupy a given diagonal, which means:

$Q(J) - Q(I) \neq J - I$ (45° diagonal)

$Q(J) - Q(I) \neq I - J$ (−45° diagonal)

These last two tests could be more simply stated as:

$ABS(Q(I) - Q(J)) \neq I - J$

Conventions for generating solutions: The following conventions should be followed:

- Always start from Q(1) = 1.
- Find an admissable position for Q(2); that is, a position where Q(2) (the queen in column 2) is not *en prise* with Q(1).
- Seek an admissible position for Q(3) and so on, until an admissible position has been found for Q(N). At this point we have a solution.

If no admissible position is found for Q(I), we will try to move Q(I − 1) to some other position satisfying the constraint that Q(I − 1) is not in a position to be taken by any of the preceding queens (Q(1), Q(2), . . . , Q(I − 2)). When this is done, we try again to find an admissible position for Q(I).

More precisely stated, the proposed algorithm is the following:

For I varying from 1 to N:

1. Set Q(I) = 1
2. Verify that the new queen Q(I) is not threatened by any of the queens that have already been positioned.
   If Q(I) is *en prise,* go to 3.
   Otherwise,
   If I < N, set I = I + 1 and go to 1.
   If I = N we have a solution, print it out and go on to 3.
3. Search for another position for Q(I)·
   Set Q(I) = Q(I) + 1
   If Q(I) ≤ N, go to 2
   If Q(I) > N, then no position will do; set I = I − 1 and go to 2.

To eliminate the solutions that can be deduced by symmetry from a solution that has already been found, we should:

- Only try Q(1) in positions 1 through N/2. This eliminates all solutions that are symmetrical with respect to the horizontal axis.
- Print no solution for which Q(1) > Q(N), because such a solution is symmetrical, relative to the vertical axis, to a solution that has already been displayed.

Flowcharts: The flowchart presented in Figure 11.6 corresponds to a subroutine that implements the algorithm described in detail above.

The flowchart in Figure 11.7 corresponds to the main program. The program listing is shown in Figure 11.8 and the resulting output is displayed in Figure 11.9.

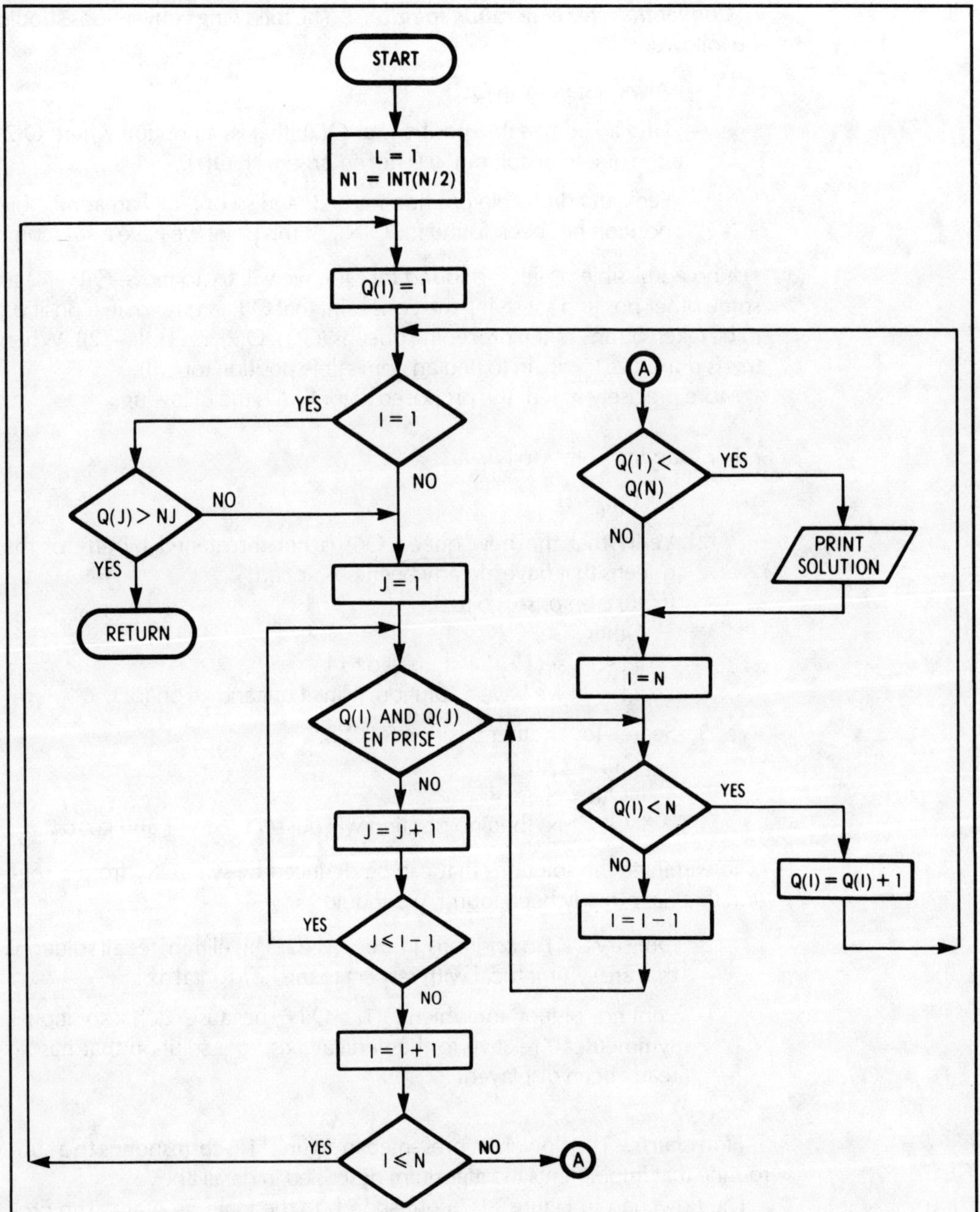

Figure 11.6: Flowchart for the Eight Queens Subroutine

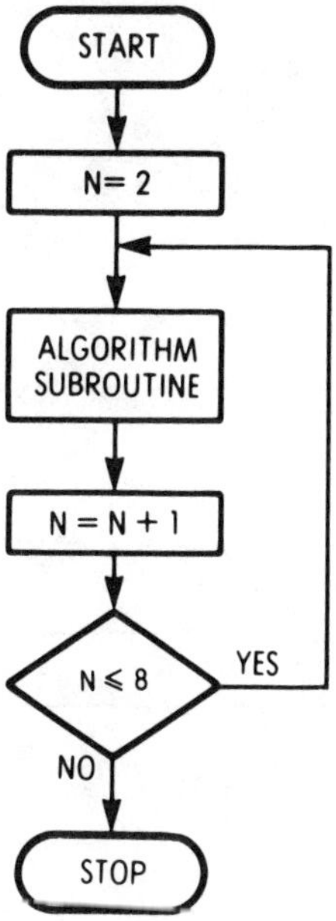

Figure 11.7: Flowchart for the Eight Queens Problem

```
100 REM GENERATION OF ALL WAYS
105 REM TO PLACE N QUEENS ON
110 REM AN N BY N BOARD
115 REM WITHOUT ANY TWO QUEENS
120 REM BEING EN PRISE.
130 DIM Q(10)
140 N9=8
150 FOR N=2 TO N9
160 S=0
165 PRINT
170 PRINT "N = ";N
175 PRINT
180 GOSUB 500
190 NEXT N
200 END
500 I=1
510 N1=INT(N/2)
520 Q(I)=1
530 IF I<>1 THEN 560
540 IF Q(1)<=N1 THEN 600
550 GOTO 690
560 FOR J=1 TO I-1
570 IF Q(I)=Q(J) THEN 640
580 IF ABS(Q(I)-Q(J))=I-J THEN 640
590 NEXT J
```

Figure 11.8: Eight Queens Program (continues)

```
600 I=I+1
610 IF I<=N THEN 510
620 IF Q(N)<=Q(1) THEN 630
625 GOSUB 700
630 I=N
640 IF Q(I)<N THEN 670
650 I=I-1
660 GOTO 640
670 Q(I)=Q(I)+1
680 GOTO 530
690 RETURN
700 FOR L=1 TO N
710 PRINT " ";Q(L);"  ";
720 NEXT L
725 PRINT
730 RETURN
740 END
```

Figure 11.8: Eight Queens Program

```
N = 2

N = 3

N = 4

 2   4   1   3

N = 5

 1   3   5   2   4
 1   4   2   5   3
 2   4   1   3   5
 2   5   3   1   4

N = 6

 2   4   6   1   3   5
 3   6   2   5   1   4

N = 7

 1   3   5   7   2   4   6
 1   4   7   3   6   2   5
 1   5   2   6   3   7   4
 1   6   4   2   7   5   3
 2   4   1   7   5   3   6
 2   4   6   1   3   5   7
 2   5   1   4   7   3   6
 2   5   3   1   7   4   6
 2   5   7   4   1   3   6
 2   6   3   7   4   1   5
 2   7   5   3   1   6   4
 3   1   6   2   5   7   4
 3   1   6   4   2   7   5
 3   6   2   5   1   4   7
 3   7   2   4   6   1   5
 3   7   4   1   5   2   6
```

Figure 11.9: Output from the Eight Queens Program (continues)

```
N = 8

1  5  8  6  3  7  2  4
1  6  8  3  7  4  2  5
1  7  4  6  8  2  5  3
1  7  5  8  2  4  6  3
2  4  6  8  3  1  7  5
2  5  7  1  3  8  6  4
2  5  7  4  1  8  6  3
2  6  1  7  4  8  3  5
2  6  8  3  1  4  7  5
2  7  3  6  8  5  1  4
2  7  5  8  1  4  6  3
2  8  6  1  3  5  7  4
3  1  7  5  8  2  4  6
3  5  2  8  1  7  4  6
3  5  7  1  4  2  8  6
3  5  8  4  1  7  2  6
3  6  2  5  8  1  7  4
3  6  2  7  1  4  8  5
3  6  2  7  5  1  8  4
3  6  8  1  5  7  2  4
3  6  8  2  4  1  7  5
3  7  2  8  5  1  4  6
3  7  2  8  6  4  1  5
3  8  4  7  1  6  2  5
4  1  5  8  2  7  3  6
4  2  5  8  6  1  3  7
4  2  7  3  6  8  1  5
4  2  8  5  7  1  3  6
4  2  8  6  1  3  5  7
4  6  1  5  2  8  3  7
4  6  8  2  7  1  3  5
4  7  3  8  2  5  1  6
4  7  5  2  6  1  3  8
4  8  1  3  6  2  7  5
4  8  5  3  1  7  2  6
```

Figure 11.9: Output from the Eight Queens Program

Conclusion

The exercises we have presented show that programming itself is not generally difficult when you first analyze the problem and then draw a flowchart. This is particlarly true in the case of the last exercise, devoted to solving the Eight Queens problem.

As we come to the end of this book we would like to leave the reader with a final piece of advice:

Before beginning to write a program:

- Make sure there is not an already existing program you can use.
- Spend sufficient time preparing the analysis and flowchart before starting to program. The initial time spent analyzing a problem is quickly regained in the coding and checkout phases.

APPENDIX A

The Alphabet of BASIC

The BASIC alphabet is made up of the following characters and symbols:

— The upper case letters	*A through Z*
— The digits	*0 through 9*
— The arithmetic symbols for:	
addition and subtraction	+ *and* −
multiplication and division	∗ *and* /
exponentiation	∧
— Parentheses	(*and*)
— The relational symbols:	
equal to	=
not equal to	<>
less than	<
less than or equal to	<=
greater than	>
greater than or equal to	>=
— The punctuation marks:	
comma and period	, *and* .
colon and semicolon	: *and* ;
question mark	?
— The special characters:	
"blank"	
quotation mark (double quote)	"
dollar sign	$

Certain implementations of BASIC use a slightly different (or extended) character set.

APPENDIX B

Main Syntax Rules

CONSTANTS AND VARIABLES

Constants: Numerical constants may be represented by:

— an integer, with or without sign
Examples: 11, −162

— a decimal number without an exponent
Examples: 3.1415917, −3., 0.12, .12

— a number with an exponent.
Examples: 1E + 5, −1.6E − 19

Note: In the last example, −1.6E − 19, the first minus sign is the sign of the number itself, and the second minus sign pertains to the exponent:

$$-1.6E-19 \text{ represents } -1.6*10^{-19}$$

Since virtually all input to computers is constrained to a single line, the exponent is set off from the rest of the number by the letter E.

The computer differentiates between the digit zero and the letter "O." The user at the keyboard must take care to make the same distinction.

Numerical Variables: There are two categories of numerical variables:

1. simple variables
2. subscripted variables (variables contained in a table or array).

Simple numerical variables are designated by their "name" (or "identifier"), which is either:

— a letter A through Z, or

— a letter followed by any number of letters and digits.
Examples: A, B, AB, FRED, ANGLE90X5 are variable names.

A program in ATARI BASIC may contain at most 128 variables.

Subscripted variables are designated by a simple variable name followed by one or two subscripts enclosed in parentheses. For example:

A(R,I), B(I), C(I + 10*K)

The subscript may be a constant, a variable, or an arithmetic expression.

Before a subscripted variable may be used, the size of the variable must be declared by a DIM instruction placed at the beginning of the program.

Example: DIM A(10,20)

ARITHMETIC EXPRESSIONS

Arithmetic expressions are built from:

— variables and constants
— arithmetic operators, +, −, *, /, ^
— standard numerical functions (described later)
— user-defined functions
— parentheses.

Parentheses serve two purposes:

1. to set off the argument(s) of a function
2. to specify the order in which expressions must be evaluated.

Examples: A + B*C will be evaluated A + (B*C)

(A + B)*C will be evaluated (A + B)*C

A + B*SIN(C + 3). In this case the parentheses set off the argument, which is C + 3.

Normally, expressions are evaluated uniformly from left to right according to "operator precedence." The descending order of precedence is:

— parentheses (highest precedence, i.e., evaluated first)
— functions
— exponentiation
— multiplication and division
— addition and subtraction (lowest precedence, i.e., carried out using the results of all operations of higher precedence).

As an example, the following expression would be evaluated in the order indicated:

```
A * (B + 3.2 * SIN (Y + 3 * Z)) + X^4 / C
```

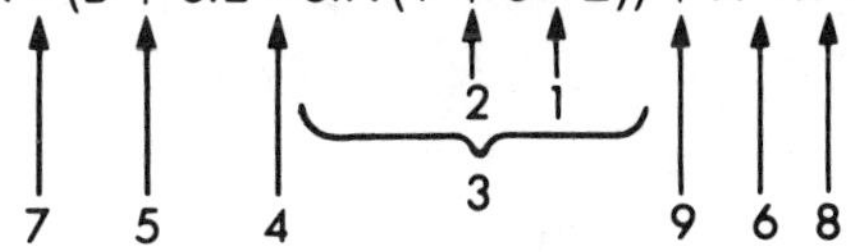

ASSIGNMENT INSTRUCTIONS

An assignment instruction should appear in the following form:

```
variable = expression
```

↑
simple variable or array element

The meaning of the instruction is to compute the value of the expression on the right of the equal sign, and store the result in the variable on the left of the equal sign. For example:

```
V = 4*3.14159*(R^3)/3
X = A
```

BRANCHING INSTRUCTIONS

Unconditional branch: The simplest form of an unconditional branch is the GOTO instruction, which might appear as:

```
GO TO L
```

or:

```
GOTO L
```

where L is a line number.

The above instruction causes the execution of the program to go to line L.

"Computed" GOTO: This instruction generally takes on the following form:

```
ON arithmetic expression GOTO L1, L2, L3, . . . LN
```

where L1, L2, . . . LN are line numbers.

During execution, this instruction would cause the expression to be evaluated. The value then obtained is truncated to an integer and used to select the branch:

- — to line L1, if the value truncates to 1
- — to line L2, if the value truncates to 2
- — to line LN, if the value truncates to N.

Example: ON 1 GOTO 100,200,600,200

If I is 1	branch to 100
If I is 2 or 4	branch to 200
If I is 3	branch to 600

Note: If the truncated value of the expression falls outside the interval [1,N], the result varies from system to system:

- — The branch may be ignored and the next instruction in sequence executed.
- — The interpreter may issue an error message.

Conditional branch: The conditioning on this type of branch is carried out using the IF instruction, which may take several forms.

First form: the simplest form of the IF instruction is:

```
IF predicate THEN L
```

where *predicate* asserts a relationship between two expressions, and L is a line number.

If the predicate is true, execution branches to line number L; otherwise, the next instruction in the sequence is executed. For example:

```
IF A < B THEN 600
IF X = Y + 1 THEN 200
IF Z^2 > X^2 + Y^2 THEN 100
```

Predicates may be constructed using the following relational symbols and combinations:

=	equal to
<>	not equal to
<	less than
<=	less than or equal to
>	greater than
>=	greater than or equal to

These relational symbols may be used with numerical variables or character strings.

Second form: This form is an improvement over the previous form. It is written as:

```
IF predicate THEN executable instruction
                                    ↑
```

This instruction may not be a FOR instruction

(For this form, THEN is optional in some BASICs.)

If the predicate is true, the instruction after the THEN is executed. If the predicate is not true, the instruction after the THEN is not executed. For example:

```
IF A < B THEN X = B
IF A < B THEN GOTO 600
```

ATARI BASIC allows more than one executable instruction after the THEN. For example:

```
IF A < B THEN X = B: Y = D
```

PROGRAM LOOPS

Program loops are created by using the FOR and NEXT instructions.

```
FOR V = E1 TO E2 STEP E3
:
:
NEXT V
```

where V is a numeric variable name and E1, E2 and E3 are arithmetic expressions.

E1 gives the initial value assigned to V

E2 gives the final value to be assigned to V

E3 gives the increment:
 If E1 < E2 then E3 must be > 0
 If E1 > E2 then E3 must be < 0

E1, E2 and E3 are evaluated before they initially enter the loop.

If the loop increment (E3) is 1, then the STEP clause can be omitted:

```
FOR V = E1 TO E2
```

For example:

```
100   FOR I = 1 TO 10
110   FOR J = 1 TO 10
120   A (I,J) = 0
130   NEXT J
140   NEXT I
```

CHARACTER STRINGS

String constants are formed by enclosing a sequence of characters in double quotes. For example:

```
"ABCD"
"THIS IS BASIC"
```

Blanks are significant within a character string. The maximum allowable length for a character string depends upon the system being used.

String variables are denoted by a variable name followed by a dollar sign. For example:

```
A$, B$, AB$, SENTRY$
```

Operations Defined on Character Strings

Comparison: A$ is said to be "less than" B$ if, in alphabetical order, A$ precedes B$. For example:

```
A$ = "JOHNNY"
B$ = "APPLESEED"
```

Here B$ is less than A$, i.e., B$ <A$.

Concatenation consists of joining two strings end to end. For example:

```
A$ = "JOHN"
B$ = " DOE"
N$ = A$ : N$(5) = B$
```

N$ takes the value "JOHN DOE".

Substrings: A section of a string may be denoted by writing its first and last indices. For example:

```
N$(4,6)
```

has the value "N D".

Special string functions: The following is a list of functions that manipulate character strings. This list may vary from one implementation to another, but it represents most of the functions available in microcomputer BASICs.

ASC(X$)	gives the numeric value of the ASCII code for X$, e.g., ASC ("A") = 65.
CHR$(I)	gives, as a string, the character whose ASCII code is I.
STR$(I)	gives a string containing the decimal value of I.

LEN(A$)	gives the length of the string A$.
VAL(A$)	gives the numeric value of the ASCII string, A$. Obviously, this function assumes that the characters of A$ actually represent a number.

INPUT/OUTPUT

In order to read "interactive" inputs (e.g., on the keyboard), the following instruction is used:

```
INPUT variable list
          ↑
  simple variables
```

The following format should be used to read data included within the program:

```
READ variable list
.
.
.
DATA numeric values separated by commas (or blanks in some
systems)
RESTORE to "rewind" (i.e., go back to the first DATA instruction for
the next READ).
```

The instruction used to print results is used in the form:

```
PRINT variable list
          ↑
     variables and constants
```

In the example

```
PRINT "X = ";X,"Y = ";Y
```

note that the separators used are a comma and a semicolon. A comma causes the next item to be printed starting in the first position of the next available tab field. A semicolon concatenates the items, i.e., the next item is printed directly afterward with no intervening spaces.

A separator at the end of a PRINT instruction suppresses the passing to a new line, i.e., a final carriage return and linefeed.

APPENDIX C

The Standard ASCII Character Set

Consult the ATARI BASIC manual for special cursor control characters (e.g. 155 = end of line).

CODE	CHAR	CODE	CHAR	CODE	CHAR	CODE	CHAR
0	NUL	32[1]		64	@	96[5]	`
1	SOH	33	!	65	A	97	a
2	STX	34	"	66	B	98	b
3	ETX	35	#	67	C	99	c
4	EOT	36	$	68	D	100	d
5	ENQ	37	%	69	E	101	e
6	ACK	38	&	70	F	102	f
7	BEL	39[2]	'	71	G	103	g
8	BS	40	(	72	H	104	h
9	TAB	41	)	73	I	105	i
10	LF	42	*	74	J	106	j
11	VT	43	+	75	K	107	k
12	FF	44[3]	,	76	L	108	l
13	CR	45	—	77	M	109	m
14	SO	46	.	78	N	110	n
15	SI	47	/	79	O	111	o
16	DLE	48	0	80	P	112	p
17	DC1	49	1	81	Q	113	q
18	DC2	50	2	82	R	114	r
19	DC3	51	3	83	S	115	s
20	DC4	52	4	84	T	116	t
21	NAK	53	5	85	U	117	u
22	SYN	54	6	86	V	118	v
23	ETB	55	7	87	W	119	w
24	CAN	56	8	88	X	120	x
25	EM	57	9	89	Y	121	y
26	SUB	58	:	90	Z	122	z
27	ESC	59	;	91	[	123	{
28	FS	60	<	92	\	124	|
29	GS	61	=	93	]	125[6]	}
30	RS	62	>	94	↑	126	~
31	US	63	?	95[4]	←	127[7]	RUBOUT

[1]space
[2]single quote
[3]comma
[4]or underline
[5]accent mark
[6]or ALT MODE
[7]or DEL

Index

The SYBEX Library

YOUR FIRST COMPUTER
by Rodnay Zaks 264 pp., 150 illustr., Ref. 0-045
The most popular introduction to small computers and their peripherals: what they do and how to buy one.

DON'T (or How to Care for Your Computer)
by Rodnay Zaks 222 pp., 100 illustr., Ref. 0-065
The correct way to handle and care for all elements of a computer system, including what to do when something doesn't work.

INTERNATIONAL MICROCOMPUTER DICTIONARY
140 pp., Ref. 0-067
All the definitions and acronyms of microcomputer jargon defined in a handy pocket-size edition. Includes translations of the most popular terms into ten languages.

FROM CHIPS TO SYSTEMS: AN INTRODUCTION TO MICROPROCESSORS
by Rodnay Zaks 558 pp., 400 illustr., Ref. 0-063
A simple and comprehensive introduction to microprocessors from both a hardware and software standpoint: what they are, how they operate, how to assemble them into a complete system.

YOUR TIMEX SINCLAIR 1000™ AND ZX81™

by Douglas Hergert 176 pp., illustr., Ref. 0-099

This book explains the set-up, operation, and capabilities of the Timex Sinclair 1000 and ZX81. Includes how to interface peripheral devices, and introduces BASIC programming.

YOUR COLOR COMPUTER

by Doug Mosher 350 pp., illustr., Ref. 0-097

Patience and humor guide the reader through purchasing, setting up, programming, and using the Radio Shack TRS-80/TDP Series 100 Color Computer. A complete introduction to the color computer.

INTRODUCTION TO WORD PROCESSING

by Hal Glatzer 216 pp., 140 illustr., Ref. 0-076

Explains in plain language what a word processor can do, how it improves productivity, how to use a word processor and how to buy one wisely.

THE FOOLPROOF GUIDE TO SCRIPSIT™

by Jeff Berner 225 pp., illustr., Ref. 0-098

Everything you need to know about SCRIPSIT—from starting out to mastering document editing. This user-friendly guide is written in plain English, with a touch of wit.

INTRODUCTION TO WORDSTAR™

by Arthur Naiman 208 pp., 30 illustr., Ref. 0-077

Makes it easy to learn how to use WordStar, a powerful word processing program for personal computers.

MASTERING VISICALC®

by Douglas Hergert 224 pp., 140 illustr., Ref. 0-090

Explains how to use the VisiCalc "electronic spreadsheet" functions and provides examples of each. Makes using this powerful program simple.

DOING BUSINESS WITH VISICALC®

by Stanley R. Trost 200 pp., Ref. 0-086

Presents accounting and management planning applications—from financial statements to master budgets; from pricing models to investment strategies.

DOING BUSINESS WITH SUPERCALC™

by Stanley R. Trost 300 pp., illustr., Ref. 0-095

Presents accounting and management planning applications—from financial statements to master budgets; from pricing models to investment strategies. This is for computers with CP/M.

VISICALC® FOR SCIENCE AND ENGINEERING

by Stanley R. Trost & Charles Pomernacki 225 pp., illustr., Ref. 0-096

More than 50 programs for solving technical problems in the science and engineering fields. Applications range from math and statistics to electrical and electronic engineering.

EXECUTIVE PLANNING WITH BASIC

by X. T. Bui 192 pp., 19 illustr., Ref. 0-083

An important collection of business management decision models in BASIC, including Inventory Management (EOQ), Critical Path Analysis and PERT, Financial Ratio Analysis, Portfolio Management, and much more.

PASCAL PROGRAMS FOR SCIENTISTS AND ENGINEERS

by Alan R. Miller 378 pp., 120 illustr., Ref. 0-058

A comprehensive collection of frequently used algorithms for scientific and technical applications, programmed in Pascal. Includes such programs as curve-fitting, integrals and statistical techniques.

BASIC PROGRAMS FOR SCIENTISTS AND ENGINEERS

by Alan R. Miller 326 pp., 120 illustr., Ref. 0-073

This second book in the "Programs for Scientists and Engineers" series provides a library of problem-solving programs while developing proficiency in BASIC.

FORTRAN PROGRAMS FOR SCIENTISTS AND ENGINEERS

by Alan R. Miller 320 pp., 120 illustr., Ref. 0-082

Third in the "Programs for Scientists and Engineers" series. Specific scientific and engineering application programs written in FORTRAN.

PROGRAMMING THE 6809

by Rodnay Zaks and William Labiak 520 pp., 150 illustr., Ref. 0-078

This book explains how to program the 6809 in assembly language. No prior programming knowledge required.

PROGRAMMING THE 6502

by Rodnay Zaks 388 pp., 160 illustr., Ref. 0-046

Assembly language programming for the 6502, from basic concepts to advanced data structures.

6502 APPLICATIONS

by Rodnay Zaks 286 pp., 200 illustr., Ref. 0-015

Real-life application techniques: the input/output book for the 6502

ADVANCED 6502 PROGRAMMING

by Rodnay Zaks 292 pp., 140 illustr., Ref. 0-089

Third in the 6502 series. Teaches more advanced programming techniques, using games as a framework for learning.

PROGRAMMING THE Z80

by Rodnay Zaks 626 pp., 200 illustr., Ref. 0-069

A complete course in programming the Z80 microprocessor and a thorough introduction to assembly language.

Z80 APPLICATIONS

by James W. Coffron 300 pp., illustr., Ref. 0-094

Covers techniques and applications for using peripheral devices with a Z80 based system.

PROGRAMMING THE Z8000

by Richard Mateosian 300 pp., 124 illustr., Ref. 0-032

How to program the Z8000 16-bit microprocessor. Includes a description of the architecture and function of the Z8000 and its family of support chips.

THE CP/M® HANDBOOK (with MP/M™)

by Rodnay Zaks 324 pp., 100 illustr., Ref. 0-048

An indispensable reference and guide to CP/M—the most widely-used operating system for small computers.

MASTERING CP/M®

by Alan R. Miller 320 pp., Ref. 0-068

For advanced CP/M users or systems programmers who want maximum use of the CP/M operating system . . . takes up where our *CP/M Handbook* leaves off.

INTRODUCTION TO THE UCSD p-SYSTEM™

by Charles W. Grant and Jon Butah 250 pp., 10 illustr., Ref. 0-061

A simple, clear introduction to the UCSD Pascal Operating System; for beginners through experienced programmers

A MICROPROGRAMMED APL IMPLEMENTATION

by Rodnay Zaks 350 pp., Ref. 0-005

An expert-level text presenting the complete conceptual analysis and design of an APL interpreter, and actual listing of the microcode.

THE APPLE® CONNECTION

by James W. Coffron 228 pp., 120 illustr., Ref. 0-085

Teaches elementary interfacing and BASIC programming of the Apple for connection to external devices and household appliances.

MICROPROCESSOR INTERFACING TECHNIQUES

by Rodnay Zaks and Austin Lesea 458 pp., 400 illustr., Ref. 0-029

Complete hardware and software interconnect techniques, including D to A conversion, peripherals, standard buses and troubleshooting.

SELF STUDY COURSES

Recorded live at seminars given by recognized professionals in the microprocessor field.

INTRODUCTORY SHORT COURSES:

Each includes two cassettes plus special coordinated workbook (2½ hours).

S10—INTRODUCTION TO PERSONAL AND BUSINESS COMPUTING

A comprehensive introduction to small computer systems for those planning to use or buy one, including peripherals and pitfalls.

S1—INTRODUCTION TO MICROPROCESSORS

How microprocessors work, including basic concepts, applications, advantages and disadvantages.

S2—PROGRAMMING MICROPROCESSORS

The companion to S1. How to program any standard microprocessor, and how it operates internally. Requires a basic understanding of microprocessors.

S3—DESIGNING A MICROPROCESSOR SYSTEM

Learn how to interconnect a complete system, wire by wire. Techniques discussed are applicable to all standard microprocessors.

INTRODUCTORY COMPREHENSIVE COURSES:

Each includes a 300-500 page seminar book and seven or eight C90 cassettes.

SB3—MICROPROCESSORS

This seminar teaches all aspects of microprocessors: from the operation of an MPU to the complete interconnect of a system. The basic hardware course (12 hours).

SB2—MICROPROCESSOR PROGRAMMING

The basic software confuse step by step through all the important aspects of microcomputer programming (10 hours).

ADVANCED COURSES:

Each includes a 300-500 page workbook and three or four C90 cassettes.

SB3—SEVERE ENVIRONMENT/MILITARY MICROPROCESSOR SYSTEMS

Complete discussion of constraints, techniques and systems for severe environmental applications, including Hughes, Raytheon, Actron and other militarized systems (6 hours).

SB5—BIT-SLICE

Learn how to build a complete system with bit slices. Also examines innovative applications of bit slice techniques (6 hours).

SB6—INDUSTRIAL MICROPROCESSOR SYSTEMS

Seminar examines actual industrial hardware and software techniques, components, programs and cost (4½ hours).

SB7—MICROPROCESSOR INTERFACING

Explains how to assemble, interface and interconnect a system (6 hours).

SOFTWARE

BAS 65™ CROSS-ASSEMBLER IN BASIC

8″ diskette, Ref. BAS 65

A complete assembler for the 6502, written in standard Microsoft BASIC under CP/M® .

8080 SIMULATORS

Turns any 6502 into an 8080. Two versions are available for APPLE II.

APPLE II cassette, Ref. S6580-APL(T)

APPLE II diskette, Ref. S6580-APL (D)

FOR A COMPLETE CATALOG OF OUR PUBLICATIONS

U.S.A.
2344 Sixth Street
Berkeley,
California 94710
Tel: (415) 848-8233
Telex: 336311

SYBEX-EUROPE
4 Place Félix-Eboué
75583 Paris Cedex 12
France
Tel: 1/347-30-20
Telex: 211801

SYBEX-VERLAG
Heyestr. 22
4000 Düsseldorf 12
West Germany
Tel: (0211) 287066
Telex: 08 588 163

SYBEX®